# POETICS,
# SPECULATION,
# AND JUDGMENT

*SUNY Series in Contemporary Continental Philosophy*

*Dennis J. Schmidt, Editor*

# POETICS, SPECULATION, AND JUDGMENT

*The Shadow of the Work of Art
from Kant to Phenomenology*

## Jacques Taminiaux

*Translated and Edited by
Michael Gendre*

*State University of New York Press*

Published by
State University of New York Press, Albany

For information, address State University of New York
Press, State University Plaza, Albany, N.Y., 12246

Production by Dana Foote
Marketing by Bernadette LaManna

Library of Congress Cataloging in Publication Data
Taminiaux, Jacques, 1928–
    Poetics, speculation, and judgment : the shadow of the work of art
from Kant to phenomenology / Jacques Taminiaux: translated and edited by Michael
    Gendre.
      p.   cm. — (SUNY series in contemporary continental
philosophy.)
    Includes bibliographical references and index.
    ISBN 0–7914–1547–3 (alk. paper). — ISBN 0–7914–1548–1 (pbk. :
alk. paper)
    1. Aesthetics, Modern—18th century.   2. Aesthetics, Modern—19th
century.   3. Aesthetics, Modern—20th century.   4. Aesthetics,
Ancient.   I. Series.
BH151.T36   1993
111'.85'0903—dc20                                                  92–35025
                                                                        CIP

10 9 8 7 6 5 4 3 2 1

# Contents

# *Preface*

I wish to express my sincere gratitude to Dennis Schmidt for his kindness in suggesting that some of my essays on philosophers and art be published in this collection.

These pieces are the result of many years of teaching at the Université de Louvain and at Boston College. Perhaps they have no greater merit than to attest to some extended readings in the authors investigated, and therefore should only claim to be reading notes. In any case, judgment should be passed by the readers themselves.

Since these texts bear on philosophers—who all attempted to be original—and since furthermore they were written over more than two decades, it is possible that collected they form a disparate assortment. At any rate, I find it useful to point out that I decided to unite them under the title *Poetics, Speculation, and Judgment* because in close proximity they allow two axes of thought to come to the fore in the philosophy of art: the speculative axis and the judicative axis. Regarding the history of philosophy from its Greek origins, these two axes are already outlined, on the one hand, in Plato's critical attitude toward the artists of his time and, on the other hand, in Aristotle's reaction against the views of his master. From the perspective of speculation adopted by Plato, art is without value and should be allowed to die if it does not lead to the ultimate knowledge of essences and of the ground aimed at by the philosophers. Such knowledge aspires to self-sufficiency and, consequently, validates a view disparaging human plurality as well as the world of appearances to which this plurality is connected. In contrast, from the perspective of judgment adopted by Artistotle, art is accepted as what it is, and is deemed to be worthy of this acceptance not because an access is being prepared in it for some metaphysics, but rather because art concerns the finite condition of human beings, their plurality, the phenomenal world that they inhabit together, and because it sheds light—if not on the impossibility of the self-sufficiency sought by metaphysicians—at least on the limits and the blind spots inherent in their pretensions to reach what is ultimate and a totality. It is striking that these two philosophical perspectives on art find themselves reproduced under various shapes and forms in modern and contemporary philosophy. In short, the essays brought together in this collection attempt to examine some modern and contemporary versions of these two perspectives—the former leading to the depreciating of art in the name of some absolute, and the second leading, in the name of human finitude, to the acknowledgment that we are taught by art.

I also wish to express my gratitude to Michael Gendre for the patience and attention he devoted to this translation.

---

The papers have been lightly edited since their first French or English publication. All words or remarks in square brackets appearing in the footnotes are translator's notes of original words.

# Speculation and Judgment

Let me formulate at the very outset the question with which this essay will be dealing: Is there a link between the way philosophers approach the political realm and the way they consider the fine arts?

That there is indeed a link is suggested at the very beginning of our philosophical tradition by the fact that the earliest political philosophy as well as the earliest philosophy of art were both articulated in one and the same text, namely, Plato's *Republic*. Whatever their divergences, most interpreters admit that this simultaneous presence is no mere coincidence. In addition they often concede that the justification for taking up these two topics together is to be found in the most decisive pages of the dialogue, namely, the story of the cave, in which Plato sets forth in a metaphorical manner his concepts of truth and of being. Concerning Plato, I propose to express the link in one word: *speculation*.

To be sure, the origin of the word *speculation* is not Greek but Latin. It stems from *speculum*, which means "mirror." Moreover, the systematic use of the word only appeared in modern philosophy, and rather late at that, namely, in German idealism. Kant's *Critique of Pure Reason* is probably the first major text in which words such as *speculation* and *speculative* are systematically and repeatedly used. But in Kant they convey a negative and derogatory connotation: They characterize ironically a way of philosophizing that trespasses the limits of the human mind. In a deliberate reaction against the Kantian emphasis on these limits, however, Hegel later grants to the same words the highest and most affirmative worth. In fact, my first intention was to focus this essay on the confrontation between Hegel and Kant regarding the political and the artistic realms, and to show that in Kant's stand toward

This paper was written in English by the author for the Dotterer Lecture given in the Department of Philosophy at the University of Pennsylvania, spring 1991.

these matters what is at stake is the predominance of judgment over speculation, whereas in Hegel it is the predominance of the latter over the former.

But since I just suggested that speculation already plays a decisive role in Plato's treatment of the political and the artistic, I would like to focus the first part of this essay on the nature of this decisive role, and what it involves for these two realms.

The Greek word for mirror—*katoptron*—is at the core of the analysis of the ontological status of artistic activity in the *Republic,* book 10. Just as a mirror can reflect and thereby imitate all the visible things that otherwise directly appear to us, likewise, says Plato, the artist can imitate all things. Such a person, however, does so by merely observing how they look, without paying attention to what they truly are. The artist never overcomes ordinary perception, he or she is attached to perceptual appearances. By contrast, the artisan, in whatever craft, tries at the outset of his productive activity—and at each step of the fabrication process—to behold the ideal pattern, the archetype, the pure form of the equipment the artisan wants to fabricate. Consequently, the artisan is in a true relationship with Ideas, whereas the artist cares only for appearances. Accordingly Plato always grants to the artisan a mediating position between those who are attached to the ordinary look of things and those who dedicate their lives to the pure *theoria,* to beholding what beings truly are, that is, to the contemplation of Ideas. This contemplation is what German idealism would later call "speculation." Plato does not say that the contemplation of Ideas is a mirroring of them; rather, he reserves the metaphor of the mirror for the description of artistic activity. But if we agree to call speculation "the beholding of Ideas," we might say that it is indeed by referring to speculation that Plato considers the artistic realm, and that it is the same reference that allows him to rank the artisan higher than the artist.

As far as the ontological structure of reality is concerned, the activity of the artist is misleading. Whereas the radiance of the realm of Ideas is what demands to be correctly seen, the artist leads us astray by making us believe that only appearances deserve contemplation. Whereas by paying attention to the activity of the artisan we are prompted to raise our seeing beyond the appearances, the artist enhances our attachment to them by glorifying them. One can even say that for Plato the true poet is the artisan. The Greek language used one and the same word to designate the productive activity of the artisan and the production of the painter, the sculptor, the epic poet, and the tragic poet. That word is *poiēsis.* Likewise one single word, *technē,* designated the "know-how" of both the artisan and the artist. Plato reacts against this linguistic use. The artisan, he claims, is the only one whose production is truly a *poiēsis,* because such a person alone holds specific Ideas in view and imitates them. By contrast, the productions of the painter, the sculptor, and the author of epic poems or of tragedy are not really *poiēsis,* because instead of trying to hold Ideas in view, they stubbornly imitate appearances. Moreover it is because of this that they can imitate everything, whereas precisely because he has to behold specific patterns and forms, the true *technitēs,* the artisan, cannot be an expert in everything: A good shoemaker cannot be at the same time a good carpenter. Compared to the true *poiēsis* of the artisan, the production of the artist is a fake: At best he is a dilettante or an amateur.

If we agree to call speculation "the contemplation of Ideas," then speculation obviously results in a privilege being given to fabrication over artistic creation. In Plato speculation acknowledges the craftsman and despises the artist.

It is extremely significant that Plato approaches the political domain in the same fashion. In other words, his view of public affairs is also ruled by the privileging of *poiēsis* as a fabrication carried out by an expert, this privileging itself depending on the supreme dignity of speculation.

But before considering how Plato looks at the political realm, let me notice that his assessment of the activity of the artisan runs against the way the Greek city-state, at the time of its blossoming—let us say at the time of Pericles—conceived of the activity and the mentality of the artisan, or of all experts. According to current scholarship, the Greek *polis,* of which Athens became the highest example, emerged as a peculiar regime or *politeia* (a word, by the way, that is in Greek the very title of Plato's *Republic*) when government started to be publicly shared among individuals who were at the same time in a position of equality and of rivalry, through the unique medium of speech. At the dawn of the *polis,* therefore, there obtained a relatedness between speech, publicity, and equality. And this cooperation became more and more forceful as the oligarchic system was replaced by democracy. The kind of speech at stake was essentially dialogical. It consisted of an exchange of opinions in a public debate between equal speakers before an audience making up its mind about the persuasive force of all the discourses in competition. In addition to characterizing this type of speech, publicity ruled everywhere in the life of the city. Its laws were written and known to everybody; its temples, as well as the statues of its gods, were visible to all; its physical center was the *agora* where all citizens met; its theaters were also open to all, and there was a public competition for the best tragedy that was staged by the city. Evidently this publicity designated a common world of appearances. It meant that all citizens had the same right of expression, that they participated equally in the sovereignty of the public assembly, and that everyone had his share in the public offices. At the time the Greeks invented many words to express all the aspects of this equality, such as *isonomia, isotimia, isēgoria, isocratia,* and so on. And they invented the verb *politeuein* to designate their political way of life, as a sharing of words and deeds, *lexis* and *praxis.*

Now, it is remarkable that in the political mode of being or *bios politikos* the activity and mentality of the artisan were held at a distance. The Greeks of the city were aware that the good *technitēs* is an expert, a specialist in a particular field. But in their view the good politician cannot and should not be an expert. In the isonomic regime, each citizen, not a limited group of professionals, must be in charge of public affairs. Those who invented the *bios politikos* were convinced that as soon as a professional mentality rules over public matters, the public realm runs the risk of losing its constitutive features: the sharing of words and deeds by all the members of the community. One does not debate with experts, one just listens to them. *Isēgoria* and expertise are not compatible. Accordingly, when the city really needed experts, such as experts in strategy, it elected them for short periods. This is why the city carefully avoided having professional civil servants, judges, tax collectors, and so on.

To be sure, the Greeks of the city knew that a continuous debate entails a good deal of unpredictability. This is why they conceived of human affairs as essentially fragile and ambiguous. In keeping with this awareness they conceived of the civic virtues not at all in terms of the strict observation of a clear rule, but as the ever-renewed search for a mean (a *mesotēs*) between extremes, midway between deficiency and excess. This sense of measure was at the heart of the Apollinian maxims in Delphi. It was also present in the background of the masterpieces of Greek tragedy, which were all created during the blossoming of Athens's democracy and staged at the cost of the city. These masterpieces were testimonies to the frailty and ambiguity of human interaction and *praxis.* If the citizens were paid by the city to attend them in the theater, it is because beholding all the ambiguities expressed by them was supposed to confirm and improve the type of knowledge specifically adjusted to human affairs, a kind of knowledge far removed indeed from the expertise of a technician. This kind of knowledge is *phronēsis.* No matter how the word is translated—as prudence, practical wisdom, judgment—what is at stake is the ability to make up one's mind about human affairs by searching again and again for a mean between extremes. The Greek word for theater, *theatron,* means a place for seeing. The Greek word for seeing is *theorein.* Prior to Plato, *theoria* meant beholding a spectacle, and the theorists par excellence were the spectators in the theater. Their contemplation included the *phronēsis* we just mentioned. Such theory did not leave the common world of appearances; it was not solitary, but inserted in human plurality and essentially tied to what appears to each individual, that is, to *doxa*, individual opinion.

These sketchy remarks allow us to return to Plato's approach to the political realm in the *Republic*. The dialogue vindicates an entirely new idea of *theoria*, which is a solitary contemplation of Ideas beyond the common world of appearances. The dialogue is an apology of a theoretical mode of being or *bios theoretikos* that no longer has anything in common with the spectators of tragedies in the theater. Against the prior beholding, the new *bios theoretikos* claims to be self-sufficient instead of being inserted in human plurality. Its aim is to overcome once and for all the ambiguities that affected the previous contemplation inasmuch as it was tied to the world of appearances and to *doxa*. Borrowing from Kant's terminology, we might say that the point of this new kind of *theoria* is to speculate, in the sense of getting a clear insight into ultimate Ideas.

Because speculation is not interested in human plurality, in *doxa*, and in the ambiguities of *praxis*, but in the clear vision of Ideas, it is inclined, by the same token, to substitute *poiēsis* for *praxis* concerning the organization of the city. Whereas tragedy allowed the fellow citizens of Pericles, who was a close friend of Sophocles, to reflect upon the ambiguities of human affairs, Plato dismisses tragical poetry precisely because it is thoroughly ambiguous. Whereas the city of Pericles held all experts in suspicion, Plato glorifies the expert. Whereas the isonomic city conceived of the civic virtues in terms of a fragile mean between extremes, Plato characterizes virtue as the strict implementation of a clear principle. Because of the excellence of *poiēsis*, Plato's city is depicted as a sort of huge workshop ruled by the principle: one person, one job. That *poiēsis* operates as a paradigm in the *Republic* is made obvious, for example, by the concept of "professional guardians"—introduced in book 2—when Socrates insists "that it is impossible for one person to do a fine job in many arts," thereby objecting to the democratic principle that each citizen is able to be in charge of any public office. This paradigm is equally obvious in the way book 2 again defines the education of the guardians in terms of the making of a reliable product with adequate means. Another example of the overall preponderance of *poiēsis* is given by the way Socrates deals with the problem of virtue in book 4. There is, he says, a virtue or excellence of a tool when it is perfectly adjusted as a means to a specific and determined goal. Likewise, he says, the virtue of the artisan is his ability to imitate a preestablished model. In his view, the main virtue of the warriors, namely, courage, should match this pattern. For the city, courage was a mean between extremes, between rashness and cowardice; for Socrates it is simply the ignorance of fear. Moreover, whereas in city life virtue was tied up with competing for excellence within human plurality, it is now taken to be self-sufficient: "A decent man is most of all sufficient unto himself for living well and, in contrast to others, has least need of another" (387d). Finally, the entire dialogue gravitates around the topic of the necessary overcoming of the common world of appearances, a topic that amounts to discarding as irrelevant an essential feature of *praxis,* since, in the public realm, *praxis* has to appear to others in relation to a common world of appearances. Everywhere the dialogue characterizes the best regime in terms of *poiēsis* against *praxis.* The very words of Socrates are evidence of this: "We made plain that each of the citizens must be brought to that which naturally suits him—one man, one job—so that each man, practicing his own, which is one, will not become many but one; and thus, you see, the whole city will naturally grow to be one and not many" (423d).

So in reference to speculation a claim is made for the substitution of the clarity of *poiēsis* for the ambiguities of *praxis* in both the political realm and the fine arts. In a good city the citizens should be like artisans, steady imitators of clear models. Likewise poetry would be tolerable if, and only if, the poet were to become, as Plato says, "the unmixed imitator of the decent." The trouble is that, since all the features of the Greek way of life—from which the very word *politics* derives—are opposed to Plato's claim, the latter implies a rejection of "politics." And since not a single masterpiece of Greek poetry ever did fit with Plato's request about poetry, his claim is tantamount to rejecting the fine arts as well.

It is well known that Aristotle reacted against Plato's views about political and artistic matters. It is no overstatement to say that he discarded the possibility of subordinating these two realms to speculation, and that he rehabilitated *phronēsis* in the philosophical treatment of them.

As far as the fine arts are concerned, his most significant text is his *Poetics.* Many interpreters agree that "the all-encompassing concept of Aristotle's *Poetics* is *mimēsis.*"[1]

This notion comes from Plato, of course. But it does not play in Aristotle the role it played in Plato's assessment of Greek tragedy. Whereas the metaphor of the mirror allowed Plato to consider the *mimēsis* carried out by the poet as a passive reflection, Aristotle defines it in relation to Greek tragedy as an active process of composition. For Plato the tragic *mimēsis* is subservient to sheer appearances. For Aristotle it brings together actions in order to compose a plot. In this composition the point is not to feature individuals such as they appear along with the qualities that constitute their specific char-

---

1. Paul Ricoeur, *Temps et récit* (Paris: Le Seuil, 1983), vol. 1, p. 58.

acter. Instead the point is the other way around, to feature an action by which individuals achieve their character and consequently certain qualities (*Poetics* 50a15). Such emphasis on the plot (*mythos*) as the principle (*archē*), the goal (*telos*) and even the soul (*psychē*) of tragedy (50a38) indicates how far re moved Aristotle is from Plato. By assigning to the plot an overwhelming importance, by claiming that it is by virtue of the plot that the dramatic heroes attain or fail to attain *eudaimonia,* or authentic individuation, Aristotle attests to his disagreement with Plato, who in the *Sophist* (242c) insisted that the first philosophical step is to discard plots, and who repeatedly in the *Republic* stressed that only in the intercourse of the soul with itself under the auspices of the Ideas can *eudaimonia* be attained. In addition, whereas no masterpiece of Greek tragedy won Plato's approval, it is as though all these masterpieces are acknowledged by Aristotle, who obviously rehabilitates the *mimēsis* that they effect. Whereas in Plato the existing artistic *mimēsis* was narrowly confined within the reflection of factual and merely particular appearances— which by nature are void of any philosophical import—Aristotle insists that the poet is concerned not with the factual but with the possible. This is why the poet, he says, is able to express universals whereas the historian tells particulars. Therefore the writing of poetry is a "philosophical activity," and one "to be taken seriously" (*Poetics* 51a36–b15).

What is at stake in this rehabilitation, in relation to Plato's views, is a new criterion—no longer speculation, but *phronēsis.* When Aristotle writes that "the plot, since it is an imitation of an action (*praxis*), should be an imitation of an action that is unified, and a whole as well, and the constituents of the plot should be so put together that, if one of them is placed elsewhere or removed, the whole is disjointed and dislocated" (51a30–35), reference is thereby made not to the pure beholding of an Idea, but to the sense of measure and proportion that was vindicated by the Apollinian maxims of Delphi and that underscored *phronēsis* as a civic virtue in the isonomic *polis.* In the same context Aristotle defines a whole as "that which has beginning, middle and end," and he indicates that these moments are not contingent events but meaningful ones. When he also suggests that the plot raises the particulars of life to a universal level, the same reference to *phronēsis* is again present, since it is one of the functions of *phronēsis* to look at the particulars of *praxis* in the light of universals, without separating in the least the latter from the former. The same reference is implicit when Aristotle characterizes the magnitude of the action in terms of an orderly arrangement and a not-accidental size. "Beauty," he says, "lies in size and arrangement, hence neither a very tiny animal can be beautiful, because our view (*theoria*) of it is blurred as it approaches that instant where perceptibility ceases, nor an enormously big one, because then the perception does not take place all at once, and the sense of oneness and wholeness is gone from the viewers' vision" (50b34ff.). Obviously this *theoria* is no longer speculation; it is the apprehension within the common world of appearances of a mean between extremes, a *mesotēs*. Beauty is now correlated to judgment. Accordingly, there is no longer any trace in this context of the privilege that Plato granted to the artisan in contrast to the poet. It could even be maintained, for that matter, that Aristotle's theory of the four causes results in some privilege being given to the artist over the artisan. The four causes indeed cooperate in all production, either natural or artificial, but only in the artistic production is the end of the product at the same time its form—a form that is there for its own sake and offered to contemplation—whereas in technical production the form is only contemplated at the start of fabrication but no longer at the end, since the product of a craft is offered to use and not to contemplation.

As far as the political realm is concerned, let me just highlight a few signs of Aristotle's resistance to Plato's views. Whereas Plato claims "that it will never be possible for a plurality of men to reasonably govern a City" and that the good regime should be in the hands of a small number because correctness belongs to the One, Aristotle insists that the city is by nature a *plēthos*, a plurality, and perishes by unifying itself in the manner of a family, and still more in the manner of a single individual, for it needs differences between its members and is resistant to being composed of identical individuals. This is why the *Nicomachean Ethics*—a sort of political treatise, says Aristotle—declines any pretension to raising political philosophy to the level of certainty of mathematics or first philosophy. It is, he says, unavoidably half way between geometry and rhetoric, which amounts to suggesting that speculation is irrelevant in the realm of human affairs.

The same text rehabilitates *phronēsis* against the monopolistic tendencies of Plato's *sophia*. Accordingly no attempt is made in it to reduce *praxis* to *poiēsis*, or to substitute the latter for the former. Instead Aristotle clearly ranks *praxis* higher than *poiēsis*. Action cannot be conflated with fabrication, and Aristotle makes clear that the disclosing aptitude relevant to the latter is irrelevant to the former. *Technē* and *phronēsis* are essentially different. To be sure, both are classified as dianoetic virtues, both include a deliberation, and they both refer to the perishable. But whereas *technē* deliberates only about the adequate means for predefined ends, *phronēsis* deliberates about its proper aim, well-doing in general, that is, the good life, which is not an intelligible Idea, but what is worth being done here and now, in relation to *kairos*. It is always in relation to a concrete situation that one has to decide about what is just or unjust, noble or vile, wise or mad, beautiful or ugly. Because it is tied to *kairos*, practical wisdom is fully temporal and concerns the irreversible process and quality of particular existences, whereas a failure in matters of *techné* does not prevent the process of fabrication from starting all over again and does not affect the very existence of the artisan. Moreover, *phronésis* is inserted within plurality and interaction, whereas it is in solitude that the artisan contemplates the patterns to be implemented. The withdrawal that is required in order to make up one's mind about particular human affairs is merely provisional. It is open to a renewed insertion within human networks, and this is why Aristotle includes discourse, mutual understanding, clemency, and even friendship among the characteristics of *phronésis.* That is why it is for him the political virtue par excellence. Finally, in contradistinction to Plato's contempt for *doxa,* Aristotle says that *phronésis* is a doxastic virtue. This does not mean that *phronésis* is trapped in the appearances and strictly attaches to the particular perspectives of individuals. On the contrary, *phronésis* is the aptitude of pondering *doxa,* which means the attitude of searching—while pondering the specifics of a particular situation—for the ever-potential universal that is the good and beautiful life. Because *phronésis* is an effort to link particulars to universals that are forever potential and never fully given beforehand, it cannot be taught by simply teaching rules or ways of implementing them. Its teaching takes place in the consideration of examples, for instance, the memorable ones that the poet relates better than the historian. There is, therefore, an obvious convergence between the way Aristotle approaches the political realm and the way he considers the fine arts. In both cases judgment prevails over speculation.

At this juncture one could perhaps object that the use of such words as speculation and judgment is misleading, for there is no strict equivalent for them in Greek, neither in Plato nor in Aristotle. Indeed, as I suggested above, Kant was the first philosopher to examine the nature of speculation. He did so in the *Critique of Pure Reason.* He was also the first one to examine the nature of judgment. He did so in the *Critique of Judgment,* a book in which his philosophy of art is unfolded.

Kant writes in the introduction to the third *Critique:* "Judgment in general is the ability to think the particular as contained under the universal. If the universal is given, then the judgment that subsumes the particular under it is determinative. But if only the particular is given and judgment has to find the universal for it, then this power is merely reflective." In other words, the judgment by which we state that this particular thing of nature or this particular work of art is beautiful or not, is not the application of a pregiven rule, principle, or law, or of a pregiven concept of beauty. Consequently this judgment is neither epistemic nor technical. Right away one can notice a kinship between Kant's characterization of the reflective judgment and Aristotle's characterization of *phronésis.* In both cases the point is to confront a particular in a universal way without help of a predefined universal. The kinship is confirmed by Kant's analysis of the aesthetic judgment as a reflective judgment. Let me recall the main points of the analysis.

Kant proceeds by comparing the aesthetic judgment with three other types of judgment, which we will agree to call (1) the cognitive judgment, (2) the judgment expressing a sensuous satisfaction, and (3) the judgment about perfection. Aesthetic judgment is irreducible to any one of these three other forms of judgment. Should something we believe to be an example of a purely aesthetic judgment show signs of compromise with any one of the others, this is so only because it is affected by some impurity and is not yet strictly aesthetic.

First, let us turn to the difference between the aesthetic judgment and the cognitive one. The cognitive judgment admits of various levels, but, whatever the level, it is always characterized by a clear aim toward an objectivity. Thus the principles of pure understanding, which are a priori cognitive judgments, make objectivity possible. Likewise, when I observe empirically that this body before me is made of this material, I refer it to a general class whose properties are all the better known as the observer is more neutral and impersonal. Objectivity and impersonality go together. By contrast, aesthetic judgment requires a personal involvement on my part. To be able to admire something demands that I, as an irreplaceable individual, am affected by it. In this sense aesthetic judgment, says Kant, is subjective. So considered, aesthetic judgment brings me no science. This is not, however, to imply that my admiration is mindless. Quite to the contrary. It implies the use of my understanding along with my imagination, but in a manner such that my mind simply plays, and from such play derives a sense of satisfaction. It does so without in the least seeking to explain the thing that so captures my attention, without seeking to uncover its formula, to define it, or to gather a concept from it. What is beautiful, says Kant, is what pleases without concepts.

Notice next how the aesthetic judgment differs from the judgment expressing the ordinary pleasure of the senses. Without question, Kant claims, there is something common both to ordinary pleasure and to aesthetic satisfaction. In the one as in the other I am involved in my affective individuality. It is I, as a sensuous individual, who am affected in both cases. But here the resemblance ends. There are three major points of differentiation separating the two forms of judgment. In ordinary sensuous pleasure, it is my own interest that is fundamentally at stake, which is to say that I subordinate the thing enjoyed to the delight that it secures for me. In contrast, the aesthetic judgment is essentially disinterested. This means that, far from being swept up in the course of my enjoyment, the thing of beauty is recognized for just how it appears. I consider it for its own sake, I contemplate it with favor, nothing more, nothing less. From this, two further points of differentiation follow. In the case of ordinary enjoyment, there occurs something like a fundamental egoism, which is well expressed by popular wisdom: To each person their own taste. But precisely because it is disinterested, aesthetic satisfaction avoids this selfish exclusiveness. In aesthetic satisfaction, instead of being locked away in my own individuality, I surpass myself toward an intersubjectivity of sorts. But there is still a third point of differentiation. It is Kant's claim that ordinary sense enjoyment finds its basis in the material realm, whereas aesthetic satisfaction is based in the formal. This means that the essential factor in ordinary pleasure is the organic state of delight in which I am immersed and to which I am subdued. In aesthetic perception, however, I am free at the very heart of the sensible, and I turn what I perceive into the occasion for a free play with sounds, colors, images, words, and so on.

There remains the demarcation of the aesthetic judgment from what I called "the judgment of perfection." This is the judgment by which I view something within the perspective of a goal or an end, and from which I derive a sense of satisfaction if I believe that the thing is perfectly adapted to the goal. This satisfaction is quite different from the aesthetic one. The satisfaction that can arise from relating something to a goal is necessarily connected to an interest, to the extent that I value the realization of the goal. Thus I am a long way from the disinterested contemplation that defines aesthetic judgment. Moreover, if I consider something from the perspective of a goal, I need some concept of this goal. But as we already know, the beautiful is without concepts. For this reason, by setting aesthetic judgment apart from the judgment about perfection, Kant stresses that the former is characterized by what he calls a "finality without end," and that the thing to which it refers manifests itself as a free beauty. A free beauty is freed of all subordination to ends, of all reference to sensuousness, and freed even of all identifiable inner rules of composition.

The aesthetic judgment is neither cognitive, nor sensuous, nor functional. We find again the traits emphasized by Aristotle, when he suggested that in order to contemplate the beautiful within the sensible realm, we have to overcome the biological cycle of pains and pleasures, as well as the utilitarian mentality, and when he insisted that *phronēsis* is not an epistemic power.

Kant was convinced that an a priori element is implied in the aesthetic judgment. This means that an element of universality and necessity is involved, not as a definable principle, of course, which would contradict the description that I summarized, but as a claim made by everyone while experiencing aesthetic satisfaction, to find in everyone else recognition of his or her appreciation. This claim, Kant says, is justified and legitimated by what he calls a "*sensus communis.*" Kant insists in section 40 that the *sensus communis* is not to be confused with common understanding, which always conceptualizes. On the other hand, it is not common in the sense of being vulgar, but in the sense of being shared.[2] He then writes the following:

> We must take *sensus communis* to mean the Idea of a sense shared by all of us, i.e., a power to judge, that, in reflecting takes account (a priori), in our own thought, of everyone else's way of representing something. . . . We do this as follows: we compare our judgment not so much with the actual as rather with the merely possible judgments of others, and thus put ourselves in the position of everyone else, merely by abstracting from the limitations that may happen to attach to our own judging; and this in turn we accomplish by leaving out as much as possible whatever is matter, i.e., sensation, charm and emotion. (*CJ*, 160) [And he says further on:] We are talking here not about the power of cognition, but about an enlarged way of thinking (in which the one who judges) overrides the private subjective conditions of his judgment, into which so many are locked, as it were, and reflects on his own judgment from a universal standpoint (transferring himself to the standpoint of others). (*CJ*, 161)

In other words: "To think from the standpoint of everyone else is the maxim of judgment."

This emphasis on the distinction between thinking and knowing demonstrates that Kant does not in the least approach the aesthetic realm in terms of speculation. To be sure, the power of thinking needs Ideas, but in contrast to Plato, Ideas in Kant's sense of the word cannot be grasped in an ultimate insight, that is, lead to a knowledge. The *sensus communis* is in some measure already actual, which means that human beings are somehow all alike, but it is at the same time only a possibility again and again open to a future of thought. But this tension between the actual and the possible is what we have seen at work in Aristotle's description of *phronēsis*. Moreover, Kant's notion of a *sensus communis* (section 40) indicates both a likeness and a renewed differentiation between human beings. Such likeness and such differ-

---

2. Immanuel Kant, *Critique of Judgment*, trans. Werner S. Pluhar (Indianapolis: Hackett Publishing Company, 1987). Hereafter cited as *CJ*.

entiation are again the very features of the plurality in which, as we have seen, Aristotle's *phronēsis* is inserted.

The same features are again insisted upon in the few paragraphs of the third *Critique* that focus on the work of art and the history of art. In sharp contrast to Plato's views about *poiēsis,* Kant argues that artistic creation cannot be based upon a pregiven rule of composition as the technical work of the craftsman. To be sure, for Kant as for Plato, there is a *mimēsis* relation between art and nature. But this relation acquires a new meaning. In Plato nature herself imitates Ideas. Not so for Kant, since we know nature not as *noumenon* but only as *phenomenon.* Moreover, when nature appears as beautiful, we may say that its very beauty points to an intelligible realm, but this realm preserves its secret. Likewise, the work of art is beautiful when it appears like nature, that is, when the origin of the work, its rule of composition, is a secret for the artist himself or herself. Regarding nature as well as art in the Kantian sense, Plato's concept of *poiēsis* is thus irrelevant. For Kant the artist is not an artist when he or she imitates preestablished rules. A true work of art is the work of a genius, who does not know beforehand the rule for his or her composition, but who receives it as an inspiration from nature. But creators are not only inspired by nature, they are also inspired by predecessors. As far as the history of art is concerned, Kant again demonstrates how far removed he is from Plato's views. Plato conceives of the historical arts as all falling away from the Ideas, and he projects an ideal art that would repeat worthy models. For Kant, by contrast, the history of art is neither a progress nor a decline, nor a repetition. For that matter, he argues not in terms of models, but in terms of inspiring examples: The creator finds inspiration in the works of the past, in that they give him or her the opportunity not merely to copy them, but to invent—with their help but beyond them—new examples. The history of art is thus, like human plurality itself, a combination of likeness and differentiation. Finally, we do find in this context a revival of sorts of Aristotle's *mesotēs.* As a work of genius, a real work of art innovates in a radical way, thereby running the risk of being meaningless or of meeting no reception whatsoever. Therefore a balance has to be found again and again between genius and taste, between the wildness of the former and the conformism of the latter. It is thanks to this balance that great works incite much thought, although they do not provide any knowledge.

About Kant's political philosophy I shall be very brief. It is well known that Kant reacted against the modern theory of natural right initiated by Thomas Hobbes. Hobbes believed that the new *mathesis universalis,* of which Galileo and Descartes were the heralds, could be transposed to human affairs. He conceived of *mathēsis* in terms of speculation, to the extent that the new science of the motions of matter was for him the true *protē philoso-phia*. This is why Hobbes, although he was thoroughly opposed to Plato's idealism, nevertheless also understood the political realm in terms of *poiēsis*, or fabrication. To him the new method, *mathēsis*, as well as the political life, were matters of making: "Geometry," he says, "is demonstrable, for the lines and figures from which we reason are drawn and described by ourselves; and civil philosophy is demonstrable, we make the commonwealth our-selves."[3] The pattern of *poiēsis* rules his entire political philosophy. This is particularly striking in his definition of language as reckoning. A reckoning, he says, implies full mastery over a sequence of defined terms, and he makes it clear that the predominant speech in public affairs should be the speech of either the scientist or the expert. The paradigm of *poiēsis* as a fully predict-able process is implied as well in Hobbes's definition of the social covenant in terms of a reckoning of predictable effects, and in his characterization of the absolute monarch as a sort of ultimate social engineer. The same para-digm is obvious in his definition of the purpose of the state: not providing a space for a public sharing of words and deeds, but protecting the safety of the private production of artifacts.

Against Hobbes Kant argues that the social contract is a regulative Idea that emanates a priori from pure practical reason. While requiring, on the one hand, inner moral autonomy, practical reason also demands, on the other hand, the rule of right in the external interactions between human beings. In this transcendental framework the social contract and, consequently, the po-litical realm are not a matter of reckoning or of calculative fabrication, in short, of *poiēsis;* they are a matter of thought. Our power of thinking, which extends beyond the limits of knowledge, demands that the state be based on three principles: (1) freedom of everyone as a human being in the pursuit of happiness, (2) equality of all under the same law, and (3) independence of everyone as a citizen, that is, as a colegislator.

Here again it could be argued not only that Kant discards as a principle the poietic bias deriving from speculation, but also that he approaches the political realm in terms of judgment, that is, of a way of thinking based on a *sensus communis*, a sense according to which human beings are at the same time all alike and all different. It is because they are all different that they have to be allowed, against despotism, freedom in their search for happiness. It is because such differentiation would result in a chaotic dissemination, if it were not accompanied by a sense of likeness, that it requires, as a counter-

3. Thomas Hobbes, *De Cive*, preface, *English Works*, ed. W. Molesworth (London: Scientia Verlag Aalen, 1839–1845).

part, that everyone be subject to the same law. And finally it is because they are all both different and alike that they must talk, express their views, and be colegislators as a result of such expression. But how could a colegislation be possible at all, without the ability of every citizen to demonstrate what the third *Critique* called "reflective judgment," that is, the ability to think from the standpoint of everyone else.

For Kant, judging is thus in every way at the core of both aesthetics and political philosophy.

It is now time to turn to Hegel. There is no need to demonstrate that his thought was speculative. He himself characterizes it with the word *speculation,* by which he means the operation through which the Absolute Spirit comes to recognize itself within all reality, a reality that encompasses the whole of nature as well as the entire history of human affairs. It is no exaggeration to claim that Hegel's concept of speculation, as the self-mirroring of Spirit, implies what I called above the "privileging of *poiēsis.*" Indeed, this self-mirroring is not immediate; it demands a mediation, a process. And this active mediation is characterized by Hegel in terms of a production: the so-called work of the negative.

This intimate association of *poiēsis* and speculation that we observed in Plato shines forth in the *Phenomenology of Spirit* in the description of the decisive transition from consciousness to self-consciousness. The transition occurs at the outcome of a life-and-death struggle, which in turn gives way to the master-slave relationship. Whereas the master merely enjoys, the slave works, thereby overcoming the immediacy of nature. The work of the slave, Hegel says, is the emergence of what he calls "the universal formative activity of the Absolute Notion."[4] Accordingly, work is understood as in Plato's theory of *poiēsis,* as a shaping activity related to an ideal realm. In Hegel, work has a speculative function: "In fashioning the thing, the bondsman's own negativity, his being-for-self, becomes an object for him . . . ; in fashioning the thing, he becomes aware that being-for-self belongs to him. . . . The shape does not become something other than himself through being made external to him; for it is precisely this shape that is his pure being-for self, which in this externality is seen by him to be the truth" (*PhS.* section 196). This obviously means that working is a self-mirroring. Once again speculation and *poiēsis* are intimately related. The relation is stressed everywhere in Hegel, and it finds its last expression in the last paragraph of the *Encyclopedia,* where Hegel says that "the eternal Idea, existing in and for

---

4. Hegel, *Phenomenology of Spirit,* trans. A. V. Miller, (Oxford: Oxford University Press, 1977), Section 196, p. 119. Hereafter cited as *PhS.*

itself, actualizes itself by eternally producing itself and enjoying itself as Absolute Spirit'' (section 577).

Not surprisingly the paradigm of *poiēsis* plays an equally decisive role in Hegel's speculative view of human affairs. As he characterizes the principle of development in the course of world history, Hegel explicitly refers to the Aristotelian concepts of *dynamis* and *energeia,* that is, to notions coined by Aristotle to account for the activity of fabrication. Since Hegel does not seem to pay attention to Aristotle's distinction between *poiēsis* and *praxis,* the transposition of a poietic scheme to history turns the latter into a process through which, with the help of specific means, a definable goal is pursued and produced, indeed a speculative goal, namely, the attainment by Spirit of its own self-awareness.

The same paradigm also governs Hegel's concept of politics. To be sure, as far as the political is concerned, a distinction should be made between his early writings and his mature thought, between his glorification of the Greek city in the former, and his celebration of the modern nation-state in the latter. However, in both cases neither the specific ambiguities of *praxis* nor the role of judgment in human affairs is really recognized by Hegel. When the early writings celebrate the ethical life of the Greek city, they define this life in terms of a living unification within differentiations, or in terms of a reconciliation between opposites. In the last writings of the Frankfurt period, this reconciliation is said to be a union of union and nonunion, or an identity of identity and not-identity, or even an *Aufhebung* of contraries. At first sight this seems to account for the Greek *mesotēs* as a balance between extremes. But in fact it does not, for Hegel's formula substitutes an ultimate sameness for what the Greeks of the city believed to be insuperable ambiguities. When he claims that the Greek citizens were united by the bond of love to the extent that everyone recognized himself in the others, he simply overlooks the essential link between *philia* and *eris* in the Greek city. Likewise, when he depicts the city as an harmonious body of which the citizens were the spontaneous and happy organs, he simply overlooks plurality and the permanent debate taking place therein. Already at this stage a speculative scheme is at work along with a poietic one, for Hegel claims that for the Greeks the city was a work of art in which they recognized the product as their own operation.

In his mature thought, Hegel no longer claimed that the Greek city was the highest political achievement. On the contrary, he claimed that the highest political achievement was the modern state, or his concept of what it should be. At this stage, the Greek city, compared to the modern state, is now said to be affected by fundamental flaws, which are summarized in one word:

*immediacy.* The Greek city, he says, achieved a merely "immediate unity of the universal and the singular,"[5] whereas the modern state is a mediated unity. I just suggested above that in Hegel's early image of the Greek city as a harmonious living body or as a living work of art there was no real recognition of the specific features of the Greek *bios politikos*, such as ambiguity, plurality, debate, *mesotēs*, *phronēsis*. In his mature thought, Hegel goes a step further: These features, he now claims, were precisely the flaws of the Greek city. He argues indeed that an immediate unity of the universal and the singular is mainly contingent, to the extent (1) that the regime is based on *doxa*, the singular perspectives of contingent individuals; (2) that the political decisions made on the basis of the expressed opinions are the outcome of a vote, that is, something contingent; and finally (3) that such decisions are essentially concerned with particular situations, that is, with contingent events. In other words, *phronēsis*, or judgment, was the fundamental flaw of the Greek city life. The essence of the *polis* is not to be found in its way of coping with the ambiguities of plural interaction but in the transparency of a poietic intercourse of an organism with itself. Accordingly, it is not in the speeches of Pericles as they are related by Thucydides, but in Plato's *Republic*, that Hegel finds, as he insists in his *Philosophy of Right*, what he takes to be "the right interpretation of Greek Ethical Life."[6] When he claims in section 185 of the *Philosophy of Right* that Plato was right in reacting against what he calls "the development of particularity . . . , a moment which appeared in the ancient world as an invasion of ethical corruption," it is almost as though *isonomia* were a disease instead of an accomplishment.

As to the modern state, it is supposed to attain a rational shape only if it succeeds in reviving, in a Christian framework and under the control of the universal class of the administrators, a hierarchic structure similar to the one described by Plato in his *Republic*. Its principle should not be as in Kant, "one person, one voice," but as in Plato's workshop, "one person, one job." We find the following in Hegel's *Philosophical Propaedeutic* (section 198): "The individuals are of more use to the State when they limit themselves to a single activity." As a matter of fact, it is possible to observe the recurrence of similar Platonic structures in Hegel's speculative concept of aesthetics. Two brief remarks will suffice to demonstrate this.

---

5. *Jenaer Systementwürfe III*, p. 262, in Hegel, *Gesammelte Werke*, ed. Rolf-Peter Horstmann (Hamburg: Meiner, 1976). vol. 8. Hereafter cited as *GW8*.

6. G. W. F. Hegel, *Philosophy of Right*, trans. T. M. Knox (Oxford: Oxford University Press, 1967), 10.

The first remark concerns Hegel's extremely significant treatment of Kant's third *Critique*. He deals extensively with it in *Faith and Knowledge*,[7] an early publication of the Jena period in which he discards Kant's distinction between thinking and knowing. In Hegel's view, the *Critique of Judgment* is the only book in which Kant proves to be almost a speculative thinker. Indeed, what Hegel calls "speculative reason" is at work in the book, inasmuch as in it Kant attempts to overcome the dualisms that were affecting his theory of knowledge as well as his practical philosophy. It is a book in which, Hegel says, Kant acknowledges an intermediary region between the empirical manifold of nature and the absolute but abstract unity of freedom (*F.K.* 86ff.), thereby recognizing that the true task of philosophy is to reach an insight into the "absolute identity of thought and being" (*F.K.*, 94). However, even in this book, Hegel says, Kant ultimately refuses to admit a science of the identity he talks about, and the most obvious symptom of such a contradictory refusal is to be found in the very title of the work. Instead of being referred to a speculative science of the Absolute (i.e., to speculative reason), the beautiful, as a realm of identity between opposites, is merely referred to reflective judgment, that is, to the strictly finite and subjective perspectives of individuals. As far as aesthetics is concerned, this reading of Kant by Hegel amounts to discarding the relevance of the activity of judging in matters of beauty. Beauty, therefore, has no essential link with human plurality and with the way individuals aim at a *sensus communis*. The true point of reference in these matters is the philosopher himself, mirroring the totality of beings.

My second and concluding remark concerns Hegel's *Aesthetics* as a philosophy of the history of fine arts. The principle upon which it is based is simple: Art is the sensible manifestation of the Idea. Because art manifests the Idea, it belongs to the sphere of the Absolute Spirit. Because such a manifestation is attached to sensibility, the fine arts are unable to express the Idea fully. Their highest accomplishment corresponds to a specific stage in the development of the Spirit, namely, ancient Greece. Afterward, Christian religion represents a higher stage of development, a stage in which artistic expression is no longer a need for the Spirit.

At first sight, these views seem to be far removed from Plato, for whom indeed the historical arts had no link whatsoever with the realm of Ideas. But upon closer inspection, it turns out that Plato is less rejected by Hegel than reappropriated in a new way. As a matter of fact the historical process, as it is depicted by Hegel, ultimately reproduces a Platonic structure. In Plato's

---

7. G. W. F. Hegel, *Faith and Knowledge*, trans. W. Cerf and H. S. Harris (Albany: SUNY Press, 1977). Hereafter cited as *F.K.*

thought it was in the name of Beauty, as the highest Idea, that the sensuous beauties of works of art were depreciated. Hegel's speculation is also a contemplation of the highest Idea. To be sure, Hegel overcomes the two-worlds theory of Plato. The Idea in his sense of the word produces and accomplishes itself within nature and history. But in this new context, it is once again, just as in Plato, in the name of an intelligible beauty that the sensuous beauties of works of art are depreciated, which means relegated in the past of the Spirit. At the end of the *Realphilosophie,* which is an early version of the mature system, we find the following: "The self-knowing Spirit knows itself in its peaceful work of art, the existing universe, and the history of the world" (*GW* 8: 286–7). In other words, true Beauty is not to be found in the historical creations of the artists; these creations are not the true works of art. The true work of art is reality itself, both natural and historical, as it is understood and mirrored by the speculative thinker, and by him alone.

*2*

# *The Critique of Judgment* and
# German Philosophy

In the present essay I want to investigate how various interpretations of the *Critique of Judgment* were carried out in their essentials, insofar as these are interpretations conducted by philosophers—not by historians of philosophy. With the suspicion that the organizers of the Kant Symposium[1] originally expected the treatment of a topic in the history of the interpretation of the third *Critique* on the Continent, after considering various philosophers, it dawned on me that there is an overlap between the history of the interpretation of this work on the Continent and the history of philosophy itself—specifically, that of German philosophy, to which I shall limit myself.

In this perspective, I take *interpretation* to mean an approach not so much historical as philosophical, consisting in keeping the texts in the forefront, so as to determine to what influence a given text bears witness, to what evolution with respect to other texts—of the same author or of his contemporaries—this text attests, and what configuration shapes its own internal coherence. What I have in mind, then, is the approach according to which a philosopher—in a debate with his forerunners—is led to consider their texts as having somewhat missed the mark of the meaning they had intended, or somewhat missed a matter they were trying to think, or—beyond the enclosure of the text within its own limits—also as opening up to a *zu-denkendes*, to a matter for thought that is not reducible to the structural configuration of those texts. As a direct consequence, the interpreter—who is a philosopher—is one who, while taking his bearings in a given text, starts thinking anew.

---

1. The Kant Symposium was held in Ottawa in October 1974. This paper was first presented at that symposium, and it was published in French in *Le regard et l'excédent* (The Hague: Nijhoff, 1977).

In the attempt to outline some of the directions for the interpretation of the third *Critique*—inasmuch as these interpretations punctuate some key moments of German philosophy since Kant—I shall try to indicate each time what part of Kant's work the interpreters selected for special attention, and what passages they retained as worthy of consideration and as thought-provoking.

Schiller is undoubtedly the first interpreter of the *Critique of Judgment,* which was published in 1790. As early as 1793, Schiller's correspondence with Körner, known under the title *"Kalliasbriefe"* (because in these letters Schiller discusses the project of a treatise on the beautiful, a project that he subsequently abandoned), bears witness to a very close meditation on Kant's work. This meditation continued to sustain his later major philosophical essays, in particular his *Letters on the Aesthetic Education of Man.*

Schiller approached Kant from the perspective of an itinerary that had already opened up its own vistas. Because of this original thinking itinerary, a central problem emerged that was bound to prescribe what kind of spirit would preside over Schiller's reception of the third *Critique.* One could formulate the terms of the problem as follows: On the one hand, Schiller takes the celebration of what he calls the "One-and-All," the omnipresent ontological power of unification and reconciliation, as the leading theme of his poetic Saying. We find evidence of this in the first poems of the *Gedanken-lyrik,* in their celebration of the gods of Greece, of joy, and of artists. Such celebration comes to the fore with a specific conception of freedom and nature—a conception very different from what one might have expected after Kant's first two *Critiques.* This freedom is not what it is for Kant, man's self-positedness enacted in his negating of immediacy. It is conceived by Schiller as the movement by which man subscribes to the affirmative force of the One-and-All and welcomes what comes to be manifested in its midst. Nature is not what it is for Kant, that is, the causal system objectified by the pure concepts of the understanding, or the antithesis of a properly human activity. It is conceived as a sort of favor granted to man, a gift calling for his approval and with which he feels a deeply rooted kinship. To this conception of freedom and nature, a conception of beauty is linked. Beauty is nothing but the very radiance of omnipresence, understood as the deeply rooted concordance of man and nature.

Beauty springs, therefore, at the juncture of nature and freedom: It is the brilliance of their harmony. Yet, on the other hand, Schiller's thought of the One-and-All is accompanied by the very vivid consciousness of all the actual signs of division and sundering. Only in the case of ancient Greece has the

One-and-All shone forth in this world. In contrast, the world in which Schiller lived revealed to him nothing but antagonisms, not only in collective, but also in individual, life. Collective life is dominated by the arbitrary power of the state and a despotic system of government by which individuals are transformed into the mere cogs and wheels of a mechanism and deprived of the free development of their lives. Individual life—which in effect is not dissociable from the collective one—is split between the egotistical and violent pursuit of sensible interests and the doctrine of moral rigorism, which treats the entire sphere of sensibility antagonistically. Schiller's central problem, therefore, is how to articulate conditions for reconciling this state of sundering—whose manifold forms he brings to the fore and castigates—and the ontology of the One-and-All that so intensely captivated his meditation on the Greek world. In the production of this articulation, neither the theoretical nor the practical part of critical philosophy can serve as a proper aid. Instead, this philosophy, for him, is evidence of the culmination of the age of sundering, in which one side is absorbed in the causal conception of nature and the other in ethical rigorism.

Nothing of the sort applies to the *Critique of Judgment*. Because the question of the articulation between nature and freedom is the backdrop against which Schiller time and again read the third *Critique*, it is clear that he welcomed it as an echo of—and support for—his own questioning. Today's readers—who view this work more as the immediate confirmation of some requirements inherent in critical philosophy than as Kant's specific interest in the beautiful or works of art—cannot fail to be struck by its enthusiastic reception by an author like Schiller, who cannot be suspected of having an interest in the technicalities of philosophical concepts,[2] as he hailed it as the most appropriate expression of the matter itself. There is nothing in the *Critique* that Schiller views as artificially originating in a theoretician, even though he expresses his disagreement with Kant on several points. In it, he suspects no reasoning by analogy, no fallacious symmetry. The reason is that, once the question formulated by Kant in the introduction was stripped of its technical character and limited to the issue of a mediation between the domain of the concept of nature and that of the concept of freedom, it found an immediate echo in Schiller's own quest. In short, the idea that art—whether it comes from nature or from man—joins together nature and freedom, was met with immediate approval by his own thought.

---

2. See the remarks made by Ernst Cassirer on the reception of the *Critique of Judgment* by Schiller and Goethe, in Ernst Cassirer, *Kants Leben und Lehre* (Berlin: B. Cassirer, 1921), 291–92, *Kant's Life and Thought*, trans. James Haden, (New Haven: Yale University Press, 1981).

In such circumstances, in his reading of the *Critique of Judgment* Schiller was bound to take his bearings in indications stressing the existence of a mediation between freedom and nature, and to direct his criticisms against whatever, in his view, was opposed to such a mediation. His reading was also bound to enable him to inscribe the third *Critique* within the perspective of a philosophy of history. For the problem of the mediation between nature and freedom involves the question of the meaning of history, that is, according to Schiller, the possibility of a reconciliation to overcome the modern reign of separation that followed the Greek reign of harmony. The Kantian essays on the philosophy of history predating the *Critique of Judgment* had already inspired his meditation on history and allowed him to write some essays on historical teleology in which he subscribed to the idea that nature receives its final end from the moral destiny of humankind, and that freedom achieves a properly natural purpose while simultaneously transforming such a purpose. Schiller was bound to be all the more eager to read carefully the third *Critique*, as this work integrates the results of Kant's historical essays within its "methodology."

A careful analysis of Schiller's text[3]—which is essentially inspired by the aesthetic part of the third *Critique*—would show that what he considered as the essentials of the work are inscribed within the synthetic perspective I have just outlined. Schiller endorses Kant's criticisms of the empirical and rationalistic approaches exposed in the analytic of the third *Critique:* The beautiful cannot be located in the mere capacity to be affected by sensations, any more than in a perfection whose essence is logical in origin. The reason is that Schiller wants to unite sensibility and spirit. It is within the same synthetic perspective that Schiller entirely subscribes to the notion of "favor" as devoid of interest and unconstrained satisfaction. "Let it be as it so wills to be," he appeals in defense of the beautiful object in a letter that we are justified in considering as a sort of commentary on the "First Moment of the Analytic of the Beautiful"; then he adds, "As soon as we judge [the beautiful object] aesthetically, we only want to know whether it is what it is by virtue of itself alone."[4] It is also in the same perspective that Schiller subscribes to the theme of universality present in the "Second Moment of the Analytic." Kant's thesis—according to which the judgment of taste postulates the universal communicability of the sensations and enlarges their very particularity toward the universal—allows the *Letters on the Aesthetic Education of Man* to find the juncture between the aesthetic problematic and the political prob-

---

3. In particular the "Kalliasbriefe" and *On the Aesthetic Education of Man*.

4. Friedrich Schiller, *On the Aesthetic Education of Man* trans. E. Wilkinson and L. Willoughby (Oxford: Oxford University Press, 1967), letter 3.

lematic: This juncture is the idea that the advent of the ideal state—which preserves the very particularity of man, his sensations, his feelings and emotions, by universalizing his behavior to the highest degree[5]—presupposes the cultivation of the aesthetic disposition of the individual, because "Beauty alone . . . we enjoy at once as individual and as genus."[6] It is also in the same spirit that the transcendental questioning into the essence of man leads Schiller, in the *Letters on the Aesthetic Education of Man,* to espouse Kant's notion of "free play" as a mediation characterizing the originary conjunction of spontaneity and receptivity at the very core of man. It is the same juncture that Schiller considers in his reappropriation of the formula about art in section 45 of the *Critique:* "Nature is beautiful if it also looks like art; and art can be called fine *(schön)* art only if we are conscious that it is art while it looks to us like nature."[7] This formula, indeed, shows with total clarity that, in Schiller's view, there is an affinity between human activity and the very movement of nature. Finally, it is for the same reason that he transcribes Kant's doctrine of the beautiful as the symbol of morality into his own formula: The beautiful is the "analogon" of practical reason.

But it is also for the same reasons that he recuses, in spite of many hesitations, the strict formalism to which Kant's doctrine of *pulchritudo vaga* seems to be confined. In Schiller's view, the distinction between free beauty and adherent beauty has no value other than methodological, it aims at delineating the domain of the logical from the aesthetic, and should not be used to relegate the beautiful to pure subjectivity—a relegation that deprives the beautiful of a charge of nature and is based only on the arbitrary decision to reduce nature beforehand to the status of an object of the understanding.

If we now consider German idealism, it is clear that in it a synthetic mode of apprehension comparable to the one regulating Schiller's relation to Kant also ruled over the reception and the interpretation of the *Critique of Judgment.* It was the case for Schelling and Hegel. Not so for Fichte, since the Fichtean attempt to find a unity of theoretical and practical reason led him to put greater and more foundational value on the practical—at least in the 1794 *Wissenschaftslehre,* which does not mention the third *Critique.* Furthermore, against the spirit of Fichte's enquiry, which led him to unconditionally

---

5. Ibid., letter 27.
6. Ibid., p. 217.
7. Immanuel Kant, *Critique of Judgment,* trans. Werner S. Pluhar (Indianapolis: Hackett Publishing Company, 1987), 174. Hereafter cited as *CJ.*

subordinate the sensible to reason, Schiller stated in a note to the *Letters on the Aesthetic Education* that "such a way of thinking is, it is true, wholly alien to the spirit of the Kantian system, but it may very well be found in the letter of it."[8]

Things are very different concerning Schelling. At the outset, his own debate with Kant and Fichte, on the one hand, and with Spinoza, on the other, is conducted under the sign of the search for absolute unity. He wrote in the *Letters on Dogmatism and Critical Philosophy*, which constitute the first step of his itinerary, "Whoever has reflected on idealism and realism, has seen by himself that both must essentially reside in the vicinity of the absolute, but that in the absolute they have to be united and cease to exist as contradictory systems."[9] According to this view, Kant's critical edifice appeared to him as both oriented toward such a focal point of absolute convergence and as precluding its actual access. To articulate this convergence and to go beyond the limitation with which critical philosophy is affected is the task that Schelling proposes to himself. Everything happens as if taking up such a task had been, according to Schelling, sketched out in the *Critique of Judgment*, concerning both the problems raised in it and the contents thematized.

Consider the introduction to the *System of Transcendental Idealism*. It is obvious that in it Schelling formulates the problems that prescribe the divisions of transcendental philosophy according to a mediating articulation similar to the one delineated by Kant in the introduction to the *Critique of Judgment*, where this *Critique* is presented as a means of uniting within a totality the two parts of philosophy. According to Schelling, the first problem consists in explaining "how representations can absolutely agree with existing objects that are quite independent from them"; this problem gives rise to the first division of transcendental philosophy, namely, theoretical philosophy, which investigates "the possibility of experience."[10] The second problem consists in explaining how objects can be modified by representations that emerge freely in us. This problem is that of free agency, which sets into motion the whole of practical philosophy. These two problems, however, bring about a contradiction: "How can we think both of [re]presentations as conforming to objects and objects as conforming to [re]presentations?"[11]

---

8. *On the Aesthetic Education*, p. 187.

9. Friedrich Schelling, Philosophische Briefe über *'Dogmatismus und Kritizismus'* (1795), in Schelling F. W. J., *Werke*, I, ed. K. F. A. Schelling, Esslingen, 1856, 9 letter.

10. Friedrich Schelling, *The System of Transcendental Idealism* trans. Peter L. Heath (University Press of Virginia, 1978), 11.

11. Ibid., 12.

Such is the principal problem encountered by transcendental philosophy: It requires the introduction of a superior philosophy that could be a middle term between the theoretical and the practical parts of philosophy. This superior problematic now gives rise to a third division of philosophy, which is teleology, or the philosophy of the ends of nature. Teleology resolves the contradiction between theoretical philosophy and practical philosophy by establishing that the activity producing the world is primordially identical to the one manifesting itself in the will, and that the only distinction between the two is that the first one produces beings at the same time consciously and unconsciously, whereas the second produces only consciously, which means that nature in its totality and in its singular products is adjusted both to ends and blind mechanism. But the demonstration of this "established harmony" between will and nature would remain incomplete if it had not been reciprocally established that the activity manifesting itself in the will is primordially identical to the one producing the world of objects—more precisely, if the identity of both activities were not manifested in the very principle of transcendental philosophy, in the ego. It pertains to the philosophy of art to show that the aesthetic activity that produces works of art is, in consciousness itself, an activity that is both conscious and unconscious. The philosophy of art is conceived as the organ of transcendental philosophy because the aesthetic intuition—understood in terms of the identification of the subjective and of the objective, and invested in objects—is as such offered to consciousness. Upon such an identification, philosophy, which is an activity reserved to a few individuals, reflects internally.

It is now becoming clearer that the configuration of *The System of Transcendental Idealism* is a reproduction of the blueprint of critical philosophy as it was described in the introduction to the *Critique of Judgment*. Its foremost problem remains, as for Kant, to find a middle term between the practical and the theoretical, and the solution to this problem involves aesthetics as much as teleology. Such a similarity in the problematics and in the access to solutions is enough to allow us to view *The System of Transcendental Idealism* as an interpretation of the *Critique of Judgment*. However, Schelling's aimed-at Absolute—which sustains his thought as he moves on after taking its bearings in the third *Critique*—turns out to interfere with key notions connected with the topic of finitude in Kant's text, and brushes this topic aside entirely. The result is the modification of all the contents under consideration by Schelling.

Whereas Kant states that the "immense gulf" between the domain of the concept of nature and that of the concept of freedom requires "a basis uniting the supra-sensible, which underlies nature, and the suprasensible which the concept of freedom contains practically," yet in such a way that "the concept of this basis does not reach cognition of it either theoretically or practically" (*CJ*, 14–15), in contrast Schelling views the basis of this unity as *pre-established harmony* that is perfectly demonstrable. Consequently, whereas in Kant's notion of teleology, the concept of natural end only aimed at a presumed unity, Schelling's teleology intends to demonstrate the necessity that nature appear as a product in keeping with an end, and deduces this necessity from the harmony necessary between the conscious and the unconscious activities. The same shift from the modality of possibility to that of necessity also characterizes the aesthetic theses that Schelling takes from Kant. Let us consider the treatment of pleasure. When Kant describes pleasure in the "Analytic of Aesthetic Judgment" as a pleasure of reflection resulting from the free play and indeterminate agreement of the imagination and the understanding, and when in the "Dialectic of Aesthetic Judgment" he correlates this pleasure to a suprasensible unity of all the faculties, he operates within the framework of the merely probably genesis of an unknown and enigmatic origin. In contrast, Schelling immediately dilates Kant's notion of reflection to enable it to grasp the identity of the objective and of the subjective: Such is the meaning of the aesthetic intuition, which is said to provide understanding of the self within a product.

Let us now consider the treatment of genius. Following an inspiration from Kant, Schelling makes genius the center of his philosophy of art. In a genius, Kant says, nature gives its rule to art, and it is only in the production of the fine arts that one can speak of a genius. To which Schelling echoes: "The product [of art] . . . is none other than the product of genius" (*STI*, 222). Like Kant, he locates the activity of the genius at the confluence of what is commonly called "art"—involving what "is exercised by consciousness, thought and reflection, and can be taught and learnt" (*STI*, 223) —and of an activity "that is without consciousness, that immediately gets involved with art without having to be learned."[12] In the same way as Kant is let in the enquiry into the faculties constituting genius to consider *Geist* as the faculty of producing, in the medium of imagination, aesthetic Ideas to which no concept is adequate, Schelling endows the artistic genius with the capacity of exposing spontaneously "an infinity which no finite understanding is capable of developing to the full" (*STI*, 225). But whereas the Kantian doctrine of the genius and of aesthetic Ideas is inscribed within the limits of finitude (a characteristic further stressed by its connection to the theme of symbolism, which undeniably is evidence of the gap between the finite and the infinite), such limits are totally disregarded by Schelling. According to *The System of Tran-*

---

12. Translation modified.

*scendental Idealism,* art, as the product of genius, "suppresses within a finite product an infinite opposition," that of the unconscious activity and of conscious activity, and thus provides the "revelation" of the wonder of absolute identity, by objectifying an "intellectual intuition"(*STI,* 232ff.), thus in complete opposition to Kant's whole effort to show that intellectual intuition is precisely not permitted to our finite condition. In the same way, finally, Schelling was inspired by Kant's historical teleology, but he translated Kant's conjectural language all at once into the demonstrative language of absolute deduction: "History, as a whole is a progressive, gradually self-disclosing revelation of the absolute" (*STI,* 211).

When Schelling transposed the *Critique of Judgment* into the registry of absolute speculation, he dispensed with an explicit debate with Kant and with the task of delineating in Kant's text what for him validated absolute identity and what prevented such a validation.

Such a task was taken up by Hegel. He addressed it in *Glauben und Wissen* (Faith and Knowledge), an essay published in the *Critical Journal of Philosophy* under the joint responsibility of Schelling and himself and amounting—to the same extent as the essay on the *Differenz*—to a justification and defense of Schelling's philosophy vis-à-vis the philosophies of the time. Because this essay was published in a journal whose papers supposedly shared a common central perspective, it goes without saying that the interpretation given by Hegel to the third *Critique* is ruled by a synthetic mode of apprehension very close to the one dominating Schelling's approach at the time. However, this it not tantamount to saying that in the essay Hegel manifested himself as a mere disciple of Schelling. In connection with his own original thinking itinerary, Hegel found that the publications of his friend Schelling combined a successful articulation and implementation of the task to which his own path led him to aspire.

In this itinerary, his debate with Kant played a major role, especially his constant rejection of the dualism inherent in the *Critique of Practical Reason.* We know that for a long time Hegel contrasted this dualism—of which he had detected analogues, or different modalities, in the Judaic religion and in Christianity—with the Greek *ēthos* of reconciliation and, thenceforth, moved to a notion of life conceived as a totality that, in order to reconcile itself with itself, sunders itself inside opposites such as the one and the many, the finite and the infinite, the subjective and the objective. With the topic of life, he associated beauty as the manifestation of this reconciliation. Thus the same synthetic modality that we noted was involved in the reception by Schiller and Schelling of the *Critique of Judgment* also seems to be deeply rooted in Hegel's itinerary. The critical exposé of Kant's philosophy in *Glauben und Wissen* credits the third *Critique* with being "the most interesting point in the

Kantian system'' because at such point ''a region is recognized that is a middle between the empirical manifold [a term that for Hegel covers ''necessity, leanings, tendencies, heteronony, nature, etc.''] and the absolute abstract unity [a term that covers ''freedom, practical reason, the law, the practical idea, etc.''].''[13] But in Hegel's view, such a recognition was equally a failure to recognize [*méconnaissance*]. Even though Kant discovered the middle term between the concepts of nature and freedom (i.e., the region of the ''identity which is the true and unique reason'' in Hegel's terms), he refused, says Hegel, to grant this identity ''any reality for knowledge'' and related it to a strictly finite and subjective capacity: reflective judgment. Hegel, therefore, views the *Critique of Judgment* as a text in which ''reason,'' that is, the intellectual intuition of the absolute identity, is present everywhere—in aesthetics, as conscious intuition, and in teleology, as unconscious intuition— yet in which this identity is expressed nowhere, because of the fixation on the phenomenal and the finite. For Hegel it is as if Kant precluded a knowledge of what he had nevertheless acknowledged. On the one hand, Kant described as ''intelligible'' the substratum of nature in us and outside of us, and therefore acknowledged it as something rational. It is in the attempt to harmonize reason with itself that Kant discovered this substratum. He provided a concept of the substratum by characterizing it as the identity of the concepts of nature and freedom. Moreover, Kant presented it as a ''solution'' to the antinomy of taste. But he spoke as though this intelligible were not so, as if this concept were not one, as if this solution did not solve anything. The reason is that, on the other hand, he had erected the opposition of the suprasensible and of the sensible into a principle. Having established thus the suprasensible as the principle of aesthetics and recognized ipso facto that beauty turns the Idea into an object of intuition, he then withdrew such an Idea from the realm of consciousness, ''and the Beautiful becomes something which is only related to the human capacity of knowing and to the harmonious play of its various faculties'' (*FK*, 88 modified).

Likewise concerning teleology, Hegel credits Kant with expressing, in section 77 of the *Critique of Judgment,* the idea of reason in terms of an ''intuitive understanding'' or of an archetype in which possibility and reality, concept and intuition, are identical, and toward which we necessarily orient ourselves. That amounts, for Hegel, to asserting the necessity of the Idea. Yet Kant stressed that we should no more than presume the notion of this intellectual intuition, because its substratum corresponds to no phenomenon. This

---

13. G. W. F. Hegel, *Faith and Knowledge* trans. W. Cerf and H. S. Harris (Albany: SUNY Press, 1977) 85. Hereafter cited as *FK*.

position amounts for Hegel to a contradictory claim regarding the problematic character of a matter whose necessity is nevertheless stated. "Kant," writes Hegel, "is considering two things: the idea of a reason for which possibility and reality are absolutely identical, and the idea of its phenomenal manifestation . . . in which possibility and reality are separated; he finds both thoughts in his intellectual experience, but, when he had to choose between the two, he was led to discount the task of thinking the rational, of thinking an intuitive spontaneity, and he leaned entirely on the side of the phenomenon" (*FK*, 89–90 modified). Thus according to Hegel, Kant was a thinker conscious both of the opposition and of the necessity of its sublation in a middle term, a thinker who qualified as subjective and finite the knowledge in which concept and intuition stand apart, only because he was also able to transcend this subjectivity and this finitude by apprehending a medium uniting both concept and intuition. In a nutshell, Kant was the paradoxical speculative thinker for whom "the supreme Idea is corrupted in the most conscious fashion" (*FK*, 92 modified).

Even after Hegel parted paths with Schelling, he continued to maintain the same interpretation of the third *Critique,* as evidenced some fifteen years later by the *Lectures on Aesthetics* and the *Lectures on the History of Philosophy.* In perfect continuity with *Glauben und Wissen* and the entire critique of the metaphysics of reflection or of subjectivity developed in this work, the *Lectures on Aesthetics* stress that Kant, "although he suggests in the abstract a solution of the contradiction of concept and reality, universality and particularity, understanding and sense, and, thereby, points to the Idea, yet, on the other hand, . . . makes the solution and reconciliation itself a purely *subjective* one, not one which is true and actual in its nature and on its own merits."[14] In the same way, the *History of Philosophy* states on the same subject: "Although Kant expresses Unity, he raises once more the subjective aspect above the concept. It is the permanent contradiction of Kantian philosophy."[15]

From Schiller to Schelling and Hegel, the theme of unification thus provides a thread for the interpretation of the third *Critique* and even allows to validate that *Critique* as a whole. In the last analysis, the theme of unification implies that of meaning: The world in which the action of men is inscribed and to which their knowledge is related is a meaningful world. In one of his reflections, Kant writes: "Die schöne Dinge zeigen an, dass der Mensch in

14. G. W. F. Hegel, *On Art, Religion, Philosophy,* ed. J. Glenn Gray (New York: Harper & Row, 1970), 89.

15. G. W. F. Hegel, *Vorlesungen über die Geschichte der Philosophie,* ed. Michelet, in idem, *Werke* (Berlin, 1833), vol. 15: 605–6.

die Welt passe'' (Beautiful things show that man is in agreement with the world).[16] Meaning is the very agreement that takes place not only between man and nature, but between man and himself, between man and the community of men. The various themes of the third *Critique* (beauty in nature, the fine arts, nature in its particularity and its totality, organism, history, ethical destiny, etc.) are all gathered together with a view to such an agreement. Such is the way in which Schiller understood the *Critique of Judgment;* Schelling and Hegel understood it in the same way and only differed from Schiller because, in spite of his speculative aspirations, he continued, in agreement with Kant, to connect meaning and finitude.

Very different was the spirit in which the *Critique of Judgment* was received in Germany after the collapse of German idealism. The reason is not that the fate of Kant's philosophy was so closely connected with idealism as to undergo the same demise. The proof can be found in the attitude of Schopenhauer, whose success coincided with the fading of the spiritual constellation within which German idealism was inscribed. In stark contrast to words of abuse, such as when he charges this movement of being ''empty talk,'' ''charlatanism,'' and ''extravagance,'' Schopenhauer showers high praise on Kant's philosophy, ''the only one with which a thorough acquaintance is positively assumed in what is to be here discovered.''[17]

Yet the positive modality of his welcoming reception is antithetical to the one expressed by the thinkers previously examined. Although Schopenhauer says that he intends to limit himself exclusively to ''reflection,'' and charges the intellectual intuition of the Post-Kantians with adorning vacuity with a rich name only because they strayed away from it, his professed return to Kant is for us far from compelling, because from Kant's work Schopenhauer rejects the entire problematic of the agreement and of meaning in which the Post-Kantians had detected the first sign of their own aspirations. Hence what Schopenhauer accepts in Kant, and what inspires him, is an opposition, a dualism, a cleavage. Whereas Schelling and Hegel credited Kant with acknowledging that unity is fundamental, but charged him with not taking this unity far enough because of his opposition between the intelligible-for-us and the intelligible-in-itself, Schopenhauer did the opposite, and credited Kant with having dissociated the phenomenon from the thing-in-itself, but charged him

---

16. Reflection 1820a in ''Reflexionen zur Anthropologie.'' *Kants Gesammelte Schriften*, Prussian Academy Edition (Berlin: Reimer de Gruyter, 1910–66), vol. 15.

17. Arthur Schopenhauer, *The World as Will and Representation*, trans. E. F. J. Payne (New York: Dover, 1969), 1:xv. Hereafter cited as *WWR*.

with maintaining a bridge from the latter to the former by calling the thing-in-itself "intelligible," in spite of its being inaccessible to us.

After translation into Schopenhauer's own horizon of thought, Kant's opposition between phenomenon and thing-in-itself resulted in the distinction between a superficial level of meaning and a deep level of absurdity: On the one hand, we have the world as representation, subjected to the formal conditions of time, space, and causality, whose general expression is given in the principle of sufficient reason; on the other hand, a profound *non-sense,* the world as will. Indeed, everything that emanates from the will, everything that becomes objective—and the world in the variety of its phenomena represents such an objectification—is immediately subjected to the principle of reason. But the will itself is not, it is groundless (*grundlos*). "In fact, the absence of all aims, of all limits, belongs to the essential nature of the will in itself which is an endless striving" (*WWR,* 164). Such a striving aims at nothing but its own perpetuation. Penetrating into the nature of the will amounts to acknowledging that at the bottom of things is blind and restless force, insatiable appetite, colossal repetition, *perpetuum mobile.*

This view, therefore, amounts to discrediting as a mirage every notion of agreement, harmony, final destination, meaning of history, peace, human community. Every natural or historical teleology is nothing but a fraud in which a blind will to live engulfs us after we have succumbed to the cycles of an ever-devouring repetition. We know that Schopenhauer articulated a specific type of soteriology out of the cleavage between meaning (stemming from the world of appearances) and non–sense (from the depths of reality). We know that, in it, art plays the role of tranquilizer of the will; we know that philosophy, by tearing the veil of Maya, shows us the way to obtaining respite from the absurd individuation process; we know that asceticism finally puts an end to the will and tears it away from universal evil.

Schopenhauer maintained that Kant provided him with the prelude to these views because of the Kantian cleavage between phenomenon and thing-in-itself, a cleavage that Schopenhauer turned into the only teaching of Kantianism (*WWR,* 417ff.). When considering the *Critique of Pure Reason,* Schopenhauer restricted its validity to the scientific demonstration of an intuition identical to the one that Plato and the Upanishads once had: Space and time, along with everything contained and organized in them according to the law of causality, must be viewed as a dream without consistency. Except for such astounding praise, Kant's work contained nothing but flaws: Scholastic language, Gothic taste for complicated symmetry, excessive use of analogies, missed appreciation for the intuitive world, unjustified division of reason between the theoretical and the practical, and unwarranted introduction of the thing-in-itself by means of causal inference.

In the end, Schopenhauer found only the "Transcendental Aesthetic" as worthy of commendation: He rejected both the "Transcendental Analytic" (because the question of the a priori synthetic judgment was based on the dissociation, which he did not accept, between intuition and thought), and the "Transcendental Dialectic" (because he denied that the essence of reason aims at the unconditional). Regarding the "Transcendental Dialectic," he commended only the distinction between the empirical and the intelligible character (while overlooking the problematic of the antinomies, which he found specious), a distinction that he translated into the cleavage between will and representation.

When considering the *Critique of Practical Reason,* he viewed the very notion of practical reason only in terms of a ridiculous taste for symmetry; he saw in the notion of unconditional duty a *contradictio in adjecto,* and in the doctrine of the supreme good a contradictory conciliation between virtue and happiness. Here again a cleavage was brought to the fore by Schopenhauer: Virtue has to do not with satisfying the will, but with renouncing it, and he credited Kant with freeing "ethics from all principles of the world of experience . . . , and [showing] quite properly that the kingdom of virtue is not of this world" (*WWR,* 523–24).

In these conditions, we should not expect Schopenhauer to praise the *Critique of Judgment* as Kant's effort to bring together what he had previously separated. Because for Schopenhauer every finality is but a phenomenal illusion that turns us into the playtoys of the objectification of the will, and because art, in contrast, frees us from such a deception, how could he see in the connection of teleological judgment to aesthetic judgment anything but a "queer combination" (*WWR,* 531)? If, according to Schopenhauer, there was a thread leading to the third *Critique,* it was contained in one word: *subjectivity.* In aesthetics and the philosophy of art, Kant is credited with opening an "entirely subjective direction" to the investigation by examining "seriously and profoundly the stimulation itself in consequence of which we call the object giving rise to it 'beautiful' " (*WWR,* 530). But he did no more than open the way.

We know that Schopenhauer was the one who followed it and that, while pretending to draw inspiration from Kant, he hardly accepted anything except the first two moments of the "Analytic of the Beautiful," In the process, he transposed the notion of a judgment "devoid of interest" within the context of his own cleavage between representation and will by defining such judgment as suspension of willing; likewise, he redefined the concept of pleasure without concept as representation independent of the principle of reason. As for teleology, it is summarized by Schopenhauer as follows: The necessity to conceive organized bodies as subjected to the principle of finality is "of subjective origin'' (*WWR*, 532). This proposition, whose true meaning is the cleavage between the veil of Maya and the blind force of the will, amounts to discarding another proposition, central in the Kantian perspective: ''The concept of freedom must realize in the sensible world the end imposed by its law.''

Can one speak of interpretation concerning an annexation so disrespectful of the text that it goes as far as pretending that the judgment of taste is nothing but ''the statement of others'' (*WWR*, 531), as if Kant had never written: ''I call beautiful the rose that I contemplate''? Yet Schopenhauer's successors thought his to be an interpretation in its own right. Everything happens as if the movement of return to Kant that began in the second half of the nineteenth century under the title ''Neo-Kantianism'' aligned itself with the mode of disjunctive apprehension characteristic of Schopenhauer's attitude toward Kant. Cassirer captured the spirit of the Neo-Kantian *Kant-Literatur* of the works devoted to the *Critique of Judgment* in his assessment:

> It has become a standard and universally admitted view to consider that analogy . . . provided Kant with the real thread leading to the discovery of the problems of the *Critique of Judgment.* They share the opinion that Kantian aesthetics was not born out of an immediate interest for the problems of art and artistic creation, and that it is not by virtue of a necessity founded in the matters themselves that this aesthetics came together in the same work with the problem of the finality of nature. In both cases, according to their view, what was really at work was rather Kant's predilection for the cleverness and artifice required in the external articulation of the system, for divisions and subdivisions of concepts, and for the coordination of the faculties of knowledge into separate 'families.'[18]

Such a view, which became established and universal in Neo-Kantianism, was gradually formulated for the first time in the appendix to the second volume of *The World as Will and Representation.* To be sure, it could be that some common aversion to German idealism played a decisive role in the alignment of the Neo-Kantians with Schopenhauer's position. Yet the Neo-Kantians felt the most profound aversion to Schopenhauer, as witnessed in the passionate polemic started against him by Hermann Cohen in *Kants*

---

18. Cassirer, *Kants Leben und Lehre,* (Berlin: B. Cassirer, 1918), 290–91.

*Begründung der Ethik.* To the question of what motivates this similarity of views concerning the *Critique of Judgment,* a common denominator between Schopenhauer and the Neo-Kantians can arguably be invoked concerning not so much what they rejected, as what they asserted: namely, what Schopenhauer used to praise under the phrase *subjective direction.*

In the concept of the subjective, however, everything initially seems to separate the Neo-Kantians and Schopenhauer. For him, subjectivity is representation, as an illusion of solidness against the abyssal backdrop of blind flux; for the Neo-Kantians, it is experience as it is elaborated with a solid content in the constitution of the science of nature. For the Neo-Kantians, drawing one's inspiration from Kant meant first of all, in contrast to Schopenhauer, elaborating a theory of science that, on the one hand, would show (in contradistinction to German idealism, scornfully labeled "romanticism") that reason evaporates into clouds of mysticism when no longer guided by experience (and experiment) in the scientific sense; and that, on the other hand, would take a stance against the positivism that immediately followed in the wake of German idealism, by showing that reason extends beyond the association of sensations and entails a prioris that cannot be produced by means of an empirical genesis. For them, accordingly, Kant had raised the issue of the philosophical foundation of science, and not at all the dissolution of its bases into the chaos of the will. But their insistence on the theory of science did not prevent the Neo-Kantians from probing into the totality of Kant's philosophy and submitting it to an exegesis—with the unquestionable merit of calling attention to the texts themselves and of analyzing them carefully. Nevertheless, concerning the interpretation of the *Critique of Judgment,* one can wonder whether the privileging of experience and the focus on relationship to beings did not bring about a new cleavage, which might indicate a similarity between Neo-Kantianism and Schopenhauer's stance with respect to the third *Critique.* This cleavage is the one obtaining between consciousness of the object and self-consciousness, or lived experience; such a cleavage is bound to overlook the problematic of the agreement of man and the world in order to focus on the problem of the unity of consciousness. As a result, the properly aesthetic (i.e., subjective) character of Kant's approach is stressed. Such was the view of Hermann Cohen, who stood as the apologist of Kant's aesthetics and for whom the problematic of the unity displayed in the *Critique of Judgment* essentially concerned self-consciousness. According to Cohen, the aesthetic consciousness (what he called the "aesthetic ego") is a feeling that is the highest form of self-consciousness because it enables us to unite the theoretical and the practical ego within the peaceful situation of a pure contemplation that overcomes the objectifying work of the theoretical attitude and the struggle inherent in the practical one. His view amounts to saying that Kant's problematic of unity concerns only the unity of the ego and the problems of "*Ichheit*"—as Cohen called them—and that nowhere is the question of the agreement of man and the world investigated. Because of its quietism, because of the theme of a joint overcoming of objectification and of struggle, because of its insistence on feeling, this interpretation, which would not acknowledge any proximity to Schopenhauer, is in fact close to the latter.

If we now turn to the contemporary era, we cannot fail to observe that Heidegger is without question the philosopher who reinvigorated the debate with Kant in an original fashion. To be sure, this debate, which is new in style, owes something to the debate conducted by Husserl with the Neo-Kantians. Husserl's doctrine of intentionality had already shattered the narrow limits within which Neo-Kantianism confined experience—conceived of as scientific experience—and had restored the object to its own consistency, previously reduced by Neo-Kantianism to a sensible multiplicity organized by the categories of the understanding. However, Husserl's constant insistence on the privileged role of the *Erkenntnislehre*, on the idea itself of philosophy as a rigorous science, and most importantly his universal and constant reference to the *cogito*, imposed a sort of continuity with Neo-Kantianism in the midst of Husserlian phenomenology. In contrast, Heidegger shatters the problematic of consciousness by insistently addressing a question that was not even raised in phenomenology: the question of Being. Conceived as the attempt to answer this question, the fundamental ontology of *Sein und Zeit* stands on a terrain quite different from that of consciousness—the terrain called *Dasein*, whose mode of being is less the immanence of self-presence than the ecstatic relation to the world and time. Man holds himself out within an ec-static relation to Being while Being is in excess of all beings and Being in return is destined to man and attunes man to himself. Finitude defines this double movement, this originary reciprocity of receptivity and spontaneity. Beyond the "Analytic of *Dasein*," the question of Being led to the deconstruction of the history of metaphysics, which shows the growing obliteration of Being and of finitude. Along both directions of the Heideggerian approach, the debate with Kant played a central role, because Kant is viewed as the first philosopher who turned metaphysics into a problem, and who connected such a problem to that of finitude.

In the framework of Heidegger's retrieval and questioning, which attempts to think what had remained unthought in metaphysics, Kant is par excellence the philosopher of the in-between, of the interval of which Heidegger says in *What Is a Thing?* that it is "an anticipation [that] reaches beyond the thing and similarly back behind us."[19] This in-between is what we can also call the ambiguous relation of the ontical and the ontological, of truth and nontruth, of Being and nothingness, and what the lecture course *Kant and the Problem of Metaphysics*[20] unravels regarding the first edition of the *Critique of Pure Reason*, specifically the doctrine of transcendental imagination as originary time. But Heidegger in that text says that after glimpsing this foundation, Kant took a step backward and attempted to save the supremacy of reason, with the result that, at the same time as he got closer to a new mode of thinking, he also remained prisoner of the modern metaphysics of subjectivity.

If we compare Heidegger's relation to Kant to the ones we considered above, we can say that its mode of reception is ruled not by any cleavage, but, on the contrary, by the theme of the fundamental mutual belonging of man and the world, of spontaneity and receptivity. Formally, this stance is much more in keeping with Schiller, Schelling, and Hegel than with Schopenhauer and the Neo-Kantians. Such an assessment is corroborated by the only text in which Heidegger expressly analyzes the *Critique of Judgment*, namely, the section "Kant's Doctrine of the Beautiful [and] Its Misinterpretation by Schopenhauer and Nietzsche" in his book on Nietzsche.

> Schopenhauer plays the leading role in the preparation and genesis of that misunderstanding of Kantian aesthetics to which Nietzsche too fell prey and which is still quite common today. One may say that Kant's *Critique of Judgment* . . . has been influential up to now only on the basis of misunderstandings, a happenstance of no little significance for the history of philosophy. Schiller alone grasped some essentials in relation to Kant's doctrine of the Beautiful."[21]

Concerning what is essential, Heidegger is somewhat terse, but what he says clears up any possible ambiguity. Taking his cue from the first moment of the "Analytic of the Beautiful," Heidegger shows that the notion of an absence of interest is introduced by Kant only as a preparatory step in the effort to delineate the comportment toward the beautiful from an attitude that would consider the being then encountered in light of something other than

---

19. Martin Heidegger, *What is a Thing?*, trans. W. B. Barton, Jr., and Vera Deutsch (New York: University Press of America, 1967), 243.

20. Martin Heidegger, *Kant and the Problem of Metaphysics*, trans. R. Taft (Bloomington: Indiana University Press, 1990).

21. Martin Heidegger, *Nietzsche*, Vol. 1, trans. David Farrell Krell (New York: Harper & Row, 1979), 107–8. Hereafter cited as *N*.

this comportment: in terms of a definition, a purpose, or a pleasure. But instead of settling with the notion that this absence of interest entails—as thought by Schopenhauer and the Neo-Kantians, as well as Nietzsche—the quietist attitude of indifference toward the thing, Heidegger argues that this "absence of interest" is the negative prelude, or counterpart, to a real and positive relation to the thing, a relation that Kant calls "favor," or "the only free liking" (*CJ*, 52). This freedom consists, says Heidegger, in contemplating the thing for its own sake in its pure appearing. According to Heidegger, it is such an appearing that is worthy of being favored, since it constitutes the essence of the beautiful, in the Kantian sense. In these conditions, the "pleasure of reflection" does not mean the internal harmony of self-consciousness, but instead—according to a phrase of Nietzsche's that Heidegger applies to Kant—"the thrill that comes of being in our world" (*N*, 112). Heidegger adds that "Kant analyzes the essence of the 'pleasure of reflection' as the basic comportment toward the beautiful, in *The Critique of Judgment*, Sections 57 and 59" (*N*, 112). And later on, he says that this interpretation "propels us toward a basic state of human being in which man for the first time arrives at the well-grounded fullness of his essence" (*N*, 113). This passage is somewhat elliptical but, if one admits that the debate Heidegger conducts with Kant elsewhere reveals in his meditation on the essence of man an approach to finite transcendence as the originary reciprocity of spontaneity and receptivity, we may well think that the "unknown unity" evoked by Kant in the "Dialectic of the Aesthetic Judgment" (sections 57 and 59) is conceived of as the root of finitude, whereas Schelling and Hegel conceived of it as absolute identity. It is in this sense that Heidegger suggests that Schiller is the only one who understood Kant.

We have now returned to the point of departure of our exploration. Hermann Cohen wrote in his *Kantian Theory of Experience*[22] that "one cannot pass judgment on Kant without, sentence after sentence, betraying what type of a world one carries in one's head." Formally, the worlds carried in the heads of the interpreters we examined can be assigned to the two categories referred to under the terms *cleavage* and *agreement,* the former designating a mode of disjunctive reception, the latter a mode of synthetic reception. Still, it must be pointed out that the interpreter could reveal his world only because the matter under interpretation called upon him to enact this very form of unveiling. In other words, our exploration now invites us to think of the *Critique of Judgment* in terms of a textual space animated by tensions arising from various poles. Although it is a text fraught with the technicality

---

22. Hermann Cohen, *Kants Theorie der Erfahrung* (Berlin, 1871), p. V.

of some scholastic language, it is also a text that simply describes phenomena. Although it is a text that founds aesthetics as the approach to the beautiful in terms of subjectivity and self-consciousness, it is also a text that splinters the subjectivity of aesthetics by locating the beautiful and art at the juncture of freedom and nature. Although it is a text that lends itself to the meditation on finitude in the Heideggerian sense, it is also a text in which we can decipher—perhaps concerning the same issues—something that might well stand as the first document of absolute metaphysics in the sense of German idealism.

To the question, then, of whether these tensions are defect or fecundity, there might be no other answer than a new question: Are not tensions inherent in the matters themselves—in the beautiful, in art, in life?

# 3

# Speculation and Difference

## On the Status of Art for Speculation in Hegel

The title of this essay lends itself to two possible lines of consideration. In both, a tension exists between two terms: *speculation* and *difference*. The first line will be at the forefront of my investigation and will involve a form of tension internal in speculative thought: This tension rules over the themes articulated by speculative thought and the impetus that sets—and keeps—it in motion in a diffuse way, without allowing the impetus to be reduced to thematic definitions. The second line will only be evoked in the conclusion and deals with the tension between speculative thought itself and what delineates it from the outside.

My topic, therefore, is the speculative concept of art, that is, the status that Hegel gave to art when he made it the first moment or degree of the Absolute Spirit. In order to outline the major features inherent in this status, I will take as my point of departure a text from the Jena period, written around 1805–6. It corresponds to the systematic manuscript edited by Rolf-Peter Horstmann in volume 8 of the *Gesammelte Werke,* bearing the title *Jenaer Systementürfe III.* The last pages of "The Philosophy of Spirit"— which forms part 2 of this manuscript—bear a title written in Hegel's handwriting: "C. Art, Religion, and Science." These pages are the first version of the triadic articulation of the Absolute Spirit later presented in the *Encyclopedia.* They have the advantage of articulating the issues with greater freshness than the subsequent exposition of the definitive system, and yet, compared to it, do not reveal any real immaturity. We are therefore justified in casting a new and close look at this fragment.

---

First published in French in *Hegels Logik der Philosophie,* Veröffentlichungen der Internationalen Hegel-Vereinigung (Stuttgart: Klett-Cotta, 1984), volume 13, *The Hegelian Logic of Philosophy,* Publications of the International Hegel Association.

The special status given to art for the sake of speculation is prescribed by the very nature of the characterization of the Spirit as Absolute. The first sentence of the text clearly indicates that this characterization is speculative:

The absolutely free Spirit, which has taken upon itself its past determinations, from now on produces another world; this world expresses the shape of its own Self [i.e., the Absoluteness of the Spirit]; a world in which its work is accomplished within itself, and in which the Absolutely free Spirit can reach to the intuition of *itself as Self*.[1]

Before investigating the evocation of the previous developments alluded to by the phrase *past determinations,* let us immediately remark that the speculative characterization of the Spirit as Absolute (i.e., its possibility of gaining access to the intuition of itself as a self within a world that it produces and to which it confers the figure of itself) is made in a language that is both precise enough to point out the importance of art for speculation, and broad enough to allow speculative thought to function as an aesthetics—even where and when it is not strictly focused on works of art. Indeed, the very use of words like *production, figure,* and *work* in characterizing the Absolute Spirit in a speculative manner already announces with sufficient clarity the speculative importance of art. These words are the indispensable terms that any philosophical enquiry into the realm of art must involve. This remark—that the given definition is broad enough to have us conclude that speculative thought can function as some sort of generalized aesthetics—will have to be substantiated by the very details of the text. And this substantiation has to originate, first and foremost, in the earlier developments (what lies upstream of this topic in the System, as opposed to what lies downstream of it in the System's subsequent unfolding), namely, in the antecedent developments alluded to in the first sentence previously quoted of the *Jenaer Systementürfe.*

## Upstream of the Speculative Characterization of the Absolute Spirit

These developments are ethical and political in nature. They concern the genesis—one that is abstract first, and concrete afterward—of the state. They show how the community of a people constituted into a state conceived

---

1. G. W. F. Hegel, *Gesammelte Werke* ed. Rolf-Peter Horstmann and Johann Heinrich Trade (Hamburg: Meiuer, 1976), 8:277. Henceforth cited as *GW*.

as a living organism is called forth both by the nature of the faculties that *in abstracto* define human individuals (who are, as such, endowed with intelligence and will) and by the actual[2] operation of the social interaction of these individuals, inasmuch as this interaction depends upon, and aims at, mutual recognition. We cannot here enter into the details of this genesis, which required that Hegel undergo a long debate with the two rival currents of the modern natural right—the empiricist current initiated by Hobbes and the transcendental one initiated by Kant. I shall limit myself to a simple presentation of this genesis.

In its outcome, recognition becomes satisfied in the general will of the people, over and beyond a first level of satisfaction reached in love and family life. The general will of the people stresses its uniqueness in a political constitution more akin to the physiological structure of a living organism than to a charter or a written document. This unique physiological constitution has an established superiority over two lower, and merely social, spheres of recognition: the economy and the legal system. Recognition is fully satisfied in this sphere, first because the corporate body of the general will of the people is in no way external to the individuals, second because the individuals animate it by relinquishing their own immediacy, and finally because the same corporate body of the general will overcomes its possible abstraction by—in a reversal of direction—entrusting the individuals with the task of being parts of its organs. This realm is no longer natural, or immediate, but spiritual, or properly ethical. That defines the reign of ethical life, *Sittlichkeit*.

This short presentation of the political developments preceding the first Hegelian theory of art as the first moment, or degree, of the Spirit does not stand in an external relationship to the speculative definition of art. Not only does Hegel, at the beginning of the presentation of the triad of the Absolute Spirit, explicitly allude to these political developments, but in addition it is clear that the speculative theory of art is foreshadowed by the theory of ethical life just mentioned.

Let us look at this issue more closely. We know that for a long time—specifically during the Tübingen years and until the beginning of the Jena period—Hegel associated the paradigm of *Sittlichkeit* with the image he had fashioned of the Greek city. Even though this image no longer functions as a paradigm in the 1805–6 text, it is still present. In his treatment of the Greek city, Hegel writes:

This is the beautiful and happy freedom of the Greeks for which they were, and still are, so much envied—the people is dissolved in the

2. [*concrète.*]

citizens, and is at the same time the unique individual, the government. The people has no interaction with anybody else but itself; the
overcoming of the singularity of the will is its immediate preserva-
tion. (*GW* 8:262)

And later on, the text contains the following assessment, in direct connection
with our topic:

> In ancient times, the *beautiful* public life was the mores of all,
> it was beauty inasmuch as it was the immediate unity of the univer-
> sal and of the singular, *a work of art* in which no part is sundered
> from the whole, but which is rather the genial unity of the Self that
> knows itself and of its exhibition [*seiner Darstellung*]. (*GW* 8:263)

I indicated earlier that, according to Hegel, the first speculative concept
of art presupposes a specific concept of the ethical and political order. On
closer inspection, this concept is, at least in part, aesthetic. The Greek city—
the site of the "beautiful ethical life"—was itself a "work of art." There is
no need here to investigate the justifications for this aesthetic concept of the
ethical and political. It seems almost certain that it owes its inception much
more to Schiller than to a methodical inventory of the institutions and of the
history of Greek cities, or even to a study of Greek political philosophies.
However, we must understand that the properly speculative theory of art be-
stows a speculative dignity upon art only with respect to the Greek city. That
means that the aesthetic concept of a certain type of ethical and political life,
namely, the life of the ancient city, loses the value of an insuperable paradigm
and model. In other words, if the speculative analysis of the political realm
brings to the fore the necessary overcoming of Greek political life, then, by
the same token, it also calls for the speculative necessity of an overcoming of
Greek art—and even of art as such. And indeed, in the Jena philosophy of the
Spirit, the properly political part (which was, as I suggested, presupposed by
the speculative theory of art) relegates the aesthetic and Greek figure of the
Spirit to the irretrievable past. In opposition to this figure, the modern epoch
is, according to Hegel, ruled by a "higher principle" and by a "deeper
Spirit": The Greek world, he says, was deficient because it lacked "the principle of absolute singularity," that is, the certainty reached by the singular
individual of "immediately holding the Absolute in his individual knowledge." In other words, the defect of the beautiful public life of the Greeks
was that, in the immediate fusion it inaugurated between the singular and the
universal, "the absolute self-knowledge of itself by the individual, the absolute being inside oneself was not present" (*GW* 8:262–63). Let us determine

the import of this increasing self-knowledge with respect to the speculative theory of art. But before taking a step inside the speculative theory, I would like to assess the meaning of the presentation made so far.

Following a first line of consideration, as pointed out earlier, the title of my inquiry focuses on a tension between what is defined thematically by speculative thought, and what—in a diffuse manner—sets it in motion. This tension is suggested, in my opinion, by the fact that the speculative theory of art is supported by a partially aesthetic theory of ethical and political life. If the speculative theory of art presupposes indeed an aesthetic definition of the ethical and political realm, we may be tempted to think that the speculative concept of art cannot be exhausted by, and limited to, what Hegel says of the fine arts and the definition he gives of their spiritual meaning. We may be tempted to think, in other words, that when the speculative theory of art names, defines, and thematizes art in the narrow sense (in the effort to categorize the works, the genres, with their history and spiritual function), it covertly supports its stance by drawing upon a much broader and more diffuse aesthetics, one not limited to the sole products of the fine arts.

How are we to characterize this other aesthetics? I shall outline a few significant features by following some indications given in the excerpts from the *Realphilosophie* quoted earlier. There it is said that the public life of the Greeks was "beautiful" and that their city was a "work of art." What is involved in the notions of beauty and the work of art? In order to answer these questions, it would be necessary to catalogue the particular themes specially treated by Hegel in his early writings at a time when he was undoubtedly fascinated by the Greek paradigm. Such an inventory would determine the topics that were then associated with notions such as beauty and the work of art. It would also itemize their connected notions. In light of the conclusions I arrived at in a previous study,[3] it is my opinion that, up until the *Differenzschrift*, Hegel associated beauty with two topics bound together in close connection: love, and the life of a free people. Hegel, moreover, associated the notion of beauty with those of life, totality, figuration, manifestation, conciliation, and enjoyment.

In what sense does love, qualified as beautiful, provide the link between these various notions? The answer is that love allows two living beings that are originally separated (at the same time from other living beings, and from life in its totality) to overcome their isolation, their separation, and their difference. They thus inaugurate between themselves a relationship not only

---

3. See my essay "The Nostalgia for Greece at the Dawn of Classical Germany," chapter 5 of this collection.

such that the conciliatory and totalizing power of life manifests itself in a relationship (and is produced therein), but also such that life derives enjoyment for itself in this manifestation and production. Saying that love is beautiful amounts to saying that life manifests its unity with itself and is satisfied in the very midst of its state of division among distinct human beings. Love, therefore, is granted special status because an *ontotheology* of life pervades it. Hegel was convinced, then, that every being is alive, that life is the divine principle that founds beings in their totality, and that life—in the midst of the self-differentiating operation resulting in the variety of living beings—divides itself from within, and does so in order to exhibit its unifying power within differentiation: Such are the essential themes of this ontotheology of life. But if love is beautiful because it is pervaded by this ontotheological process of "the union of union and nonunion" (*Systemfragment*, 1800, 348). the same process is what defines beauty in the last analysis. It is no exaggeration to claim that an aesthetic theme presides over this ontotheology of life, because it belongs to the essence of life to produce itself in the midst of living beings that, in spite of their difference and separation from life, are nevertheless its *work*, and through which its power of union over the nonunion is exercised. We find, therefore, two properly aesthetic components: the moment of the *figuration within works* and the moment of *enjoyment*, as characteristics of the ontotheological process of life. More precisely, the properly aesthetic dimension of this ontotheology consists in this, that life produces itself in living works wherein it enjoys itself. The enjoyment taken by life in the work—as the manifestation of its self-sameness—is the specifically aesthetic structure that clearly presides over this ontotheology.

If such is the meaning involved in, and entailed by, the notion of beauty in the writings that, from a distance, prepare the ground for the Hegelian philosophy of the Spirit, we have reason to suspect that—notwithstanding the shift from a philosophy of life to a philosophy of the Spirit—the same notion of beauty is still present in the 1805–6 project of a system in which Hegel characterizes the public life of the Greeks as beautiful. Their life is beautiful because each of the members of the city—by virtue of the fact that he is simultaneously a singular individual and a public individual, or citizen—encounters in the public sphere nothing but *his own work*, and therefore derives an enjoyment from his direct link with the universal.

What can we say of the notion of the work of art used by Hegel to describe the very organization of the Greek city? Although the early writings (from Tübingen, Berne, and Frankfurt) do not, to my knowledge, grant to love (or to the family, where this love finds a representation through its procreation) the status of a work of art, we nevertheless find in them frequent allusions to the artistic genius of the Greek city as such. The reason for such a disparity seems to be the following: As an interindividual relationship, love does not elevate the beauty that affects it to the level of the artistic genius because it operates within a restricted totality, one still engulfed within nature. In contradistinction, Hegel claims, the ethical life of the Greek city is artistic because it is animated by an encompassing movement of genuine totalization, and because the unity of the singular and the universal is no longer exhibited at a natural level, but at the level of an institution. Moreover, this institution involves more than the limited conciliation that obtains in love, and concerns the absolute essence of a people. Consequently, the ethical life of this people is completely religious, completely artistic, even before giving itself any sort of figurative representation in any specific art form. All these themes—first present in the Frankfurt meditations, then rearticulated in the early writings from the Jena period, in a language that owes much to Schelling—find a later echo in the 1805–6 *Realphilosophie*, in which the beautiful public life of the Greeks is described as a work of art and as "a genial unity of the Self which knows itself, and of its exposition (*Darstellung*)" (*GW* 8:263).

However, this genial unity—which still served in many respects as a paradigm in the essay on "Natural Right" and in the *System of Ethical Life*—is from 1805–6 on definitely relegated to the irretrievable past and replaced by a properly modern configuration of the political sphere, one that we shall soon investigate. But before attempting this, I want to find out what effects the rejection of the Greek model had on the speculative treatment of art as the first moment, or degree, of the Absolute Spirit. Yet even before this, let me summarize the results we have obtained in the course of this incursion into the presuppositions of the speculative theory of art: Upstream of this conception, we have detected a notion of art that extends beyond the production of works of art in the strict sense, and the notion of an aesthetic schema of such sweeping extension that its sphere exceeds that of the works of art—by encompassing the theory of ethical and political life, and by sustaining an entire ontotheology. Of course, such a discovery may now prompt us to raise tentatively the hypothesis that such a notion, and schema, could reoccur under different guises downstream of the speculative theory of art in the narrow sense. Let us provisionally leave this question unanswered and, for now, try to investigate the speculative theory when it deals explicitly with the theme of art.

### The Center of the Speculative Theory of Art

The thematic definition of art articulated by the speculative theory is closely associated with the preceding ethico-political theory. The link between the two can be expressed as follows: In the political constitution that is the site of ethical life, what is being produced is the Absolute Spirit itself, which, in its products, finds a content in conformity with itself, that is, a "spiritual content," but this production takes place in "the form of the object" and not in the form of knowledge (*GW* 8:278). But we saw that the political constitution can have two configurations: the Greek one, which although immediate, is irretrievably a thing of the past, or the modern one, which is mediated and reveals a northern origin. In conformity with these two configurations, the Absolute Spirit (inasmuch as it concerns itself with knowledge) brings about its self-production under two species of knowledge, one ancient and one modern. The first one is the religion of art, the second is the religion of the Spirit, or Christianity. Art corresponds to the cognitive aiming at the Absolute Spirit when it is linked to a religion, namely, the religion of art. Art, then, is defined as an immediate knowledge that a subsequent mediated knowledge has to overcome. This mediated knowledge is Christianity. In the context of the speculative thematization, art can therefore have no other definition than that of the merely immediate knowledge "which the Absolute Spirit has of itself as Absolute Spirit" (*GW* 8:280). The content of art is, indeed, the Absolute Spirit, that is, the "self-production of self as life conscious of itself as such and reflected within itself" (*GW* 8: 280). Yet art's content in its full richness cannot be grasped by art proper, because the knowledge reached by art is immediate.

The speculative theory is therefore *based upon the principle of the necessary overcoming of art*. Such a necessity depends on this, that immediacy as such is inherently contradictory. This contradiction is brought to light by Hegel in three areas: the *typological* aspect of the artistic genres, the *chronological* aspect of the epochs of art, and the *systematic* aspect of an analysis of the levels reached by the works of art themselves and of the faculties involved in their production and reception.

If we consider the typological aspect of the artistic genres, the contradiction is connected to the fact that art "oscillates," as Hegel says, between a spatial figure and a temporal interiority, between plastic art and music, between intuitive immobility and disappearing movement. If we consider the chronological aspect, Hegel distinguishes three stages: First comes the religion of nature, the epoch "inspired by the Hindu Bacchus"; second, the beautiful religion, the epoch of "absolute art" in which "the content is equal to the form"; third, the level of "modern formalism" or of "intellectual beauty." This sequence anticipates the later sequence *symbolism-classicism-romanticism* articulated in the *Lectures on Aesthetics*. In each period there is a contradiction. In the first period, the "I" is dominated by the awesome power of nature, and the self cannot therefore initiate its self-production.

What the second period offers to view is "a game without fundamental significance or depth," or a game in which there is no other depth than "the unknown Destiny." What art loses, therefore, on this level corresponding to the Greek world, it gains in sensual intuition. In the third stage, an intellectually reflected meaning prevails upon the sensible figure. Hegel expresses the contradiction of this sequence as follows:

> Art is in this contradiction with itself, which consists—when it is autonomous—in necessarily expanding towards the allegorical (wherein it disappears as individual work), and—if the meaning is totally absorbed in the individuality—in a meaning that is not being expressed.(*GW* 8:279)

Finally, from a *systematic* point of view, art suffers from the limitations of the specific element of its means of expression. Such a means is sensibility, nonmediated intuition, a finite medium, which as such can never grasp the infinite, but can only aim at it from a distance, because the infinite is held captive in the singular entity expressed within the medium. Moreover, although the activity of the artist indeed originates in a life conscious of itself, this life never reaches beyond the limits of its singularity, because the satisfaction of others is only receptivity, not productivity, and therefore such a satisfaction is without a self (*selbstlos*).

Altogether, therefore, these considerations about the speculative theory of art point to the necessity of the overcoming of art. Hegel writes: "Beauty is the veil which covers truth much more than the exhibition of truth" (*GW* 8:279). Consequently, even when we understand art as the absolute art of the beautiful religion that corresponds to the beautiful ethical life of the Greeks, the truth of art can be found not in itself, but in another religion, the absolute religion, or Christianity, in which "profundity comes to the light of day" (*GW* 8:281) as the very self-certainty of the Spirit. This absolute religion is no longer aesthetic, because it has rejected the medium of intuition to adopt the element of thought, and art is no longer necessary to it.

By and large, this speculative theory of art may be viewed—in spite of the impression it may give of being merely a draft—as containing the essentials of what the *Encyclopedia* would later express on these issues. A detailed confrontation of both texts would show evidence of this continuity, but such is not my goal here. Rather, the issue is one of detecting the logic of the speculative theory of art and of assessing how this theory is set in place by the rejection of the Greek ethico-political model. We are now in the position to note that the rejection of this model entails some consequences for that logic. The principle of the necessary overcoming of art for the sake of the speculative theory repeats the necessary overcoming of the ethico-political level of the Greek model. The highest summit of art, absolute art or Greek art, suffers from the same defect as the political configuration in which it developed: It was an immediacy without depth.

## Downstream of the Speculative Theory of Art

I have suggested above that the speculative theory of art was preceded by, and contained in, an aesthetic theory of the ethical life. I pointed out that in its genesis this aesthetic theory of the ethical life, which is aligned with the Greek model, is based—more or less explicitly—upon an ontotheology of life that is itself ruled by an aesthetic schema: the satisfaction of self-sameness in the work. The question left unaddressed earlier—so as to allow us to consider the speculative theory of art—was whether this schema could play any role downstream of the speculative theory of art. Rephrased: Are there traces of the aesthetic schema in the developments subsequent to the speculative theory of art, that is, in the ones in keeping with religion and science?

Let us first consider the speculative theory of absolute religion, that is, Christianity. Just as the speculative theory of art unfolds in strict parallelism to a specific concept of the Greek city, similarly, the speculative theory of the Christian religion unfolds in strict parallelism to a specific concept of the modern state. In the modern state we no longer find the immediate unity of the singular and of the universal characteristic of the ancient city. In the 1805–6 text, Hegel describes the modern state as a hierarchy of corporate orders, or estates (*Stände*), crowned by hereditary monarchy. The estates are the organs of the modern body politic. They include, from the bottom up, the peasantry, the various types of guilds and the traders, and, at the highest rank, the corporate orders devoted to the universal: the businessmen, the scientists, and the military. The specific articulation of the modern body politic has now overcome the immediate configuration of the Greek city, because each of the various corporate orders devotes itself to one task only. More precisely, that unity has disappeared from existence, from *Dasein;* it is no longer here. But the unity is restored at another level, the level of self-consciousness.

Along with the freedom to think for himself, an individual taken from whatever corporate order in the modern body politic is granted the capacity to transcend the limits of this order and to raise himself to the level of a universal sense of duty—something that escapes the peculiarities attached to the mentality of each *Stand*. But, for Hegel, this universal sense of morality remains empty and formal if religion is not to supply it with a content. In the Christian religion, "the Spirit is reconciled with its world." Not only is it the

case that "each one reaches to this intuition of itself as a universal Self" because "each one is for God as much as every other one," but also, in each
individual, "religion satisfies his confidence that the events of the world and
nature are reconciled with the Spirit and that there is—in these events—no
discordance, no unreconciled necessity devoid of selfhood" (281–82). The
properly speculative content of religion consists in the fact that the same negativity requires both the sacrifice of the abstraction of pure being for the sake
of actual existence (creation and incarnation) and the sacrifice of the immediacy of actual existence (the passion of Christ) to allow the advent of the
Spirit reconciled with its world.

Now we can notice that the speculative structure of the Christian religion
is strictly isomorphic to the very constitution of the modern state. The modern state, indeed, never stops sacrificing its own abstraction as an institution
for the sake of the existence of its corporate orders and of the individuals that
compose them. But conversely it never stops requiring that the individuals
divest themselves of their mischievous immediacy in order to animate the
spiritual universality of the state body. This divestment might go so far as the
supreme sacrifice required of the warrior. In such a case, his death is redeemed by the state, because it is the state that metamorphoses this death into
the survival of its own absolute power.

The fact that God is both the "spirit of the community" or effectiveness,
existence (*Dasein*), and effectiveness that is sacrificed and redeemed,[4] such
is the speculative feature of the Christian religion that forms the strict counterpart of the spiritual character of the modern state. It is the same thing to
claim that "the Spirit of the community is the State of the Church" and that
"the Church is the State elevated in the thoughts" (*GW* 8:284). There is,
therefore, a synthetic link between the church and the state.

Is the aesthetic schema previously mentioned present in these developments? We are bound to acknowledge that it hardly manifests itself in the text
devoted to religion. Only in a marginal note do we find an aesthetic connotation: It concerns the act of worshiping, conceived as "composure that
knows itself in the essence." The note says: "[Worshipping] takes pleasure in
body and blood being sacrificed daily within the community" (*GW* 8:283).
But this looming emergence of an aesthetic connotation is immediately can-
celed by another note that says: "In this silent gathering, satisfaction is not
present" (*GW* 8:284). This contradiction does not stem from Hegel's inat-
tention, because—inasmuch as religion's mode of thinking is deficient with
respect to its content—the deficiency stressed by Hegel at its core results in

---

4. [*sursumée.*]

such a contradiction. This mode of thinking is representation, *Vorstellung*, which divides what speculation is required to unite. Representation as such is not adjusted to grasp the speculative content of religion. Whereas reconciliation with this world should prevail, representation divides the real into this world and the otherworldly, and thus generates a nostalgia for the heavens and a suffering.

What the religious representation, however, cannot grasp, science can envisage in "evidence," because "it has the same content as religion but in the form of the concept" (*GW* 8:286). And it is at this level that the aesthetic motif resurfaces with every vigor. Because religion is a mode of thinking absorbed in the mode of sundering, characteristic of representation, it cannot have access to immediacy after undergoing mediation. Hegel writes: "Religion is the thinking spirit, such, however, that is does not think *itself;* not itself—therefore, this Spirit is not equal to itself, it is not immediacy" (*GW* 8:286). In contrast, "the knowledge of philosophy is restored immediacy" (*GW* 9:286). Philosophy unfolds by means of mediation, it moves in the medium of the concept, but at its highest point philosophy is the divestment of itself and the return to immediacy. Concerning this return, the Hegelian text reintroduces the aesthetic motif without any hesitation: "It is as immediacy that the spirit knows itself. . . . The Spirit is its own *peaceful* work of art— *universe as it is* and *world-history*" (*GW* 8:287).

The diffuse and encompassing significance of the aesthetic schema is therefore operative both downstream and upstream of the speculative theory of art in the narrow sense. Because this schema is the ultimate clue to the universe—nature and world-history, and the coming to self of the Spirit—we can wonder whether it does not end up dominating the entire system. It might be objected that the approach I have taken here is based on an early draft of the system. I do not dismiss that point, but would call attention to the last words of the definitive version of the system. In section 577 of the *Encyclopedia,* we read the following:

> It is the eternal Idea, existing in-and-for-itself, that actualizes itself, eternally produces itself and eternally enjoys itself as Absolute Spirit.

The self-production and self-enjoyment mentioned in this sentence are, as we know, characteristics of the aesthetic schema.

But if the speculative identity of art, in the narrow sense of the works and of their history, is both preceded and followed by itself—on the one hand in the form of the ancient city, and on the other hand as nature and history, in which the peaceful artistic productivity of the Spirit is set-into-work—we can wonder whether this speculative identity has not been deferred and, as it were, thrown into a play of endless displacements. Concerning what lies upstream of the speculative theory of art, we can wonder whether aesthetics does not subsume and absorb ethics. Concerning what is downstream of the speculative theory of art, we may suspect that aesthetics absorbs logic. Concerning the center of this speculative theory of art, we can wonder whether ultimately this schema of art does not, paradoxically, require the overcoming of art. As a consequence, true art might not reside where one might expect it, namely, in the works of art and in their history: It lies in beings in their totality, inasmuch as the Spirit has turned this totality into its work in order to enjoy itself, or to reach the satisfaction of its self.

But my topic has now reached a point at which it rebounds, where it lends itself to a second hearing, which no longer involves those shifts internal in speculative thinking, but the tension operative between speculative thought and this thought's other. Such a direction may be now opened up by an inquiry into what I have been calling the "aesthetic schema" of speculative thinking. We can call attention to this schema from the perspective of the history of ideas. Or we can address it by raising questions about its relevance in the topics over which it rules.

If we consider the history of ideas, it is not doubtful that this schema is linked to the modern world and the modern reign of subjectivity as self-consciousness. On this point, it is significant that the Tübingen fragments—the first Hegelian texts where we find the trace of this schema—celebrate the beautiful religion of the Greeks by crediting it with being a "subjective religion" and thus by projecting upon it a specifically modern concept, one vastly different from the Greek concept of *hypokeimenon*.

If we consider the aesthetic schema from the perspective of the topics over which it rules, it might be necessary to call into question the pertinence of the aesthetic theme of a satisfaction in the manifestation of self-sameness within the production of the ownmost work. This question has bearings upon the ethical relation, upon *logos*, and upon art. Concerning the ethical relation, it will be asked whether the all-too-famous concept of recognition—elaborated by Hegel at Jena in the wake of a new reading of Fichte—might not be so exclusively focused on self-satisfaction that, in the actual confrontation of individuals with one another, it precludes the acknowledgment of the imperious distance kept by the other person. Concerning politics, we should ask whether the concept of satisfaction of the self does not punctuate a real denial of the intrinsic conflictual nature of the political realm. Concerning the *logos*, we should ask, similarly, whether this schema does not ring in the demise of the source of the *logos*—the unending renewal of what Jean-Luc Nancy has termed "the sharing of voices" (*le partage des voix*).[5] Concerning art, finally, we should ask whether this aesthetic schema does not contribute to obliterating what, from time immemorial, has always been art's resource, its bursting forth from the powers of the earth, its connectedness with the unnameable, its relationship to the surprising, to the enigmatic, and to what, always, is and remains outside.

---

5. See Jean-Luc Nancy, *Le partage des voix* (Paris: Galilée, 1982).

# 4

# Between the Aesthetic Attitude and the Death of Art

The hypothesis I would like to put to the test here can be simply formulated as follows: What today is being produced and revealed in the plastic arts is as if inscribed within a magnetic field between two poles—two poles that Kant and Hegel, two philosophers of the first order, identified, and upon which they reflected as early as the dawn of contemporary times.

To be sure, such a formula is to be dispensed with a great deal of caution. For I am not claiming that Kant, on the one hand, and Hegel, on the other, actually influenced, in some way or other, the various currents and movements defining the scene of the contemporary arts. The question is not one of influence, direct or indirect, obvious or hidden. The formulation of my hypothesis only suggests that, as philosophers—that is, as men whose thinking is animated by the most exacting demand for the universal and the fundamental—Kant and Hegel were both able, albeit in ways quite diverging, to grasp the very foundations of their time and to unearth something directly connected to the ultimate meaning of the contemporary artistic project. And this is true in spite of the fact that several decades separated both from the first steps belonging to the typically contemporary artistic enterprise, whose unfolding, one may suspect, they were far from imagining.

After this word of caution, let us consider each in turn. What we owe to Kant is the fact that he circumscribed, and carefully analyzed, what we can call the "aesthetic attitude" as a comportment and a specific intentionality. The expression *aesthetic attitude* is not from Kant, but it can be appropriately used with reference to what he describes. Kant was the first to propose that in the general economy of the faculties and of the activities of the human

---

This essay was first published in French in *Recoupements*, (Brussels: Ousia, 1982).

mind—generally speaking, manifesting themselves in a capacity for cognition, on the one hand, and for desire, on the other hand—there is room for a capacity and activity irreducible to either knowing or desiring: It is the aesthetic attitude, or, to use Kant's words, the faculty of *judging aesthetically*. This faculty is exercised by each of us—in more or less pure a form—when in front of the thing of nature or the products of art, we stand to acknowledge their beauty, to appreciate them and to hail them as beautiful.

Let us consider the specific and irreducible traits of this attitude, as they are brought to the fore by Kant in the work containing his entire reflection on these matters, the *Critique of Judgment*. The word *critique* found in the title has obviously no negative connotation. It simply means an examination aiming at discerning the specificity of something. But from the outset, we are entitled to deem it significant and meaningful that Kant inscribes his inquiry within the framework of an examination of the faculty of judgment. In what sense is this significant and meaningful for our topic? The reason is that art, considered in light of the approach sought by Kant, falls within the competence of the activity of one individual who raises himself or herself to be its judge. This means, in other words, that the products of art fall under the rightful jurisdiction of a self, an ego, an individual who appreciates them and turns them into a matter for his or her own judgment. Now, considered in the perspective of the history of ideas, this approach—referring artworks to a subject who judges them—strictly comes with a date. It strictly comes with a date, because it presupposes undoubtedly the emergence of the ego and its self-positing as the absolutely privileged point of reference.

This emergence of the self and of subjectivity ushered in the modern era. It received it theoretical expression in Descartes's theory of method, which posits the "I think" (*ego cogito*) as the foundation for knowledge, but also had been in the offing as early as the fifteenth and sixteenth centuries—specifically in the revolution of thinking that made the birth of modern physics possible. This emergence had also been prepared by the mental revolution that made the birth of modern painting possible, namely, with the discovery of pictorial *perspective*, that is, the creation of a plastic space *de jure* polarized by an ideal focus, namely, the pure gaze of a viewer. The essential reference to the ego that defines the framework of Kantian aesthetics reveals Kant as the heir of a movement of thought intricately connected to the very foundations of the modern era. Just as it is vain to look for a statement similar to the one formulated by Galileo about inertia in the physics of the Greeks and the medievals, it would be pointless to seek the equivalent of what—since the eighteenth century—has come to be called "aesthetics" in the Greek philosophy thought or in the theological speculation of the medievals.

The very word *aesthetics,* in its designation of the discipline dealing with beautiful things and works of art referred to an *ego* that stands to be their judge, was coined in the eighteenth century. To be sure, in the Greek philosophers and in the medievals, a highly elaborate meditation on beautiful things and on works of art can be found, but this meditation was first and foremost poietic and not aesthetic. In other words, it reflected on the rules presiding over the production of the works rather than on their contemplation. Moreover, these rules received their pivotal justification either from an ontological order or from a concept of human affairs, or from the relationship of resemblance that linked the creatures to the creator for the medievals. Such a pivot, then, was not subjectivity. In order for works of art to start being ascribed to aesthetics, the ego—the *cogito* in the broadest sense—necessarily had to become the center of reference under the form of an ego that derives pleasure from them. Kant's originality on this point consists in assigning irreducible properties to the pleasure that accompanies the perception and the appreciation of beautiful things. Kant highlights this irreducibility by confronting the aesthetic attitude—or more precisely the aesthetic judgment—with other types of judgments.

Let us consider this confrontation, whose internal logic we expect to contain many consequences for the contemporary history of artistic production. Kant distinguishes very rigorously the aesthetic judgment from three other types of judgment, which—not in direct observance of his exact terminology, but in consideration of his spirit—we might refer to as (1) the judgment of cognition, (2) the judgment on the agreeable, and (3) the judgment of purposiveness (or of perfection).

The aesthetic judgment is not reducible to any one of these three judgments, and if it is possible that something in what we take to be a pure aesthetic judgment reveals some compromise with one or another of the three judgments, it is because our judgment is burdened with impurity, that is, it is not yet strictly aesthetic.

Let us first examine in what way aesthetic judgment is different from the judgment of cognition. The judgment of cognition admits of several levels. On the most elementary level, it can be the simple observation of a fact that shows itself here and now. On a higher level, it can be the empirical determination of a relationship between two separate facts. Finally, it can be a properly scientific judgment by which I enunciate a measurable relationship (a law) between a given phenomenon and another one (e.g., that all bodies are attracted to one another by a force whose measure is directly proportional to their mass and indirectly proportional to the square of their distance). Whatever the distinction between these three levels, what characterizes the judgment of cognition in every case is the fact that it aims at a specific *ob-*

*jectivity*. When I say that this body in front of me is made of lead, pewter, or platinum, I connect it to a general class of bodies whose properties are all the better known as the people observing them occupy a neutral ground and make themselves impersonal judges—a point clearly evidenced by the fact that scientific verification is practiced by means of totally impersonal instruments of measure. To claim objectivity means to claim impersonality.

In contradistinction, the aesthetic judgment requires that I be involved individually and personally. In order to be able to admire this or that thing, it is necessary that I be the one who, as an irreplaceable individual, is affected by it. In this sense, the aesthetic judgment is said to be *subjective*, in opposition to the objectivity aimed at in the judgment of cognition. What I grasp of the thing is referred not to the neutral ground of objectivity, but to my affective individuality. Thus considered, the aesthetic judgment presents nothing that I can, properly speaking, know. It presents me with no knowledge of anything. This does not mean that my admiration for the beautiful object is mindless. Quite the contrary. It truly implies the exercise of my intellect, but in such a way that my mind simply plays and satisfies itself in such a play—without in any way seeking to explain the thing that keeps my attention captive, without seeking to uncover its formula or to define its meaning, in short, without ever providing me with a concept of it. Kant says that the beautiful is *what pleases apart from concept* (Introduction, vii).

Let us now examine in what sense the aesthetic judgment is different from the judgment on the agreeable or, if one prefers, from the ordinary pleasure of the senses. Between the ordinary pleasure and the aesthetic attitude, Kant claims, there undoubtedly exists a common element. In both cases, I am involved with my affective individuality: In both cases, I am the one whose individual sensibility is affected. But the resemblance goes no further, and it would be entirely wrong to reduce the aesthetic judgment to a judgment on the agreeable on the basis of this resemblance, thereby equating the two. For three major differences separate these two judgments:

1. In ordinary sensuous pleasure, whether visual, auditory, gustatory, olfactory, or erotic, I am fundamentally *interested,* which amounts to saying that I subordinate the thing enjoyed to the satisfaction that it gives me. The thing is, in a manner of speaking, nothing but an opportunity for the voluptuousness I get from it: As a means aimed at giving me pleasure, it might almost lose its being and fade away in my enjoyment. The thing is but a means in the service of such a goal, even though, conversely, I too can be said to depend on the thing insofar as I value the pleasure I derive from it. It is precisely this relationship of mutual dependency, in the final analysis centered on my interest, that does not obtain in the aesthetic attitude. The latter,

Kant says, is *disinterested*. This means that, far from being absorbed in the process of my enjoyment, the beautiful thing (or the work of art) is recognized for just what it is. Instead of seeing it from the perspective of my satisfaction, I let it appear for its own sake: I consider it, I contemplate it— nothing more, nothing less. From this characteristic, two other differences follow.

2. In the case of ordinary pleasure, which, by definition, is interested, the current interest concerns me exclusively as a unique individual. This situation speaks of a fundamental selfishness of pleasure. Such a selfishness is adequately described by a popular saying, "To each, his or her own taste." But precisely because aesthetic satisfaction is disinterested, it avoids this egoistic exclusiveness. Inasmuch as I am disinterested, I am no longer caught in my own individuality. Instead, I surpass myself in reaching out, so to speak, to something universal. Of this overcoming, Kant finds a sign in the fact that the person who recognizes the beauty of a thing, or of a work, invites others to share in the discovery and feels some kind of regret if the others do not partake in it as he or she does; yet nothing of the kind occurs if this person discovers that others have different culinary tastes.

3. But there is yet another difference, perhaps more difficult to grasp because it introduces a technical distinction—the distinction between content and form, between the material and the formal. Kant stresses that ordinary sensuous pleasure is of the *material* order, whereas the aesthetic one is of the *formal* one. This means that, in ordinary pleasures, the crucial point is the organic well-being into which I am immersed; to put it bluntly, in this type of pleasure I am nothing but my body. Such is not the case at all for aesthetic judgment. The sensuous factor is certainly essential to it, which is to say that I am involved in the act of perceiving, of being "all eyes" and "all ears." But precisely because this perception is disinterested, it makes it possible for me not to be immersed in my body, not to be identified with a pure emotion, or a pure passion. In other words, it makes it possible for me to be free in the very midst of the sensible. My being free in the very midst of the sensible elicits the opportunity of free play with the perceived. Whereas I do not play with what compels or awakens my desires or passions, I play with what I perceive aesthetically, and the beautiful thing to me is a play of sounds, of lines, of colors, of relationships, and so on. Kant has such a play in view— with all the connotations of gratuitousness and freedom specific to the realm of playfulness—when he stresses that aesthetic perception is formal, not material.

Now it remains for us to distinguish the aesthetic judgment from what, for the sake of brevity, we called earlier "judgment of purposiveness." In such a judgment I consider a situation, an event, or a thing within the perspective of a goal or an end, whether the end be of a moral, or of a merely technical, nature. It happens that I feel some satisfaction when considering something in light of a goal or end. Thus I can experience satisfaction in face of a given event that, in my view, seems to promote justice or freedom. Likewise, I can feel satisfaction when considering the appropriateness of an instrument to the given use I intend to make of it. But in both cases, the satisfaction is very different from the one inherent in the aesthetic attitude or judgment. The reason is that a satisfaction resulting from comparing or contrasting a thing to a goal is necessarily linked to an interest. This interest is certainly quite different from the one previously considered, because at stake here is not an aiming at my own egoistic pleasure, but rather the striving for a noble ideal or for some efficiency or usefulness. Yet this is still an interest, in that I do value the realization of these goals. To that extent, I subordinate the given thing to the objective, to the realization with which it seems to concur, and therefore I am far removed from the pure, disinterested contemplation that defined the aesthetic judgment.

Aesthetic judgment requires a total disengagement from all function-oriented activities. Moreover, when I look at something with some end in mind, I am bound to incorporate in my view a definition of what this thing will promote, or of that to which it will be useful, or of its essence. But as we already know, the beautiful is without concepts. Consequently, to dissociate the aesthetic judgment from the judgment of purposiveness, Kant stresses that this judgment is paradoxically characterized by what he calls "a purposiveness without a purpose," and that the thing considered in this judgment manifests itself as "a free beauty." Purposiveness without a purpose means that, between the beautiful thing and myself, there is indeed a concordance or affinity, but that this affinity, in me, concerns nothing determinate—neither the feelings stemming from my sensibility, nor my voluptuousness, nor an end that I assign to my volition, nor a meaning or definition that would satisfy my intellect.

A free beauty, that to which the pure aesthetic judgment directs itself, is freed of all subordination to ends, of all appeal to voluptuousness, of all conceptually definable meaning, and even of any specifiable immanent rule— that is, of any recognizable formula involved in its composition. It is indicative of the purism of this notion that, when Kant wants to give artistic examples of free beauty, he can find them only on the fringes and at the margins of the artistic production of his time. He cannot find any in the painting of his days, because at that time painting was too representative and figurative, and therefore under the constraint of given models: the human face, landscapes, allegorical or historical scenes. He cannot find any in the literary arts, which at that time were more or less constrained by criteria of established meaningfulness.[1] Neither can he find any in architecture, which by essence cannot be dissociated from some functionality, private or public, secular or religious. He can find them only in music—when music, theme-free and text-free, is akin to pure improvisation—and in the most remote margins of the plastic arts: for example, in the volutes or foliated scrolls used to decorate wallpapers, or in the secondary motifs used to ornament the frames of paintings, because there the imagination is left free to run its course without interference from the intellect and the business of defining, naming, and explaining what is being seen.

Let us now step back from this presentation of the Kantian theses to reflect on the consequences they entail. In general, purism is the striking feature of the attitude defined by Kant. As pure and free contemplation, the aesthetic attitude concerns things that do not require explaining, that even resist *all cognition*, that are in no way an opportunity for *voluptuousness*, and that in no way permit an integration to an *end*. Free beauties are neither true nor false, because they escape cognition; neither pleasant nor unpleasant, because they extend beyond every ordinary pleasure or desire; neither useful nor useless, neither perfect nor imperfect, because they are outside the realm of ends and goals. I indicated at the beginning that it would be vain to look to a direct influence of Kant over the artistic production of his time. But still it is possible to view the real history of such production—from romanticism to some recent currents—as unfolding the logical consequences of the attitude analyzed by Kant with such a concern for purity. In other words, Kant meditated on an attitude that was only in the process of emerging, and that, as soon as it became foundational for the artistic production itself, would tend to promote aesthetic purism within the works themselves.

This attitude is in fact what provides the foundation for the entirely new institution of the museum of fine arts, which appeared at that time and turned out to play a decisive role in the subsequent course of plastic production. For such an institution to become possible, it was necessary to approach the artworks of the past with an attitude different from the one that had presided over their production at the time of their creation. For at the time when they were sculpted, the Greek bas-reliefs were not aesthetic objects, but expressions of the power and glory of the city, or tributes to the divinities that protected it. A Romanesque crucifix in the Romanesque age was not an aesthetic object, but the picture of the sufferings of Christ, and the support of an attitude of piety. The portrait of a Dutch burgher, as in one of those painted by Franz Hals, was not at the time of its production an aesthetic object, but pre-

1. [*des signifiés.*]

cisely the portrait of a leading citizen—it bore witness to the social success and prestige attached to the individual. An endless list of examples could be adduced here. In order for works of this kind, whatever the diversity, to be brought together in the same place and unified under the common denominator of one gaze, a totally new attitude had to be adopted: It consisted in grasping in them nothing but what is offered to—and intended by—a pure aesthetic judgment by means of dissociating these works form what they initially taught, that is, from the knowledge they provided within their world of origin, and from the social, political, or religious purposiveness they fulfilled therein.

The role played by the institution of the museum was to be absolutely crucial throughout the contemporary era down to our times—a role that André Malraux, in particular, brought to light in his *Musée imaginaire*. Thanks to the museum, art becomes conscious of itself as art, correspondences between productions become manifest at both ends of the spectrum of time and space. Artists start to create less with the intention of expressing, celebrating, or denouncing a world than with that of situating themselves vis-à-vis paintings and sculptures of other artists, from the past or the present. The historical process of the production of works or art acquires some sort of *autonomy:* It is a sequence that, in a sense, is always primarily related to itself, some sort of chain whose individual links, in their very uniqueness, are connected to the ones preceding them. Impressionism defines itself in contrast to naturalism, fauvism in contrast to impressionism, cubism in contrast to Cézanne's painting; expressionism defines itself over against impressionism, geometrical abstraction against all the above, lyrical abstraction against geometrical abstraction, 'pop' art against all various abstractions, conceptual art against 'pop' art and hyperrealism, and so on.

In addition to the fact that these diverse links reveal the autonomy of the specific movement of artistic production and therefore, by virtue of this autonomy, also exhibit the presence of the specific attitude called "aesthetic" by Kant, it is now possible to understand the various links of this sequence as *new variations on the constitutive characteristics of the aesthetic attitude*—namely, the absence of cognition, of voluptuousness, and of function-oriented activity. In its first steps, the adventure embarked upon by abstract art can be viewed as the implementation of the requirements specific to these various constitutive characteristics. If a painting, no matter how far removed from the common way of perceiving, as in the case of cubist paintings, still allows us to recognize definable and otherwise knowable elements—for instance, a pipe, a glass, a newspaper, a bottle—then it cannot help but maintain some links to the realms of knowledge and function-oriented activity: Everyone knows what a glass is, and what it is used for.

Abstract art appears, notably with Kandinsky, when these elements of knowledge and functionality are put aside, when the painting is nothing but a *composition* of lines, of nonidentifiable shapes and of colors. But here too the fact that such compositions still use colors, and create harmony in the general movement and relationships they bring together, generates a pleasure that is not without recalling the agreeable satisfaction one gets in the real world from a warm, glowing, or high-spirited decor. Purism, then, consists in refusing such a satisfaction, as too much akin to daily gratifications, and in eliminating colors with their load of symbolism and eroticism—keeping in the end no more than the black and white: This, precisely, is what Malevitch's suprematism set out to do.

But respect for the requirements of the aesthetic attitude is bound by no clear-cut limits or privileged form. Just as one can eliminate from the work anything that reminds us of anything else, anything that pleases, anything that calls to mind the realm of usefulness—thereby keeping the work free of knowledge, of voluptuousness, of functionalism—one can also conversely introduce all of these dimensions massively in order to subvert them. Thus, when Duchamp took manufactured products (the well-known "ready-made," such as a bottle holder or a bicycle wheel) and placed them as sculptures in the exhibition room, his decision, though based on a radical refusal of the aesthetic object, turned out, as a result of the very fact of the exhibition, to reinforce a constitutive character of the aesthetic realm, namely, non functionality. Since these objects were no longer used for any purpose, they exhibited a sort of self-destruction of functionality, thereby becoming strange objects of contemplation. In the same manner today, when the so-called conceptual artists show in their works the pages of a dictionary or some computer data printouts, they metamorphose the tools of knowledge into enigmatic things that exhibit a sort of self-negation of the concept—very much in line with the requirements of the aesthetic attitude.

To the list of traits just mentioned—generalized museum collecting, an autonomous history of the plastic productions, countless variations using the constitutive characteristics of the aesthetic attitude—we should include another item, which some authors have called "the tradition of the new," that is, the constraint and obligation to be original in the same way as the predecessors were, but differently from them, since otherwise there would be no originality.

But now the time has come to consider Hegel, who, I claimed, identified the other pole of the magnetic field of contemporary art.

This other pole is the *death of art*. Hegel is the first to have introduced the idea that art was mortal and destined to die. Before tracing the steps and transformations of this idea within contemporary art, let us attempt to delineate its meaning in the context of Hegel's thought. Even a quick overview of Hegel's monumental aesthetics will soon make it clear to us that Hegel's thinking on the matter does not stem from the *aesthetic attitude* as it had been defined by Kant. The reason is not that this attitude is not examined by Hegel (for it is, but in order to be criticized), but that the center of gravity of the Hegelian aesthetics is not the pure aesthetic gaze of an ideal and disinterested viewer, pivotal in the Kantian analyses. The center of gravity is now the very history of the arts. Whereas Kant's aesthetics centers on the description of one of the attitudes of the mind, now it is with respect to a *philosophy of history*, and in this perspective only, that Hegel can claim that art is destined to die. Generally speaking, Hegel's philosophy of history considers the temporal destiny of humankind as a global odyssey that, after passing through formative periods (the Orient, Greece, and the Christian world), is now on its way to completion in modernity itself. Such a completion is the reign of reason. This reign is achieved when the real turns out to be entirely penetrated with rationality and when, conversely, rationality is not at all a sort of ideal to reach, a wish to be fulfilled, but instead when the ideal coincides entirely with reality itself. Such a reign is both practical and theoretical. Practically, that is, regarding the activity of men, it is realized in a specifically modern political framework: the constitutional and bureaucratic state. Theoretically, that is, with respect to knowledge, it is realized in science—which, in the sense considered by Hegel, means his own philosophical system.

For Hegel, the entire history of humankind is oriented toward such a completion. What men sought in their works, in their beliefs, in their institutions, in their thoughts, is the reign of rationality that is supposed to reach its absolute form at the time of Hegel. Thus the history of humankind is a progressive maturing of the absolute rationality, a progressive maturing within which art occupies a specific place, yet a place that is no more than a preliminary degree—the higher degrees being the Christian religion and modern philosophy. More precisely, art was an essential step in the maturing process of the absolute rationality, exclusively within a world that has now completely disappeared: the ancient Greek world.

Let us try to consider this view in greater detail. For Hegel, absolute rationality is reached only when there is no longer contradiction between opposites that usually seem to be antithetical, such as the human and the divine, the finite and the infinite, the relative and the absolute, the many and the one, time and eternity, the subject and the object, the other and the same. It is reached when these antitheses fuse into one another and when this fusion-identification is understood as such. In the last resort, such an identification can be fully understood only in the Hegelian system itself—but, according to Hegel, the entire history of humankind had been aiming at, and pursuing, such an identification. Greek civilization, which was a civilization entirely artistic, consisted in a certain type of apprehension of this identification. This apprehension was sensible and plastic. The Greek statues, the Greek temples bear witness to a sensible apprehension of the identity of opposites, that is, of the Absolute itself, the very ground of beings. The Greek plastic arts inaugurated a mutual penetration, a conciliation, an identification of nature and culture, since their works glorify the natural reality of the human body—but under a cultural form, because these are works made by human beings. They inaugurated a mutual penetration and an identification of the human and the divine, for they feature deities under human shapes: Apollo, Athena, Zeus, Aphrodite. They inaugurated also a conciliation of external space and of the interiority of consciousness, since they were the objects of a cult, the receiving ends of sacrifices and of spiritual expressions of piety. Greek art, which for Hegel culminated in plastic works, is therefore interpreted by him as the holding together, and an expression, of the identity of opposites. Yet—for a restriction comes to play—both apprehension and expression suffered from being bound to the individuated forms of the statues that realize the unity of the human and the divine, of the relative and the absolute, merely in an external intuition, in a corporeal figure. Hegel writes:

> As art, classical [i.e., Greek] art reaches the highest summits; its flaw is to be one art only, one art short of anything else—nothing else beyond it. In a next development, art attempts to reach a higher level. It becomes what was called Romantic or Christian art. In Christianity, a dissociation took place between truth and representation of the senses. The Greek god is inseparable from the intuition; it represents the visible unity of human nature and divine nature. But this unity is of a sensible nature, whereas in Christianity it is conceived in the Spirit and in Truth.[2]

The Christian religion—the highest one, according to Hegel—is the second degree in the temporal series of the striving to grasp the absolute unity. But because the Christian apprehension of the identity of the opposites is of an internal and spiritual kind, art is no longer indispensable to it. Yet there is

---

2. G. W. F. Hegel, *Sämtliche Werke* (Berlin: H. Glockner, 1927–30), vol. 12, p. 118–9. Hereafter cited as *SW*.

a history of Christianity, a history that is one of increasing spiritualization—reaching its culmination in the Reformation only. Such is the perspective in which Hegel interprets the history of Christian art as a movement that consists in removing itself, more and more unambiguously, from the sensible exteriority into the interiority of conscience and of spiritual feeling. But precisely because in Christianity the Absolute is Spirit and can be apprehended only within the Spirit, as evidenced in the teaching of the Resurrection and of the Pentecost, the plastic arts come to play a role less important than the literary, or the musical, arts, which are arts of interiority. Whatever the nuances, the Hegelian thesis is that the farther spiritualization has progressed, the less art is important, and that the history of art in the Christian age exhibits the effort of art to overcome itself in the direction of something that is no longer art, that is, the effort to apprehend the spiritual by means of the sensible, an effort that inevitably turns the sensible into something inessential. The essential in the painting of the Christian era consists, therefore, not in the fact that it is painting, but in that it signifies a spiritual content that cannot but escape it.

Religion, however, even when it is radically internalized as in the Reformed church, is still not the highest degree of the Spirit. The highest degree is no longer religious, but secular. It is only reached in the reign of the politico-scientific rationality that we mentioned earlier as characteristic of the modern world. At such a level, art is no longer essential to the Spirit, it carries out a marginal activity with respect to the actualization of spiritual freedom, which in effect takes place in the political realm and in science. Indeed, a peripheral testimony of this liberation is what Hegel describes in the art emerging at that time—Romantic art—about which he says:

> The artist stops being dominated . . . by a given content, by a given form, he dominates the one and the other and keeps his freedom of choice and production untouched . . . , he has made a clean slate [*tabula rasa*] of all subjects and of the forms of his production (*SW* 12:120–2)

But this artistic freedom is something formal and relatively insignificant when confronted with the concrete existence of freedom in the state and its theoretical reflection, namely, philosophy itself as the science of sciences.

Thus, the first formulation of the idea of the *death of art* is inscribed within a philosophy of history that is inextricably a philosophy of *absolute knowledge,* in which nothing enigmatic or secret is left in the real. The real, as the whole, once and for all, has revealed its secret.

The aesthetics of the death of art, one notices easily, diverges radically from Kantian aesthetics. Whereas Kantian aesthetics, centered as it is on the aesthetic attitude, suggests that art can become properly aesthetic only when dissociated from knowledge and purposiveness, Hegelian aesthetics maintains that art is legitimately art only inasmuch as it is a necessary path to knowledge and an attempt to apprehend the Absolute—inasmuch, therefore, as it is inscribed within a purposiveness. Whereas Kantian aesthetics, again because of its center in the aesthetic attitude, suggests that the arts have their entire life ahead of them, Hegel's maintains that their life is now behind them, in Greek antiquity.

But the paradox is that the Hegelian theory of the death of art—notwithstanding its radical divergence from the Kantian one—touches upon something central in the contemporary artistic approach, something as central as the Kantian theory of the aesthetic attitude. For since the First World War and the appearance of Dadaism in Zurich, Berlin, and New York, we have witnessed periodic announcements of the imminent demise of art—in various manifestos and demonstrations carried out by the artists themselves, who aimed at exhibiting the terminal and certain obsolescence of the plastic arts. One heard of art openings at which the destruction of works was performed, of the exhibition of litter, of empty rooms, of lacerated canvases, or of the disparagement of masterpieces conducted under various forms. These anti-artistic manifestations turn out to be in line with the Hegelian definition of the contemporary era, in which art is destined to die, because unshackled freedom has rid it, in one fell swoop, of all subject matters and of all forms.

To be sure, such manifestations do not expressly claim a Hegelian legacy. We said before that the issue is not Hegel's influence over them, but whether it is legitimate to suspect that their unfolding takes place according to a logic somewhat analogous to that of Hegelianism, i.e., that the various forms of the contemporary denial of art follow, unbeknownst to them, a line of reasoning implicitly based on Hegelian premises.

In this movement some say, for example, that the aesthetic attitude presiding over today's art exhibitions, over the work of a majority of artists, and over the attitude of the viewers is the reign of the most extreme form of arbitrary fancy, the reign of dispersion and isolation of individuals—while they claim that art can only live in a climate of unanimity and social consensus. This view amounts to revitalizing the Hegelian opposition between the Greek world and the eras that followed it.

Another option is for these antiartistic movements to reproach the aesthetic attitude with being subjective and abstract, and with fostering—by means of the contemplative joy it creates—the illusion that everything is well and good as it is, and that the world is currently in good order, when in fact it abounds with contradictions. Often such movements will claim their affiliation with the Marxist criticism of capitalism and with the Marxist project of a society transparent to itself and free of contradictions. They thus inscribe themselves in the Hegelian posterity, by the mediation of Marx, and—more deeply, although implicitly—share with Hegel an approach to art aiming at *interpreting it with respect to the completion of rationality*—a completion that no longer is in keeping with art, that art even hides or hinders, and that is much more in keeping with the political realm and a self-proclaimed final knowledge of the meaning of history.

To be sure, such movements can take many shapes and forms. At times, they are seen to massively oppose artistic activity because they view it as perpetuating—and masking at the same time—an irrational social system based on individual profit-making that transforms everything into sellable merchandise; at other times, they will produce works whose critical, negative, and challenging load is supposed to be instrumental in implementing the ultimate rational politico-theoretical order. Whatever the variations, one can suspect that they all share in aiming at an ultimate rationality, at a reign of transparency present at the core of the Hegelian idea of absolute knowledge.

In another option, these antiartistic movements will contend that art has used up all its possibilities, that it cannot but repeat itself, and that, therefore, it has become a vain occupation: Such was already the way in which Hegel reasoned concerning the art of his time.

Another possibility consists in claiming that art has always contributed to the belief that the world is meaningful, coherent, and rational, that art has always supported religious or human values—be it under the contemporary, somewhat flimsy, form of the freedom of the artist—but that such a view is an illusion because the world, history, and reality as a whole are devoid of any meaning. It will not, then, be in the name of a final achievement of rationality that art will be criticized, but on the contrary in the name of the definitive impossibility of any rationality. This attitude might have been that of Marcel Duchamp. One can also suspect that it carries along with it unassimilated chunks of Hegelianism, because not only does this position decree that art is a thing of the past, but more deeply it pretends to be all-encompassing. It was from the perspective of a totality of meaning that Hegel was reasoning. Now this new reasoning, conducted from the perspective of a totality of meaninglessness, might be nothing but an inversion of signs. At any rate, we can suspect the notion that everything is meaningless of being a form of disappointment concerning the possibility of a total implementation of meaning, and, therefore, concerning our entire culture—if it is true that this culture aims at being always more and more rational.

Perhaps this short outline has confirmed that the antithetical themes of the aesthetic attitude and of the death of art really strike at the core of the contemporary plastic production. To be sure, it has happened that these themes have presided over productions that, apparently, take a stance one against the other—that is, either over ever-more-purified works, or over non-works, destructive gestures, and productions that wanted to be scandalous. But paradoxically, it has also happened that works produced with a view to inducing a negative charge became very rapidly aesthetic objects, as in the case of Duchamp's ready-mades. This is the reason why I first talked about a magnetic field.

Such is perhaps the paradox upon which we have to meditate. If it turns out that this paradox is not marginal, but generalized, if it turns out that the same works (or "gestures," or "interventions," as some like to call them today) point to the intersection of these two themes, if it turns out that they function, so to speak, both as testimonies to the death of art and as renewed calls to the aesthetic attitude, the paradox might very well invite us to a new confrontation between what we referred to, at the beginning, as the "two poles" of today's art production.

By way of a conclusion let me attempt a few steps in this direction. It is perceptible that there is a paradox in the fact that the death of art and the aesthetic attitude encroach upon one another only if one grants unreservedly that the tension between these two themes is a radical one. For this tension to be so, its poles must not lend themselves to any integration whatsoever. In a sense, integration always looms ahead, at least judging from the confrontation that we conducted in these pages. If the aesthetic attitude—the Kantian aesthetic judgment—were reduced to the features that we distinguished previously, namely, the absence of knowledge, of voluptuousness, and of functionality, it would still be amenable to a speculative dialectic in Hegelian style. Speculative dialectic can very well find confirmation of its own idea in the fact that works lend themselves to a judgment defined in terms of such features, in the fact that they find their justification in this judgment, as in a standard whose requirements are endless. The constant innovations imposed by such a standard seem to be accounted for by Hegel when he characterizes contemporary art as the "*tabula rasa*" of all subject matters and forms. Does not Hegel, by granting an unlimited freedom of choice and of production to the modern artist, account for the fact that the absence of knowledge, of voluptuousness, or of function-related activity determines a very specific, properly aesthetic, freedom, such as the one that is at the core of Kant's aesthetic judgment? Hence can't the motif of the aesthetic attitude be integrated with that of the death of art?

In this integration, speculative dialectics only has to show the *insignificance* of the aesthetic attitude with respect to the absolute actualization—under a theoretico-practical guise—of the identity of the real and of the rational. Although, according to Kant, the aesthetic attitude is defined by the negative features pointed out earlier, it is possible for Hegel to integrate this attitude in his system by limiting its application to the contemporary era and by showing that the attitude at stake amounts to the implicit admission that knowledge, satisfaction, and purposiveness could not possibly be reached in the aesthetic realm, because, by definition, this realm cannot transcend the limits of the sensible and of the individuation of the works, of the artists, and of the connoisseurs. But from a Hegelian viewpoint the persistent attempt in the artistic sphere to find freedom in the lack of knowledge or of purposiveness is the *a contrario* proof that such a completion takes place beyond the aesthetic realm.

The endless freedom of play in aesthetics would then be a concession made by the Spirit to the individual's whims, inasmuch as the Spirit has the absolute knowledge of itself and enjoys being a self in the ultimate completion of its ends. If it is true that self-enjoyment in the absolute knowledge of the completion of Spirit defines freedom in the Hegelian sense, then aesthetic freedom in the Kantian sense is like a small mirror in which absolute freedom is refracted and gets confirmed within the limits of the individual.

Is the tension about which we were talking abolished? Not at all, if we strive to delineate it more clearly. Speculative dialectic can integrate the aesthetic attitude only insofar as the metaphysics of absolute subjectivity, or of the completion of freedom, sees its own anticipation foreshadowed—be it in a refracted, a blurred, or an inverted image—at the core of aesthetic freedom. But the whole question is whether there might not be within the nature of aesthetic freedom something that resists such an integration. In other words, the question is whether, in the freedom that Kant had assigned to subjectivity and to the harmonious play of its faculties, there might not be something that eludes the power of subjectivity and a fortiori the empire of absolute subjectivity.

Of such an evasion we find only very tenuous signs in Kant's text. Heidegger has taught us to meditate on the import that these signs have beyond the metaphysics to which they belong. Let me call attention to two signs among the most striking ones. In a kind of positive counterpart to the negative features on which we focused—absence of knowledge, of voluptuousness, of purposiveness—Kant calls upon the beautiful word *favor* (*Gunst*) to capture the specificity of the properly aesthetic freedom. Favoring the free manifestation of what it welcomes, aesthetic freedom consists, in, so to speak, letting the phenomenon be within itself, for its own sake, without subordinating it to our concepts, our desires, our pleasure. The fact that Kant grants an ultimate status to such freedom, the fact that he detects in it the indication that we are attuned to the world, suggests to us that, deeper than the correlation of subject and object, freedom consists in being open to the very unconcealing of the world, an unconcealing that precedes and exceeds the theoretical, practical, and hedonistic powers of the ego.

At this point the aesthetic attitude overcomes itself, if it is true that the modernity that witnessed its rise, and that reflected upon it, never desisted in defining it as a modality of subjectivity in the ego-logical sense. On this point—however infinitely small and unapparent it might be—Kant evades Hegel and the circle of absolute subjectivity. He evades him just as much—and this is the second sign he provides us with—when, specifically treating the work of art, he detects in it a rootedness in nature that escapes all knowledge, all mastery derived from rules, all craftsmanship. To be sure, Kant does not explicitly state that this rootedness within nature has something to do with the very unconcealing of the world and stands at the very core of the unveiling as the abyssal secret constituting its source; yet this is perhaps suggested by him with sufficient vigor for us to conclude that on this point the order of subjectivity in the ego-logical sense is being superseded.

In these two points—which, I believe, are converging—the tension with speculative dialectic encounters a new resurgence and finds renewed power. What the metaphysics of absolute subjectivity can never integrate, as it deals with the death of art, that is, with what it takes to be the arbitrary repetition of its insignificance—the perpetuation of the *tabula rasa*—and only recognizes in this a minor and marginal concession of the Spirit certain of itself, certain of its own absoluteness, and certain of the completion within itself of all meaning—what such a metaphysics can never integrate is precisely what this insignificance points to: the ever-again-renewed enigma of unconcealment. It is an enigma imperceptible to metaphysics, for which Kant, in spite of his divining it, did not have a word.

More deeply than the tension between the aesthetic attitude and the death of art, the intersection of these two themes at the core of contemporary art seems to indicate to us, if we are willing to question radically what is at stake in them, a tension between the enigma of unconcealing and the ever-renewed certainty of subjectivity in the modern sense. If it is the case that a tension is discernible in the works themselves and that they derive their life from it, this would indicate that everything in them confirming the completion of metaphysics (the unbridled aiming at new impressions, at new intensities, at new images, at new challenges), everything confirming the total availability of beings to a will that plays the game of losing itself therein, only to better refine the pursuit of its self-identity within all beings, everything confirming the absolute will to knowledge and enjoyment, all this would *by the same token* make the admission of the abyssal enigma, that is, of a fundamental powerlessness within the very confirmation of subjectivity.

# 5

# The Nostalgia for Greece at the Dawn of Classical Germany

Let me formulate two questions at the outset of this essay:

1. Under what conditions can one speak of nostalgia, as applied to the bygone age of ancient Greece?
2. What are we to understand by the expression *German classicism*, once it is granted that it is set in motion historically by a certain nostalgia for Greece?

Only by answering these two questions without delay shall I be able to delineate my topic with some rigor.

Assuming, as I do, that the expression *German classicism* applies to Goethe's works, to Schiller's, and to the great poems of Hölderlin, I shall try to determine under what conditions it is possible to talk about nostalgia, concerning their works at the time they were being produced.

*Le Dictionnaire étymologique de la langue française* by Bloch and Von Wartburg indicates that the word *nostalgie* appeared in French around the middle of the eighteenth century; it was derived from a Latin medical term (*nostalgia*) created in 1678 by the Swiss physician Hofer by combining the Greek words *nostos* (return) and *algos* (suffering) and modeled after other words ending in *-algia*, so as to translate the Swiss German word *Heimweh*,

---

This essay was first published in French in the journal of the Hölderlin-*Gesellschaft* (Hölderlin Society) in an issue bearing the title *Turm-Vorträge 1987/88, Hölderlin und die Griechen*, ed. Valérie Lawitschka, Hölderlinturm, Tübingen, 1988. In the original, the quotations were in German, the translations are mine (Trans.).

homesickness, a sickness then quite prevalent in the Swiss living abroad, especially the mercenaries. The feelings of suffering in exile and painful longing for the return to a world where one belongs are the most obvious characteristics of nostalgia. We can, therefore, speak of nostalgia for Greece only when these characteristics—suffering in exile and longing for a homecoming—determine the very approach to the Greek world. Yet, since this suffering and aspiration aim at a bygone world—one that has disappeared in the past and is not merely distant in space—it goes without saying that both features presuppose a confrontation between past and present and will be strengthened by considerations that, in the wake of this confrontation, depreciate the present time.

But in order for nostalgia to emerge, it is not sufficient that such a confrontation should merely take place and result in granting a privilege to the past. Any quarrel between the ancients and the moderns, any depreciation of the moderns when compared with the ancients, does not, by itself, entail nostalgia for the ancients. For the feeling of suffering in exile or the painful aspiration to a return will not lead to a radical depreciating of the moderns when compared with the ancients if, simultaneously, such comparison brings the certainty that the latter are imperishable models—examples whose imitation still remains possible, inasmuch as, focusing on what determined their excellence, one may draw one's inspiration from them. When this certainty is present, the admiration bestowed upon the ancients can no doubt give rise to very harsh polemics against the moderns, but it does not entail that the current world appears as one of exile. In that sense, no one could claim that Winckelmann's work bears witness to a nostalgia for Greece.

No matter how much Winckelmann criticized the excesses of the baroque and rococo eras or denounced the platitude of realism, he nevertheless did not doubt that the world of his times was capable of raising itself to the greatness of the ancients by imitating them. In other words, we must ask the question, Does it make sense to speak of nostalgia, so long as the very possibility of such a restoration is taken for granted? Concerning this point, we have to admit that the psychological vocabulary used so far is inadequate, if not misleading. This vocabulary is inadequate because the core of the phenomenon I want to investigate is in no way limited to states of suffering and aspiration, and to their expression. It is misleading because it may give the impression that the topic of nostalgia is one belonging to psychology and akin to melancholy and depression, when in fact it accompanies a lucid and thoughtful analysis of both past and present—an analysis that probes into the foundations of two modes of existence. Nostalgia begins when this analysis reveals, at the heart of the present epoch, a radical rupture from what made the value of the mode of being of the ancients and shows this rupture or sundering as the very principle ruling over the current mode of existence and its manifold aspects. It goes without saying that the perception of such a rupture is bound to generate the suffering of exile and the aspiration for a return only in connection with the concurrent conviction that true life is absent from the present, and that only the Greek mode of existence was fully human and corresponded truly to the requirements of a wholly human way of life.

In summary, for any era, it makes sense to speak of a nostalgia for a bygone epoch, and of the affliction in being separated from it, only against the backdrop of a confrontation comparing in depth past and present, and showing that, regarding the conditions of authentic life, the present is deficient.

If such is indeed the answer we can give to the first of the preliminary questions I raised, it now delineates more clearly my field of investigation. Long is the list of those in eighteenth-century Germany who celebrated the excellence of the Greeks, but their celebration was not accompanied by nostalgia, properly speaking, so long as it dealt with a limited aspect of life or so long as, even when aiming at the totality of Greek existence, it did not imply the acknowledgment of a radical discontinuity between the ancient and modern modes of existence. Such are in fact the features that characterize Winckelmann's celebration of the excellence of the Greeks. To a large extent, he celebrates limited aspects of life and focuses on the formation of taste for the creation of works of painting and sculpture. And even if Winckelmann's analyses of the spirit presiding over the Greek plastic works are far from being only formal, as he draws on Homer's and Pindar's poetry, Plato's and Aristotle 's thinking, and even if he never tires of praising the athletic and ethical education of the ancients, their works, and their festivals, he does not doubt that his own Saxony could be in the position of reopening the doors to "the purest sources of art. . . . Dresden [the city] will henceforth be the Athens of artists."[1]

Likewise, we can also dismiss the possibility of talking about the nostalgia for Greece in the case of Lessing, whose Laocoön is directly inspired by his mediation on Winckelmann's *"Gedancken über die Nachahmung der Griechischen Werke in der Malerey und Bildhauer-Kunst"* (*Thoughts on the Imitation of Greek Works in Painting and in Sculpture*). The reasons are that Lessing applies Winckelmann's Greek ideals only to sculpture and painting, that the care with which he differentiates the plastic arts from those of speech leads him to view poetry as essentially connected to action, and that, on this score, he deems that Shakespeare, not the ancients, should be taken as the

---

1. "reinsten Quellen der Kunst: . . . Dressden wird nunmehr Athen für Künstler." Johann Joachim Winckelmann, "Gedanken über die Nachahmung der Griechischen Wercke in der Mahlerey und Bildhauer-Kunst," in *Kleinere Schriften*, (Berlin: Walter Rehm, 1968), 29.

model. In addition, Lessing's dramas draw their subject matter from the life
of his time, and we hardly see mention of the Greeks, either in his writings
on philosophy of religion, because they tend to treat the religious as something entirely internal, or in his *Erziehung des Menschengeschlechts* (*The Education of Humankind*), which distinguishes only three epochs—the Old
Testament, the New Testament, and the demand for justice specific to modern
rationality—or even in the formula *Hen kai Pan* (One-and-All) that had been
attributed to him by Jacobi in the account of their last conversation—since in
the context the formula was of Spinozistic inspiration.

There is no nostalgia, either, in Herder, another admirer of Winckelmann. What he finds fascinating in Winckelmann is less the celebration of
Greece than the enthusiasm with which Winckelmann attempts to celebrate
it, and the example offered by his very exuberance—in contrast to the cold-
ness of a narrow rationalism—concerning the possibility of a union between
the understanding and the heart. But for Herder, Greece is not endowed with
any special privilege: Christianity is for him the most perfect form of pantheism, because, according to him, it teaches us to acknowledge the divine in
all the facts of nature and in all events involving human beings. Moreover,
one does not see clearly how nostalgia could be combined with his organicist
conviction that each people is like a leaf in the great living tree of humankind, whose growth is progressing toward a higher stage.

We are therefore brought back to the classical authors whose names I
mentioned earlier: Goethe, Schiller, and Hölderlin himself.


Can we talk about nostalgia for Greece in Goethe? I do not think so. To
be sure, a Hellenic inspiration runs throughout his writings. We need only
mention such titles as *Iphigenia, Prometheus, Pandora,* and *Achilles.* Moreover, a profound unity of spirit involving admiration for the ancients played a
considerable role in the powerful bond that united him to Schiller. Finally,
those of Goethe's writings that elicit the greatest sense of his vivid presence
are ones, like his *Gespräche mit Eckermann* (*Conversations with Eckermann*), abounding with allusions to the Greeks and bearing witness to his unending and tireless reading of their works. But an admiration felt for the
Greeks, by itself, does not entail nostalgia. First, in Goethe this admiration
brings no exclusive privilege, since he says:

> I owe much to the Greeks and the French, I have become infinitely
> indebted to Shakespeare, Sterne, and Goldsmith. This alone, how-
> ever, does not cite all the sources of my culture; it would go on in-
> definitely and wouldn't even be necessary. The important thing is

that one should have a soul that loves the truth and takes this truth wherever the soul finds it.[2]

Moreover, the very fact that the young Goethe could, in agreement with Herder, think that Winckelmann was a Greek who happened to be born in the eighteenth century, gives us a hint that for Goethe, between the Greeks and the moderns there is no radical discontinuity, because a modern can be the equal of an ancient. At any rate, it does suggest that Goethe's relationship to the Greeks involves no rupture and does not originate in a man living in spiritual exile, and that the ancients are for him models that can be used for the inspiration of the present—and toward whom, in art or life, we can move closer without any major obstacle. Such is indeed the view expressed by Goethe in his late discussions with Eckermann. In them, he says that the Greeks remain models in art, in both the plastic and the poetic arts, because they oppose the false realism consisting in copying the common empirical realm and recounting historical events. The Greeks always strip the empirical realm of the countless superfluous aspects and raise what is human to the truth and beauty of the Idea. Goethe told Eckermann that

in our need for something exemplary we must constantly return to the Greeks whose works always portray a beautiful human being.[3]

Not only are the Greeks still models for art, they are so, too, for life:

Only a noble person, in whose soul God has placed the potential for future greatness of character and spirit, will—by means of acquaintance and intimate dealings with the mighty creatures of Greek and Roman times—develop most wonderfully, and with each day grow to similar greatness.[4]

---

2. "Ich verdanke den Griechen und Franzoschen viel, ich bin Shakespeare, Sterne und Goldsmith Unendliches schuldig geworden. Allein damit sind die Quellen meiner Kultur nicht nachgewiesen; es würde ins Grenzenlosee gehen und wäre auch nicht nötig. Die Hauptsache ist, dass man eine Seele habe, die das Wahre liebt und die es aufnimmt, wo sie es findet." Johan Peter Eckermann, *Gespräche mit Goethe in den letzten Jahren seines Lebens,* (Wiesbaden, Fritz Bergemann: 1955), 281 (16 December 1828).

3. " . . . im Bedürfnis von etwas Musterhaftem müssen wir immer zu den alten Griechen zurückgehen, in deren Werken stets der schöne Mensch dargestellt ist." Ibid., 212 (31 January 1827).

4. "Allein ein elder Mensch, in dessen Seele Gott die Fähigkeit künftiger Charaktergrösse und Geisteshoheit gelegt, wird duch die Bekanntschaft und den vertraulichen Umgang mit den

Modernity, therefore, is not an age of exile. It is in no way impossible in today's world for individuals of excellence to equal the Greeks. In addition, the conflict between excellence and lowliness belongs to all ages, and it is "from all quarters that excellent, brave, beautiful, and good men with a splendid demeanor come to greet us." Thanks to them, "the praise sung by humankind has not ceased: Harmonious streams are spread throughout all times and all parts of the earth." I said previously that the nostalgia for Greece was supported by a penetrating analysis of the way of life of the ancients in contrast to that of the moderns—an analysis that exhibited a radical break from everything making the worth of the ancients' mode of existence and showed that this rupture or sundering is at the very foundation of the moderns' way of life and determines its manifold aspects.

It seems to me that among the classics of German literature, we only encounter such an analysis in Schiller and Hölderlin. However, it is also correct to point out that, in the classics of German thought, this theme is also present in the young Hegel. Let me consider Schiller, who takes us into the heart of the matter.

At the outset, we can point out that two components of nostalgia—the feeling of living in exile and the aspiration to a return—are present in Schiller's first dramas, which draw their inspiration from Jean-Jacques Rousseau, more specifically from the Rousseauistic idea that culture and the political order of the eighteenth century evince the greatest disparity with the state of nature, that is, with the condition to which human beings initially belong. Both components are also implicitly contained in the *Theosophie des Julius* (*Theosophy of Julius*) with his opposition to the philosophies of the day, whose central point of reference is the ego. This opposition is maintained by Schiller in the name of a thought of *Vereinigung,* whose principle is the ubiquity of one single divine stream[5] from which originate the affinity of all beings and their communion in the welcoming and unfolding of the free manifestation of the One-and-All. This is what is celebrated in the famous "Hymn to Joy" ("An die Freude"). We can also detect the presence of these two components in Schiller's subsequent writings on the philosophy of history. Influenced by Rousseau, but also tributary to Kant's ethics and the essays in which Kant proposes as plausible conjecture a teleological reading of history, Schiller's writings decipher the historical destiny of humankind both

---

erhabenen Naturen griechischer und römischer Vorzeit sich auf das herrlichste entwickeln und mit jedem Tage zusehends zu ähnlicher Grösse heranwachsen." Ibid., 573 (1 April 1827).

    5. [*courant divin.*]

as an exile from the state of innocence (*Stand der Unschuld*), the true human homeland, and as a return toward this lost homeland from the depths of exile. The exile is characterized by the conflict between nature and freedom, that is, the immediacy of the senses and the moral law that reason imposes upon itself. The return will be the reconciliation between nature and the rule of reason for the will. Such a teleology of the return is somewhat condensed in the famous epigram:

> Do you seek the highest, the greatest? A plant can teach you. What
> it is unconsciously, you must be deliberately—that's what it is![6]

The nostalgia for Greece appears when Schiller, who spent the better part of 1788 absorbed in a feverish and enthusiastic reading of Homer and the Greek tragic poets, substitutes the image of ancient Greece to the Rousseauistic state of nature. From then on, the features of the true state of nature are revealed not by the noble primitive, or *sauvage,* living in a Rousseauistic forest, but by the ancient Greek individual. What are these features? What instigated Schiller's rapture in front of the Hellenic world?

First, obviously, is the Greek concept of the divine: In the light of the gods of Greece, everything appeared differently from how it appears today:

> How entirely different, so different was it there.[7]

Nature, in those days, was animated by the fullness of life (*Lebensfülle*)[8] and endowed with nobility, since everything reflected the trace of the divine. The links that united human beings to nature were bonds of love entirely permeated with joy: Stars, rocks, woods, and brooks spoke enchanted words to everyone. In sharp contrast, nature in the modern sense is devoid of soul— empty, inert, and unenchanted.

With the moderns, however, it is not nature alone that has been afflicted with a metamorphosis. Human existence, too, underwent a complete change. In Greece, the celestial ones often came down to earth, where they met the race of Deucalion, allowing every worldly joy to be ennobled by the Graces and the Muses. Because

---

6. "Suchst du das Höchste, das Grösste? Die Pflanze kann es dich lehren. Was sie Willenlos ist, sey du es wollend—das ists!" Friedrich Schiller, *Schillers Werke, Nationalausgabe,* (Weimar: Julius Petersen and Gerhard Fricke (1943), 1:259. Hereafter abbreviated *NA.*
7. "Wie ganz anders, ander was es da."*NA,* 21:363, v. 6.
8. Ibid., v. 11.

> Between humans, gods, and heroes,
> Love tied a pretty band,[9]

everywhere virtue was not in hiding. Because it did not require that one renounce this life but seek to ennoble it, and make it more beautiful, virtue was shining forth and celebrated:

> Higher prizes strengthened then the wrestler
> On Virtue's strenuous path,
> Achievers of great deeds,
> Climbed upward to the blessed ones.[10]

If we turn to the moderns, we notice in contrast that a cloak of shame has been thrown on life, and that the characteristics of virtue are a harsh gravity and stern renouncement.

Finally, the limitation that is intrinsic in existence, its mortality, was not accompanied in Greece by dread and the fear of a ruthless judge:

> Back then, no horrifying skeleton stepped up
> To the bed of the dying. A kiss
> Took the last bit of life from the lips,
> A wise one lowered his torch.[11]

Perhaps no text expresses more clearly the nostalgia for Greece than this poem, because the confrontation it sustains between the Greek and the modern worlds is not limited to a specific aspect of life[12], but is global and rad-

---

9. "Zwischen Menschen, Göttern und Heroen
   Knüpfte Amor einen schönen Bund."
Ibid., 364, v. 37–38.
10. "Höh're Preise stärkten da den Ringer
    Auf der Tugend arbeitvoller Bahn,
    Grosser Thaten herrliche Vollbringer
    Klimmten zu den Seligen hinan."
Ibid., 365, v. 81–84.
11. "Damals trat kein grässliches Geripppe
    Vor das Bett des Sterbenden. Ein Kuss
    Nahm das letzte Leben von der Lippe,
    Seine Fackel senkt' ein Genius."
Ibid., v. 65–68.
12. [*sectorielle*.]

ical: Both worlds, indeed, are opposed to each other as radically as heat and cold, light and darkness, color and dullness, fullness and emptiness, life and death.

And the longing expressed in this mood is indeed an aspiration to a return:

Bygone Golden Age of Nature![13]

and the suffering of exile:

Yes, they returned home and everything beautiful
Everything great they took away with them,
All colors, all sounds of life,
And for us remained only the soulless word.[14]

Finally, it is striking that this poem that speaks of nostalgia should evoke nothing else but that. No way out remains open, no remedy is suggested, since it concludes with a complaint about the fatality of exile, loss, and fall:

What is to live forever in song
Must die in life.[15]

Schiller's later work, both poetic and philosophical, would display many variations on the themes I just mentioned. In this sense, his later work was characterized by nostalgia for Greece. But a work limited to nostalgia would not be able to expand beyond the register of regret and sorrow.

As it turns out, Schiller is not at all limited to such a registry. It is to be expected that nostalgia, as an evil, might induce the search for the means to escape it. Because it is the characteristic of the nostalgia for Greece to be rooted in a profound confrontation between past and present—something

---

13. "Holdes Blüthenalter der Natur!"
Ibid., 366, v. 90.
   14. "Ja sie kehrten heim und alles schöne
      Alles Hohe nahmen sie mit fort,
      Alle Farben, alle Lebenstöne,
      Und uns blieb nur das entseelte Wort."
Ibid., 367, v. 121–24.
   15. "Was unsterblich im Gesang soll leben
      Muss im Leben untergehen."
Ibid., v. 127–28.

evidenced in the poem previously quoted—it is natural that such a nostalgia should sustain an activity of thinking, and an insistent interrogation on the conditions of possibility for transforming the exile into a meaningful dwelling place.

If we look at this more closely, Schiller's terms in this questioning are laid down in the last distich of the poem "Die Götter Griechenlandes": *Gesang* and *Leben*, song and life. The terms are laid down, but the question is not raised yet. The question is, What is the role of singing,[16] poetry, and art vis-à-vis life? This question opens for us the possibility of surmounting the inevitability of exile. But for this question to be articulated as a problem, it was required that Schiller immerse himself in the study of Kant with no less fervor than in his previous reading of the Greek poets.

It seems to me certain that such an inquiry, which allowed for Schiller's great philosophical essays, is tantamount to a debate between Kant's teaching and the nostalgia for Greece. In a sense, this debate had already been anticipated to some extent by the reappropriation by Schiller of Kant's essays on the philosophy of history. Schiller had indeed detected in these essays the first overcoming of the tension between the trial of exile and the hope of return. To live in exile means to have lost one's homeland as the location to which one belongs by nature, it means that one has experienced a rupture with nature. Such a sundering seems to be validated by Kant's philosophy and, in it, justified both theoretically and practically. Kant offers here a theoretical justification, because the only cognizable nature, according to the *Critique of Pure Reason,* is the silent mechanism of the objects of modern physics, with which no relationship of mutual belonging, harmony, and friendship should be expected. He offers a practical justification also, because what is highest in a human being, that is, freedom and moral nobility, is conquered only by this individual's own permanent sundering from nature itself, that is, from the spontaneous tendencies found in his or her sensibility.

On both accounts, Kant provides a justification for the exile, his teaching authenticates the sundering between nature and human freedom. But such is not the case for Kant's philosophy of history. The attention Schiller pays to Kant's philosophy of history allows him to detect in it a return to nature back from exile. Kant's essays on history suggest that history could be deciphered as the implementation of a design by which nature uses mechanism and the brutal clash of forces to further the progress of freedom. They also suggest, in addition, that such progress announces the final metamorphosis of freedom into nature, and the mutual reconciliation of the two.

---

16. [*le chant.*]

But it is above all an original reappropriation of the *Critique of Judgment* that allows Schiller to articulate the philosophical investigation aiming at overcoming the tension between the trial of exile and the hope of a return, aiming therefore at overcoming the nostalgia for Greece, since Greece was seen by him as revealing the features of the true state of nature. Schiller writes to Körner:

> Kant's *Critique of Judgment* which I have acquired for myself fascinates me with its lucid ingenious content and has created in me the greatest desire to steadily learn more about his philosophy.[17]

It is impossible to consider here in their complexity the results of Schiller's meticulous assimilation of Kant's thought, which provided the opportunity of a long correspondence with Körner and was the impulse from which soon emerged a succession of essays: *Anmuth und Würde* (*Grace and Dignity*), *Über die ästhetische Erziehung der Menschen* (*On the Aesthetic Education of Man*), and *Über naive und sentimentalische Dichtung* (*On Naive and Sentimental Poetry*). I shall limit myself to the first two of these essays.

What the treatise on *Anmuth und Würde* validates in Kant's critique of aesthetic judgment is the notion of aesthetic freedom. In Kant, this notion means that the favor (*Gunst*) with which we contemplate the beautiful thing is the only free satisfaction, in the sense that it is subjected neither to the requirements of our impulses, nor to technical constraints, nor to a moral imperative. Schiller appropriates this notion and transforms it by conferring upon it an ethical meaning absent in Kant. Schiller's aesthetic freedom is the privilege of the beautiful soul in which tendencies and duty have been reconciled. Such beauty stands far apart from the enslavement to sensuous drives and is also far removed from the submission to pure reason. It is, nevertheless, nothing interior, since it shines forth and makes itself visible in grace. But the beautiful soul is in no way identifiable with a sort of spontaneous innocence, because it does not give itself over to nature. In nature, there is a harsh and violent element against which the beautiful soul is capable of resisting with heroism, thus attesting to its dignity. On this score, the

---

17. "[Kants] 'Kritik der Urteilskraft' die ich mir selbst angeschafft habe, reisst mich hin durch ihren lichtvollen geistreichen Inhalt und hat mir das grösste Verlangen beigebracht, mich nach und nach in seine Philosophie hineinzuarbeiten." Friedrich Schiller, *Schillers Briefe, Kritische Gesamtausgabe*, vols. 1–7, ed. Fritz Jonas (Stuttgart/Leipzig/Berlin/Wien) 3:136 (Letter from 3 March 1791).

Greek notion of excellence (*aretē*), of the *bios kalos k'agathos*, provides
the standard that Schiller interprets in light of transformed Kantian notions.
He writes:

> To the Greeks, nature was never just nature and so they were not
> embarrassed to honor her; to them, sensibility was never just sensi-
> bility so they were not afraid of being measured by its standards.[18]

Therefore, there must have been a time in history when the *bios* itself,
human existence, bathed in beauty. It is this beauty of the human *bios* that
Greek art celebrated.

As a consequence, the question soon arose from Schiller of the destiny of
beauty and art after the disappearance of the Greek world. But let us note
already that the topics of exile and homeland are at the core of the treatise
*Grace and Dignity*, as in the little essay "On the Sublime" written soon
thereafter (1793) in response to the caustic remarks Schiller heard from Kant
for having introduced the "Graces" into the ethical world. Schiller says expressly that, by submitting itself to the only imperative of pure practical reason, existence is deprived of beauty: It is the existence of an individual in
exile (*Fremdling*). However, he adds that our true homeland (*unser wahres
Vaterland*) remains no less lost if we are ruled by our senses.

The question of the destiny of beauty and art after the disappearance of
the Greek world is central in the letters *Über die ästhetische Erziehung des
Menschen* (*On the Aesthetic Education of Man*), a work that is the joint cor-
onation of Schiller's ethico-aesthetic reflection and philosophy of history.

The general problem of these letters is well known. In the closing years
of the eighteenth century, at a time when the world had just heard the ringing
of the Declaration of the Rights of Man and the Citizen, the whole epoch
aspired to see an end to the political system of despotism—originally based
on a natural mechanism—and the beginnings of a new one based upon the
law that reason gives to itself. From the *Naturstaat*[19] justified by Hobbes to
the *Vernunftstaat* justified by Kant, we have, according to Schiller, a muta-
tion called for by the entire epoch. But it is precisely against this opposition
between nature and reason that he takes a stand. In the final analysis, such an
opposition rests on an erroneous conception of freedom. Schiller proposes to
separate the concept of freedom both from the latitude granted to the imme-

---

18. "Dem Griechen ist die Natur nie bloss Natur, darum darf er auch nicht erröthen, sie zu
ehren; ihm ist die Vernunft niemals bloss Vernunft, darum darf er auch nicht zittern, unter ihren
Maassstab zu treten." *NA*, 20:254.

19. Ibid., 314ff. (letter 3).

diate desires (this view corresponds to the theoreticians of what Schiller calls *Naturstaat*) and from a pure freedom radically opposed to such desires and impulses (this corresponds to the freedom of pure practical reason); thus conceived as equally removed from the empirical character defining the first and from the intelligible character defining the second, Schiller insists, true freedom consists in a "third" character, both natural and moral, a character termed "total" because it unifies all the faculties of a human being.

This notion gives Schiller the opportunity to contrast the Greek and the modern worlds. Greek man is opposed, he wrote in the sixth letter, to modern man,

> since the latter receives his form from all-unifying nature, the former from all-separating intellect.[20]

It is in Greece that the third character manifested itself in the purest fashion:

> At once full of form and content, philosophizing and educating, tender and vigorous, we see how she [nature] unifies the youth of fantasy with the manhood of sensibility in one glorious humanity.[21]

In contrast, everything in the moderns bears the seal of sundering:[22] separation and independence of the sciences, sundering between the social classes and tasks, sundering between intuition and speculation, sundering between state and church, between law and customs, or mores, but also between enjoyment and work, between means and end, between effort and satisfaction, between theoretical and practical spirit. In the modern era, the world is scattered into an infinite series of bits of experience, both theoretical and practical, because both nature and the human community are reducible to the many cogs and wheels that make up a machine.

If his *Letters* had not gone beyond such an observation, he would have been limited to the expression of the nostalgia for Greece. Such was not the case. Schiller's search for the principle of the modern reign of separation and sundering seems to lead to what, in line with Rousseau, he calls "art"

---

20. "Weil jenem die alles vereinende Natur, diesem der alles trennende Verstand seine Formen ertheilen." Ibid., 322 (letter 6).

21. "Zugleich voll Form und voll Fülle, zugliech philosophirend und bildend, zugleich zart und energisch sehen wir sie die Jugend der Phantasie mit der Männlichkeit der Vernunft in einer herrlichen Menschheit vereinigen." Ibid., 321 (letter 6).

22. Ibid., 322f. (letter 6).

(*Kunst*) in the sense of artifice, that is, reckoning and dominating reason by means of which *homo faber* secures for himself the mastery of certain effects. The preponderance of this reckoning and dominating approach—which could simply be called a "utilitarian" mentality—explains the evil of modernity for Schiller. But what the use-oriented craftsmanship has destroyed, an art of a higher type, a "noble art" can restore. Such art is "fine art" (*die schöne Kunst*).[23] Whereas, by means of artifice, we do no more than escape the violence of nature, by means of fine art, we evade it on one side, but on the other one must "return to its simplicity, truth, fullness," (*zu ihrer Einfalt, Wahrheit und Fülle zurückkehren*).[24] At this juncture, a new way will present itself for the overcoming of the nostalgia of Greece: the aesthetic education of man. Because the memory of the artistic summit of Greece is not lost as modern beautiful works continue to draw inspiration from them, and because a noble art is possible in all epochs, the restoration of a total character is possible. The meditation on the ways to operate this restoration brings Schiller to develop a whole ontology of human existence. This ontology is expressed in notions borrowed from Reinhold: *Formtrieb* (drive to form) and *sinnlicher Trieb* (sensuous drive).[25] It states that both tendencies of spontaneity and receptivity correspond to the essence of the human being only if they are strictly reciprocal:

> In one word: only insofar as man is independent, is reality beyond him and is he receptive; only insofar as he is receptive is reality within him and is he a thinking force [creature].[26]

Such a reciprocity depends on a third tendency, the *Spieltrieb*,[27] a play tendency that attempts

> to receive in such a way as he himself would have conceived, and to receive in such a way as his mind wishes to receive.[28]

This *Spieltrieb* is encountered in the experience of beauty.

---

23. Ibid., 323 (letter 9).
24. Ibid., 329 (letter 7).
25. Ibid., 345f. (letter 12).
26. "Mit einem Wort: nur insofern er selbständig ist, ist Realität ausser ihm, ist er empfänglich; nur insofern er empfänglich ist, ist Realität in ihm, ist er eine denkende Kraft." Ibid., 352 (letter 13).
27. Ibid., 353f. (letter 14).
28. "So zu empfangen, wie er selbst hervogebracht hätte, und so hervorzubringen, wie der Sinn zu empfangen trachtet." Ibid., 354 (letter 14).

The notion of play is at the heart of Kant's analytic of the beautiful. Schiller borrows this notion from Kant, while assigning it to a range absent in its text of origin because he now links it to a faculty, the *Spieltrieb*, seen by him as the foundation of the essence of the human being.

> man only plays where he is man in the full meaning of the word, and he is completely man where he plays.[29]

On this point, too, an original reappropriation of Kant has been superimposed on the reflection on Greece—as it can be claimed that Schiller understands his *Spieltrieb* along the lines of the Greek *scholē*, leisure.

In a previous attempt I made to follow as precisely as possible Schiller's reflection along his itinerary, it appeared to me that his thought was not without an element of hesitation and inconsequence.[30] At times, beauty seems to be linked to the intrinsically finite character of human existence and to be a condition of humankind; at other times, it seems to be a transcendent idea that corresponds to an aspiration to the divine and the abolition of every limit. At times, it seems to be bound to counteract the notion of an unconditional *Sollen* (Ought), in Kant's and Fichte's sense; at other times, it seems to be itself object of a *Sollen*. At times, it seems to announce the metamorphosis of life, the unfolding of its deepest virtualities; at other times, it seems to be reserved to a sort of enclave sheltered from life, the shelter of the good appearance (*Schein*).[31]

Concerning art, on the one hand, it seems to be the sufficient condition for the restoration of the "total" character; on the other hand, it seems to be quite insufficient, because Schiller deplores that the beauty of works is twofold: alternatively energetic, thus sustaining the *Formtrieb*, and soothing, thus sustaining the *sinnlichen Trieb*.

At a deeper level, this meditation on the conditions for overcoming nostalgia occasionally leads to a sort of serene, and therefore nostalgia-free, acceptance of the beauty of finitude, that is, of a mixed condition involving at the same time receptivity and spontaneity. But it also occasionally leads to a sort of inverted nostalgia, under the form of an aesthetic transposition of Kant's *Sollen*, that is, an unlimited aspiration not toward a presence behind

---

29. "Der Mensch spielt nur, wo er in voller Bedeutung des Worts Mensch ist, und er ist nur da ganz Mensch, wo er spielt." Ibid., 359 (letter 15).

30. Jacques Taminiaux, *La Nostalgie de la Grèce à l'aube de l'idéalisme allemand* (The Hague: Nijhoff, 1967).

31. *NA*, 399ff. (letter 26).

us, but to the quasi-Platonic pure Idea of beauty, and to a presence inaccessible in life—as is expressed in the magnificent poem "Das Ideal und das Leben." Finally, his meditation, at times, leads beyond Kant and Fichte, but also beyond the Greeks, to a sort of anticipation of the absolute speculation of Schelling and Hegel, which does not involve any nostalgia for Greece because such a speculation considers the history of the world as an *Aufhebung* of both the naive Greek unity and the modes of sundering present in modernity.

In order to conclude this presentation of the spiritual constellation within which the nostalgia for Greece came to be inscribed for Schiller, I would like to call to mind a word of Nietzsche, who had read Schiller both attentively and critically. Nietzsche wrote in *The Origin of Tragedy* concerning the Apollinian gods of Olympus that they are "like roses born from thorny bushes" (*wie Rosen aus dornigen Gebüsch hervorstechen*).[32] It does not seem to me implausible that in the image of Greece that Schiller had made for himself—the nostalgic image that emerges, in the last analysis, from the poem on the gods of Greece—the roses hide the thorny bush. I mean that Greek existence had appeared to Schiller in the clear brightness shining forth from the gods as entirely permeated with light, harmony, and beauty. The possibility that such brightness could overlook a dull counterpart of shadows is an idea that Schiller never seems to have entertained.

In contrast, this possibility was perceived by Hölderlin with unparalleled acuteness. Let me, therefore, assess how Hölderlin reacted to the Schillerian nostalgia. That the young Hölderlin held Schiller in veneration is a well-known fact. It is obvious that his first poems and their topics—love, joy, freedom, and beauty—are quite closely akin to Schiller's celebration of the free unfolding of omnipresence, especially in "An die Freude," and of the spontaneous and harmonious correspondence of the Greek world to the *Hen kai Pan* (One-and-All).

As is the case in Schiller, Hölderlin's fervent admiration for the Greek world is accompanied by a feeling of irrevocable exile:

Let, O Parcae, the scissors be heard,
For my heart belongs to the dead![33]

---

32. Freidrich Nietzsche, *Kritische Gesamtausgabe*, ed. G. Colli and M. Montinari (Berlin/New York, 1972), 32.

33. "Lasst o Parzen, lasst die Schere tönen,
    Denn mein Herz gehört den Todten an!"
*Stuttgarter Ausgabe* of Hölderlin, *Sàintliche Werke*, ed. Freidrich Beyzner, 180, v. 55–6. Hereafter cited as *StA*. "Griechenland," 180, v. 55–56.

The antithesis between Greece and modernity, along with the antithesis between homeland and exile, shapes the space within which nostalgia occurs. This tension gives their specific tonality to the first poems of Hölderlin. On the one hand, we have omnipresence; on the other hand, the growing wasteland.

But soon this massive antithesis will be subjected to corrections, because the aspiration to a return—a major component of nostalgia—instead of being taken for granted, becomes an object of interrogation, whereas for Schiller its legitimacy never seems to have been questioned. This is confirmed, it seems to me, when one follows carefully the successive versions of *Hyperion*. There is, in my view, a sort of paradox in the cycle of Hyperion. On the one hand, this cycle is entirely permeated with a nostalgia for Greece. On the other hand, it allows the emergence, as early as the beginning, of some significant reservations concerning such a nostalgia.

The nostalgia for Greece was in the first poems the nostalgia emerging from a state of indigence and sundering toward an accord with the One-and-All.

If we consider the first version of the novel, that is, the "Thalia"-Fragment, we will easily agree that nostalgia looms prominently in the text. The preface to this fragment indicates that the novel describes some of the essential directions by means of which humankind can regain its essence. These directions are first the fusion within the One-and-All, then the domination of the One-and-All. The first corresponds to the nostalgia for Greece, the second to pure practical rationality as in Kant and, even more so, in Fichte. To these two, Hölderlin adds the evocation of a supreme formation that would consist in a return of the completed culture to the simplicity of an agreement with nature.

The first of these directions is at the center of the "Thalia"-Fragment. It corresponds very closely to the nostalgia for Greece expressed in the first poems. But in contradistinction to these poems, which can do no more than express the élan toward the plenitude of omnipresence and the unhappy consciousness of separation and sundering, Hyperion's itinerary points toward an overcoming of these themes. After speaking of the impulse that pushes him toward nature—fully living and free of sundering—Hyperion writes to his confidant Bellarmin:

> Blessed he . . . who has survived this trial by the fire of the heart, who has learned to comprehend the sighing of the creature, the feeling of paradise lost.[34]

---

34. "Wohl dem, . . . der sie überstanden hat, diese Feuerprobe des Herzens, der es verstehen gelernt hat, das Seufzen der Kreatur, das Gefühl des verlorenen Paradieses." StA III:165.

Such words show the emergence of a distance, or at least of a reserve, vis-à-vis nostalgia itself. This reserve can have two outcomes. One corresponds to the third of the paths mentioned in the preface, that is, the idea that the sorrow of exile is inscribed inside a teleology of reconciliation. This conception is present when Hyperion celebrates Homer's memory:

> Let pass on what passes on, I exclaimed among the inspired ones, it passes on in order to return, it ages in order to become more youthful, it separates itself in order to reunite itself more fervently, it dies in order to become more alive.[35]

To this we find a response or an echo in the words of one of his companions:

> Thus wither the beautiful youthful myths of the ancient world, the poetry of Homer and his times . . . , but the seed that lay within them emerges in autumn as ripe fruit. The simplicity and innocence of the first era dies so that it may return in completed form.[36]

But on the other hand, the novel does not conclude at all with such a teleology of reconciliation, serene and without nostalgia. It concludes—and this is the second outcome—on a sort of questioning mood fraught with expectation. Hyperion says:

> From inside the grove I felt reminded, from the depths of land and sea I felt questioned, why don't you love me?[37]

This amounts to the suggestion that blazing omnipresence, either under the form of a paradise lost or of a *telos* to come, is not the proper element for mortals. To this blaring and blazing, the last pages of the first version sub-

---

35. "Lasst vergehen, was vergeht, rief ich unter die Begeisterten, es vergeht, um wieder-zukehren, es altert, um sich zu verjüngen, es trennt sich, um inniger zu vereinigen, es stirbt, um lebendiger zu leben." StA III:180.

36. "So verblühen die schönen jugendlichen Myrthen [Mythen] der Vorwelt, die Dichtungen Homers und seiner Zeiten, aber der Keim der in ihnen lag, gehet als reife Frucht hervor im Herbste. Die Einfalt und Unschuld der ersten Zeit erstirbt, dass sie wiederkehre in her vollendeten Bildung." Ibid. StA III:180.

37. "Aus dem Innern des Hains schien es mich zu mahnen, aus den Tiefen der Erde und des Meers mir zuzurufen, warum liebst du nicht mich?" StA III:183.

stitute an area of shadows that is not presented as defective, as lesser in being, as an evil, but as a propitious element. Twice Hyperion says:

> My heart feels good in this twilight. Is this our element, this twilight?[38]

One should not be so rash as to conclude that the whole of Hölderlin's subsequent itinerary is contained in an embryonic form in the "Thalia"-Fragment. I only intended to suggest that, coming as early as this writing, a reservation is uttered concerning Schiller's confusion between the destiny of mortals and the serene brightness of the Olympian gods.

This reservation determines a relationship to the Greeks other than nostalgia, if it is granted that this nostalgia developed its own features and was fully expressed for the first time in Schiller's hymn to the gods of Greece. Of this different relationship, which is no longer one of aspiration to the full brightness of omnipresence, but one of meditation on the element of twilight and penumbra,[39] it seems to me that Hölderlin had made a very early acknowledgment to Neuffer, the friend to whom he had said, shortly before—at the time of the first poems—that the *Hen kai Pan* and Greece were the "flames of true life." Let us consider the words of this declaration:

> Indeed, I was silent even toward you since I gave you, more than to others, cause to suspect within me an unhappiness about all that was not sterling or gold, to suspect a continuous moaning that this world was not Arcadia. But I have now more or less outgrown this childish cowardice.[40]

Such an overcoming is the overcoming of the Schillerian antithesis between the brightness of Greece and the darkness of the modern age. It inaugurates a relationship with the Greeks no longer under the seal of the nostalgia for *Hen kai Pan,* but under that of the sober meditation on *Hen diapheron heauto* (self-differentiating Oneness).

---

38. "Meinem Herzen ist wohl in dieser Dämmerung. Ist sie unser Element, diese Dämmerung?" StA III:184.

39. [*la pénombre.*]

40. "Ich schwieg indes auch gegen Dich, wiel ich besonders Dir nur zu viel Veranlassung gab, in mir einen Unmuth über alles zu vermuten, das nicht versilbert und vergoldet ist, eien ewigen Jammer, darüber, dass die Welt kein Arkadien ist. Über diese kindische Feigheit bin ich aber so ziemlich weg." (Letter to Neuffer dated 10 October 1794). StA VI:136.)

Its focus of interest is to be no longer the gods of Olympus, but the tragedies.

Hölderlin would discover that the impulse toward *Pan*, is hostile to the human being, and that, instead, one has to purify oneself from wanting to fuse into the limitless Oneness of gods and mortals.

Such a meditation no longer opposes the plenitude of omnipresence to the indigence of sundering; it links the two together, as is attested to in the following passage, from a slightly later version of *Hyperion*, the prose version of the "Metrische Fassung,"[41] with which I shall conclude:

Let me speak as human. When our originally limitless being first began to suffer and the free, full power felt its first constraints, when indigence appeared alongside abundance, then it is that love began. You ask when that was? Plato says: on the day when Aphrodite was born. So at the point when the beautiful world began for us, when we gained consciousness, at such point we became finite.

Now we feel deeply the limits of our being and the bridled power rebels impatiently against its constraints, and yet there is something in us that willingly keeps these constraints—for, if the divine within us were not constrained by some resistance, then we would not know of anything outside us, and thus nothing about ourselves, and to know nothing about oneself, not to feel oneself and to be destroyed is to us the same thing.

---

41. "Lass mich menschlich sprechen. Als unser ursprünglich unendliches Wesen zum erstenmale leidend ward und die freie volle Kraft die ersten Schranken empfand, als die Armuth mit dem Überflusse sich paarte, da ward die Liebe. Fragst du, wann das war? Plato sagt: Am Tage da Aphrodite geboren ward. Also da, als die schöne Welt für uns anfieng, da wir zum Bewusstsein kamen, da wurden wir endlich.

Nun fülen wir teif die Beschränkung unseres Wesens, und die gehemmte Kraft sträubt sich ungeduldig gegen ihre Fesseln, und doch ist etwas in uns dad diese Fesseln gerne behält—denn würde das Göttliche in uns von keinem Widerstande beschränkt, so wüssten wir von nichts ausser uns, und so auch von uns selbst nichts, und von sich nichts zu wissen, sich nicht zu fülen, und vernichtet seyn, ist für uns Eines." StA III:192ff.

# 6

# Fire and the Young Hölderlin

It is a well-known fact that, until the composition of *Empedocles*, Hölderlin maintained links of close friendship with Hegel and Schelling, his two friends from the Tübingen Stift. It is also well-known that he was an assiduous auditor of Fichte's lectures at Jena, that he read Kant with fervor, and that, for a long time, he felt the most extreme veneration for Schiller, whose influence furthermore turned out to loom large in the shaping of Hegel's thought.

My topic is not one that overlooks the philosophical coordinates of Hölderlin's itinerary; instead, it aims at putting to the test my reading of Hölderlin's itinerary up to the threshold of his poetic maturity in the *Elegies* and the *Hymns*, by focusing on a precise theme: the young poet's complex attitude toward fire.

Precisely, fire, in the young Hölderlin, is quite obviously the very first theme of *The Death of Empedocles*, a tragedy set on that threshold. For it is in Etna's inferno that the destiny of the Greek sage on whom Hölderlin meditates closes and gains its meaning.

What meaning is this? This question raises a problem because this work by Hölderlin, whose central theme is fire, was never completed. We have three consecutive versions of *Empedocles*, which are all drafts, accompanied by four philosophical fragments, all unfinished too. Fire, therefore, infuses at the core of the tragedy a question that the tragedy does not bring to a resolution. It is as though Hölderlin, who was attracted to fire as the hero had been, turned out to be unable to justify this form of destiny and, so to speak, was compelled to an invincible reserve vis-à-vis the element of fire and what it symbolizes. Why this attraction? Why this reserve?

---

First published in *Le regard et l'excédent* (The Hague: Nijhoff, 1977).

It seems to me that both attraction and reserve are given the proper expression in a small ode entitled "Empedocles" dating from 1798, the year when Hölderlin first conceived the theme of his tragedy during his Frankfurt stay:

Life, you look for it, and still again look for it, when
flaring and blazing
from the Earth's depths Divine Fire springs forth for you,
and you, aflutter with desire,
throw yourself in Etna's blaze.
For a queen's vanity, pearls were also lost to wine.
Little did it matter. But why, poet,
did you sacrifice your wealth
and throw it over into the boiling crater?
Yet to me you are sacred, as the Earth's power
that plunged you under, intrepid victim,
and if love did not hold me back,
unhesitatingly into the depths I would trail the hero.[1]

I shall take my clue from this poem. It tells us that fire is divine, that it is the power of the earth, that it is life itself. It also says that fire is the goal of a pursuit now identified to the movement of desire; the comparison with the queen connects this desire to pride, to temerity, in short to some excess. Finally, the poem expresses a twofold reticence vis-à-vis fire: The full and divine life of fire, the object of an unbounded desire, is not the element of poetic Saying. Neither is this divine life the goal of love. On the contrary, love is what saves the poet from an infinite worship of Empedocles.

What is fire, then, if it arouses, on the one hand, such a violent desire and, on the other hand, such a reserve, originating both in poetic Saying and love?

In order to answer these questions, I will have to describe in outline Hölderlin's itinerary from the first poems to *Empedocles*.

Hölderlin's first poems present a first delineation of fire. The fire that is celebrated therein with no less fervor than grandiloquence is closely connected to the "beautiful divine spark, daughter of the Elysian Fields,"[2] the

---

1. Friedrich Hölderlin, *Sämtliche Werke*, historical-critical ed., 6 vol., ed. Norbert von Hellingrath, Friedrich Seebass and Ludwig von Pigenot (Berlin: Propyläen-Verlag, 1913–23), 6 vols. Hereafter cited as *SW*.
2. Schiller, *Nationalausgabe*, NA, 1:169.

very one celebrated by Schiller in the "Hymn to Joy" and in "The Gods of Greece." In their glorification of love, joy, and freedom, the early poems of Hölderlin all gravitate around the same center, which we can characterize as the free unfolding of the One-and-All.

When, for example, the young poet speaks of love, he does not consider a human, all-too-human, feeling, but rather the world, or nature. Nature, in turn, is not considered as a domain of beings coexisting with other domains, such as freedom or culture, but as the original and absolute unity, as the indivisible realm of omnipresence. Love is one of the modes—one of the laws—of this realm:

Faithful to love's holy laws
The world freely dispenses its sacred life.
(*SW*, 1:144–45)

Fully permeated by a Schillerian inspiration and by themes closely related to the pantheism of the *Theosophie des Julius,* Hölderlin's early poetry also stands as the lyrical equivalent of Hegel's *Tübingenfragment* and gives currency to the motto Hegel had discovered in Lessing and inscribed in the poet's workbook as the seal of their fellowship, *Hen kai Pan,* One-and-All. For Hölderlin, as for Schiller and Hegel, upon Greece is bestowed the unique and exemplary privilege of being spontaneously and authentically attuned to the spirit of the One-and-All.

The One-and-All and Greece define in Hölderlin's first poems the realm of fire or, as he says in a letter to his friend Neuffer, the "flame of my true life" (*SW*, 1:284).

But true life has now deserted this world, the true homeland has fled the earth, a situation he expresses thus: "My heart belongs to the dead" (*SW*, 1:166). His fervent identification with Greece, the guardian of the One-and-All and daughter of nature, is permeated with a feeling of irrevocable absence. The holy enthusiasm that burned in Greece has now turned to ashes, the gods have deserted the world, the golden age of fervent and simple heroes is no longer. Ours is the age of stone in which man and things are subjected to the empire of necessity, in which nature is the slave of man, in which man is the slave of another man, or of a God that stifles him, or of morals under which life suffocates. To the poet caught in the extreme opposition of this age of stone and what Hölderlin calls "the part of fire in me," in the depths of his exile, no other allotment is granted than the aspiration to the fire of omnipresence, in which resides the true homeland and the authentic element of man.

This pursuit of presence, of the homeland, which is originally an aspiration to the fiery element, is a characteristic of the *Hyperion* cycle, which is usually presented as the traveling phase of Hölderlin's itinerary, a traveling phase thanks to which—or should I say following which, namely, after his venturing through a foreign land—the poet would have been able, by initiating the turn to what is called the "patriotic" or "native," to discover what was his ownmost. I will attempt to show, against this usual presentation, that at the outset this traveling phase meant less a complete plunge into the foreign than a discovery—made early, and undergoing an expansion into its depths—of the ground of the homeland, namely, of finitude, which is a term whose meaning can only be clarified by exploring the very words of the poet.

But if it is true, on the one hand, that the traveling phase is set in motion by the decision to return within the divine omnipresence symbolized by fire, and if it is true, on the other hand, that the outcome of the travel is not a divine realm but finitude, it becomes necessary to show that the goal initially sought by the traveler changed along his path, and that the paths he took turned out to be inadequate or impractical, with the result that what he found en route was not what he had sought, and what he was seeking originally did not match what actually in the end he did find.

In this extremely complex course, whose meandering I cannot survey here, I would like to call attention, in their essentials, to three basic paths that correspond to the limits of my topic in the sense that all three answer a certain call from fire, although in each one, fire presents a different aspect.

These three paths seem to be indicated as early as the first preface to *Hyperion*, the "Thalia"-fragment, in which Hölderlin characterizes his novel as the description of some of the "essential orientations" of the path thanks to which man gains access to his essence. It seems to me that two of these pointers are invoked when the author states that "man's dream is to be both in everything and above everything" (*SW*, 2:53–54).

The dream to be in everything defines what Hölderlin calls "the tendency to covet everything." Such is the first path, in which desire wants to be in everything and to fuse into the whole.

The dream to be above everything defines what Hölderlin calls the "tendency to dominate everything." This is the second path, that of domination of the whole.

But Hölderlin also says that covetousness and domination are "dangerous" and suggests that authentic realization takes place at an equal distance from both, in a state he characterizes as one of "highest formation," in which the simplicity of a harmonious agreement of man with himself and with every other thing—a concordance that primordially was granted by nature—would be reproduced by means of human agency, and of the organization that man is capable of giving himself. This indicates the third orientation, that of the completion of nature and the return of it in completed culture.

Each of these three paths, I would point out, corresponds to one aspect of fire, but while Hölderlin remains attracted to each of them, he avoids being entirely committed to one, this reserve allowing him to lead the way into a meditation on finitude. Furthermore, when he explicitly formulated this meditation for the first time, he associated it with a particular conception of love, and when he explored it in its depths, it was associated with a particular conception of poetic language. With this, we can cast some light on the ode mentioned above, because both love and poetic Saying were what prevented the poet from walking in the footsteps of Empedocles.

## I.

The first path, the aspiration to be everything, is illustrated in the "Thalia"-fragment. The novel is composed of letters sent by Hyperion to his confidant, Bellarmin. The tone presiding over most of these letters is one of impatience and impetuous aspiration to the One-and-All. Hyperion claims to be weary of every determinateness, of every separation, of every limit, of every succession: "That which for me is not Everything, Everything eternally, is nothing for me" (*SW*, 2:54). In refusal of anything partial, temporal, perishable, of anything which in life or thought is marked by a lack, he "aspires to abolish the impediment of finitude" (*SW*, 2:54). And in a sense the entire fragment is animated by the turbulent opposition of the strife toward plenitude and the unhappy condition in the realm of separation, solitude, differentiation, and indigence. Such is the opposition—where one term elicits exaltation and the other loathing, each following the other in rapid succession—ruling over Hyperion's love relationship with Melite. The woman—whose name is changed to Diotima in the definitive version of the novel—is like the incarnation of the undivided plenitude of the One-and-All celebrated by Hölderlin in his first poetry. And Hyperion now celebrates his beloved in the very same terms used in that poetry to glorify Greece or the living nature. For it is because of her plenitude that the beloved precipitates in her lover the feeling of the most extreme destitution, with the result that turmoil immediately walks in the wake of enchantment. "When the notion occurred to me that the sovereign object of my love was so sovereign as not having to bother about me, despair was to overwhelm me" (*SW*, 2:65). In this context, it can be noticed that love and the desire to be All coincide; they follow the same trajectory. For both are led to overcome destitution by aiming at plenitude and at union with the One-and-All. "We are nothing, what we aim at is All" (*SW* 2:53).

Yet it is toward an overcoming of the opposition between indigence and plenitude that Hyperion's itinerary points. Precisely at this juncture we encounter both the theme of fire and that of a distancing from it. "Fortunate," writes Hyperion after speaking of the irrepressible élan he feels toward the living nature, and undivided presence, "fortunate the one whose heart has overcome the test of fire, and who finally understands the sigh of the creature and the regret for a paradise lost" (SW, 2:54). The test of fire is, indeed, the test of the élan toward the One-and-All in which desire and love are engulfed. Overcoming the test of fire amounts, therefore, to overcoming this élan, which incessantly alternates between nostalgia and impetuousness. But regarding what is entailed in the overcoming of the test, and of the opposition presupposed by it, the novel remains indecisive.

On the one hand, beyond alternating ecstatic fusion and dereliction, it seems to sketch the outline of a reconciliation[3] that would take upon itself the contradiction of union and separation, of plenitude and destitution. It is thus in the direction of the third orientation suggested in the preface that the narrative seems to move—a path that is given only in outline as a sort of dialectical reversal before the time, and thus similar to those anticipations found in the philosophies of history of Rousseau and Kant. This path is suggested in the following passage, where Hyperion celebrates Homer's memory:

> Let come to pass what is coming to pass, beings come to pass only
> to come back, they grow old only to be rejuvenated, they separate
> from each other only to be united more closely, they perish only to
> live a richer life. (SW, 2:76)

An echo of this passage can be found in the words of one companion:

> Thus wither away the beautiful myths of a young world, the poetry
> of Homer and his contemporaries, the prophecies, and the vistas,
> but the seeds they contained will be a ripened fruit in the autumn.
> The innocence and the simplicity of origins fade away so as to re-
> appear in the completion of culture, and the holy peace of paradise
> dissipates, so as to allow the blossoming of what was a mere gift of
> Nature into man's conquest and property. (SW, 2:76)

The ordeal of separation would then be inscribed in a teleology of reconciliation. This ordeal would be calling for a final completion of the origin, of

---

3. [accomplissement.]

nature, in the midst of culture or completed subjectivity, following a process described by Schiller in some of his poems and soon to be thematized in *The Letters on the Aesthetic Education of Man* and *Naive and Sentimental Poetry,* and also later adopted by Hegel as the fundamental schema of his philosophy of history. Yet, on the other hand, *Hyperion* does not close on the celebration of the glorious path of the final reconciliation of nature and culture. Although such a path is not expressly discarded, the last pages of the novel rather stress a sort of restraint. The theme of the last letter is that of questioning, of the silence of listening and awaiting: "An exhortation," says Hyperion, "seemed to rise from the depths of the earth, and a call to swell from the sea, Why do you disdain me?" (*SW,* 2:80–81). Thus, faithfulness to the earth seems to take precedence over the impetuosity of the élan toward fire. The gigantic blaze previously sought makes room for the penumbra, which is described no longer as an evil, but as the propitious "element." "My heart," says Hyperion twice, "is at peace in this penumbra. Might this be our element? But why cannot it bring me sleep?" (*SW,* 2:81).

The novel remains, therefore, suspended not over the theme of the élan toward fire, but over that of a distance held with respect to this element. However, everything happens as though there were two forms of distance, two ways of overcoming the test of fire. In outline, the first could be roughly presented as follows: There is no reason to oppose the omnipresence of the One-and-All to finite determinations, and, first, to sustain this opposition in constant oscillation between the surging élan and its plunge, because this opposition is the promise of a superior reconciliation. The second form of the test of fire could be considered, in contrast, the resolute acceptance of finitude as an ever-unsatisfactory, yet propitious, realm. It is toward the meditation on finitude that, after his first novel, Hölderlin turned his attention.

Before considering this new phase, we can pause after this exploration and try to summarize it by keeping in view the little ode that we quoted earlier. It said to us that fire, described as the plenitude of life, is the correlate of desire, taken at its greatest amplitude. But on the other hand, it also said that fire is an element appropriate neither to poetic Saying nor to love, and this was the reason why the poet refrained from yielding to the call of fire while being deeply receptive to it. If we confront the first version of *Hyperion* with this ode, we can say that the correlation of desire and fire is clearly stated in it. Concerning the distancing from fire, it is indeed a direction of the work, but is suggested only in an irresolute manner in the name of a sort of teleology of history, and later in the name of a thought of the in-between, at which point the novel ends hesitatingly. But neither poetic Saying nor love is connected to this reserve. On the contrary, speech, considered from the perspective of the élan toward the One-and-All, is deemed superfluous and hindering: "Words," Hyperion says in one of the first letters, "are clouds that hide Hera" (*SW*, 2:57). Likewise, the tale of Hyperion's passion for Melite seems to require that love fuse with the One-and-All.

## II.

We have a different situation in the very next phase of Hölderlin's itinerary, namely, in the drafts leading to the definitive version of the novel. We have now a meditation directly centered on the question of finitude, in connection with a new notion of love, whose trajectory now diverges from the élan toward the One-and-All. Such a meditation is equally removed from the longing for omnipresence—the first path previously considered—and from the second path, as we shall see, of domination.

It is attested by Hölderlin's correspondence at the time, that he was striving to get away from the path of nostalgia and of desire, and consequently to overcome the dualism that previously opposed the One-and-All and nothingness, the infinite omnipresence and a wasted finite. I shall limit myself to a quotation from a letter by Hölderlin to his friend Neuffer, the same to whom he had disclosed earlier that *Hen kai Pan* (the One-and-All) and Greece were "the flame of his true life." Hölderlin now writes: "I only gave you too many opportunities to suspect in me a dissatisfaction with everything that is not pure gold or silver, a never-ending desperation at not finding this world in the like of Arcadia. I am now beginning to overcome this childish cowardice" (*SW*, 1:346).

This overcoming of the dualistic intransigence now makes room, not at all for the acceptance of what Hölderlin used to call "indigence," which he contrasted to the beautiful plenitude of omnipresence, but for the acknowledgment of a sort of secret kinship between the two. With this acknowledgment a new conception of love is associated. The text of one of the *Hyperion* drafts, the *Metrische Fassung*, expresses this relationship:

When our originally limitless being first began to suffer and the free, full power felt its first constraints, when indigence appeared alongside abundance, then it is that love began. You ask when that was? Plato says: on the day when Aphrodite was born. So at the point when the beautiful world began for us, when we gained consciousness, at such point we became finite. Now we feel deeply the limits of our being and the bridled power rebels impatiently against its constraints, and yet there is something in us that willingly keeps these constraints—for, if the divine within us were not constrained by some resistance, then we would not know of anything outside us, and thus nothing about ourselves, and to know nothing about oneself, not to feel oneself and to be destroyed is to us the same thing. (*SW*, 2:495).

In Hölderlin's text these words are spoken by a sage encountered by the young Hyperion in one of his travels and whose words tell Hyperion of his own straying. But according to the narrative made by Hyperion of his trip, it appears that he went astray by following one of the paths indicated in the first preface to the novel, not the path of desire and nostalgia that we just considered, but the path of conquest and domination. This second path differs from the first one in the sense that it is oriented not toward the return to the lost omnipresence of undivided nature, but instead toward the ultimate victory of the Spirit over nature. We need only to look at some of Hyperion's pronouncements to understand how he progressed along that way:

Schooling from Fate and the sages had made me tyrannical towards nature. Because I refused to trust in what I had received from her hand, no love could grow in me any longer. Pure and free spirit, I thought, could never be reconciled with the senses and their world, and joy thus only existed in victory. Impatient as I was to restore freedom in our being, I rejoiced in the struggle that reason wages against the irrational. . . . I wanted to dominate nature. . . . I had become almost deaf to the sweet melodies of human life, to what belongs to a home and childhood. I used to find it incomprehensible that years ago I had liked Homer. I was traveling and wished to travel endlessly. (*SW*, 2:493)

In the impetuous struggle against everything that is nature, in reason's pursuit of equality with itself by domination over everything that it is not, there lies the second aspect of fire. It is the "fire of the victorious spirit," as Hölderlin calls it in *The Young Hyperion*, which is a slightly later text that for the most part repeats the themes and terms of the *Metrische Fassung* (*SW*, 2:507).

There can be no doubt that by opposing the path on which, in his description, Hyperion walked under the schooling of sages, Hölderlin takes aim at Kant's practical philosophy and at the Fichtean developments of it. And it would be particularly easy to show that the theme of the wandering traveler who breaks all previous links with nature is extremely close to another wandering figure, that of Abraham—soon thereafter described by Hegel as an eternal wanderer on the boundless earth, whose first step was to reject the beautiful harmonies of his childhood, to persevere in an attitude of hostile opposition toward all things and in his appeal to an ideal being to perpetuate the only possible relationship to nature as soon as she was envisaged as hostile: the relationship of domination. And just like Hölderlin, Hegel was directing criticisms at the Kantian ethics.[4]

But Fichte is, as much as Kant, intended by Hölderlin, and it is undoubtedly in light of those reflections occasioned in Hölderlin by his study of the philosopher of Jena that we can best attempt to understand the idea of the kinship of plenitude and indigence that seems to define the thought of finitude. The principle of Fichte's doctrine, as it was being exposed at the time in *The Foundations of the Doctrine of Science* and in the lectures *The Vocation of the Scholar*, is the absolute primacy of practical reason, the definition of consciousness and Being in terms of pure freedom and pure activity. Fichte's ambition on the theoretical level is to show that natural consciousness falls into an illusion when it believes that objects impose themselves upon it from the outside, an illusion that has the non-ego from the outside actively interfering in the ego. Denouncing this illusion amounts to showing that it is consciousness that imposes this passivity upon itself, to retrieving in the manifold of natural consciousness the unity of transcendental consciousness from which the manifold can be deduced. But this deduction cannot end on the theoretical level: It encounters the opacity of the non-ego, and it is to the practical level of moral action that the quest for pure freedom and pure activity now shifts. But neither is the non-ego incorporated in the ego on this level. The ego is constrained—in the attempt to become pure activity—to undergo a process of infinite effort and of relentless destruction of what in it is nature or passivity. Moral action is, then, some sort of terror; it is the aiming by the finite ego at a pure, and always ideal, unity that forces it to consider the non-ego as an obstacle, against which violence is constantly required.

The fact that such a thought moves within the element of fire can be confirmed by the assessment made by Jules Vuillemin, one of today's main commentators on Fichte:

> Moral action in Fichte is the fire that devours the moments of time and the individuals. Being is in the ashes remaining after the struggle. The ashes testify that there was a struggle, but it belongs to

---

4. See *Hegels theologische Jugendschriften* (Tübingen: H. Nohl, 1907), 245ff. *Early Theological Writings*, trans. T. M. Knox (Philadelphia: University of Pennsylvania Press, 1975), 186ff.

the dead to bury the dead. Fire, which is pure act and ungraspable [element], only asserts itself in the absolute nothingness of every determined being. Loving nature and finitude does not devolve on us.[5]

At this juncture, it seems to me, Hölderlin comes forth to assert against Fichte that loving nature and finitude devolves on us. His attitude toward Fichte, as expressed in the *Hyperion* drafts and in his correspondence, can be summarized in the following terms:

> Fichte's absolute Ego is supposed to contain all reality; it is everything, and outside of it, nothing exists. For this absolute Ego, there is no object. Yet a consciousness without an object is not conceivable, and consequently the Absolute Ego is for us as if it did not exist. (*SW*, 2:315–16)

Far from rallying around the absolute ego, Hölderlin stresses the finite ego, which Fichte fails to overcome. But giving credence to the finite ego amounts to relinquishing the concept of nature as the ego's pure negative, because it is only in the perspective of returning to the absolute ego that nature is reduced to being nothing but a permanent obstacle. If, on the contrary, the finite ego is in such need of the non-ego that negating the latter would entail abolishing the ego itself as a conscious being, then nature is no longer our enemy, she is our resource. Under these conditions, the true lesson from Fichte's philosophy, as Hölderlin understands it, teaches—albeit *a contrario*—that we do not have to become pure spontaneity to the detriment of all receptivity, but that there lies at the very foundation of consciousness a sort of reciprocity of spontaneity and receptivity. "If nothing were contrary to us," Hölderlin writes, "there would be no object for us" and we would be nothing, so that "limitation is necessary to a conscious being" (*SW* 2:326–7). But it is not sufficient for us to be limited in order to be conscious, and Hölderlin adds: "Infinite activity, unlimited in its tendency, is also necessary to a conscious being, because if we did not long to be infinite, we would never feel anything that is different from us, we would know nothing, and, consequently, we would have no consciousness" (*SW*, 2:326–27).

In other words, for a world to be manifested to our eyes, it is necessary that an infinite power of negation should mysteriously animate us. On this point, Hölderlin asserts that Fichte was right. But precisely because sponta-

---

5. Jules Vuillemin, "Fichte," in *Les philosophes célèbres*, ed. Maurice Merleau-Ponty (Paris: Mazenod, 1956).

neity is the element reciprocal of receptivity and is only meaningful in connection with the world that it brings to emergence—against Fichte—one
must say that this infinite power is less destructive than disclosing. Far from
annihilating the world, the power of negation is what unveils it, what allows
us to be adjusted to what is unveiled.

I believe that one can understand by means of Hölderlin's interpretation
of Fichte both his reserve toward the "fire of the victorious spirit" and the
meaning of words denoting a Platonic inspiration in one of Hyperion's
interlocutors.

No more than the fire of nostalgia and desire, is the fire of domination
propitious to man. In either case, it is the link of spontaneity and receptivity
that is broken, it is the difference inscribed at the heart of man that unilat-
erally is abolished. And it is precisely this link that Hölderlin had in view
when Hyperion's interlocutor is made to say that access to consciousness is
the admission into finitude—something that does not mean a fall from divine
plenitude into pure and simple indigence, because this admission into finitude
is also the revelation of the beauty of the world and because it is in finitude that love originates. From this, we see that love is not pure and simple
nostalgia of plenitude (as is the case in Plato's *Symposium* interpreted by the
tradition), but both the withdrawal in the name of *Poros* from the limit ascribed to love by *Penia* and the affection for this limit. Accordingly, *The
Young Hyperion* says that love, who inherited from his father the tendency of
overstepping all boundaries and from his mother the tendency of abiding by
them, transforms into an accord the struggle of these tendencies "indispensable to each other" (*SW*, 2:507). Accordingly, also, as we see in the same
work, love is led astray when it wants to mask the conflict from which it was
born, and remains authentic to its origin only when maintaining these opposites in their difference, as alliance that it secures by avoiding the fascination
of the unlimited and the satisfaction with the limit. "*Non coerceri maximo,
contineri tamen a minimo*" (Be not constrained by the greatest, yet be
touched by the smallest) (*SW*, 2:54).

## III.

The third path corresponding to the third aspect of fire remains to be
explored. That path had already been evoked in the first preface to *Hyperion*,
where it pointed toward a sort of supreme reconciliation of nature and culture, between immediate omnipresence and the mediation that is part and
parcel of human activity. But in this preface, it is not asserted at all that this
path is dangerous. Far from being described as an excess to be avoided, this
path is described as reconciliation of what remains univocal both in the path

of covetousness or the path of the élan toward the One-and-All, and in the path of the domination over everything. It seems to me that this third path is presented with greatest clarity in the tragedy *Empedocles,* more particularly in the theoretical reflections that accompany the elaboration of the work and seek to justify its foundations. But the successive transformations of this uncompleted tragedy and certain reflections from the theoretical pages show that this path, which exerted a fascination upon Hölderlin, also exceeds every measure. It is associated with fire as a result of this lack of measure, and is contested in the name of finitude.

More precisely, it is a new attention paid to language that inhibits the temptations originally exerted on Hölderlin by fire.

This third path plunges into metaphysics. It is directed toward the absolute metaphysics being elaborated at this period by Hölderlin's closest companions from the Tübingen Stift, Schelling and Hegel, the very same ones whose thought, like his, had been kindled by the motto *Hen kai Pan.* That Hölderlin experienced the temptation of a sort of absolute idealism can be substantiated by many signs predating the time of *Empedocles,* especially in his correspondence. Consider the following ambitious project mentioned in a 1795 letter to Schiller:

> I am trying to show that the unification of the subject and of the object in an Absolute Ego (whatever name one chooses to apply to it)—an inescapable requirement for every system—can be achieved at the theoretical or practical levels only as an infinite approximation, as in the squaring of the circle, but is however possible in an intellectual aesthetic intuition. (*SW,* 2:344)

Here too, the relation to Fichte is what transpires, but a very different relation from the one that we mentioned above. Indeed, instead of opposing the finite ego to Fichte's absolute ego, it seems as though, in this text, Hölderlin wanted to go farther than Fichte, by bringing to completion absolute idealism left incomplete by Fichte because on the theoretical level he did not succeed in the absolute recuperation of the non-ego in the ego and because on the practical level he went no further that an infinite requirement, a *Sollen* (an Ought) that can never bridge the gap between the finite ego and the pure activity it pursues. In other words, Hölderlin was aiming at conquering a sphere within which the absolute synthesis could be completed, whereas this identity was ever refused to the spheres of knowledge and action. Accordingly, he claims that there is an aesthetic-intellectual intuition in which beauty is revealed as absolute identity of the object and of the subject, of nature and consciousness or human activity.

Certain passages from the definitive version of *Hyperion* confirm this point. Thus, in evoking a final return to the Greek origin: "There will be one, only one, beauty: humankind and nature will be identified within universal divinity" (*SW* 2:200). But other passages in the novel closely associate beauty with finitude, that is, with the ambiguity of man, constituted by the conflict between an aspiration toward the unlimited and an attachment to the limit, with the result that, when Hölderlin states that Heraclitus's words, *Hen diapheron eauto,* self-differentiating One, define the essence of beauty, it is not clear whether what Hölderlin means is a sort of speculative unity of the opposites, or whether, at the core of Being, he points at an insurmountable movement of differentiation—to which, in man, would correspond a correlative tension between two antagonistic aspirations. In addition, the nostalgia of the *Hen kai Pan* remains one of the constants in the novel.

But let me now consider Empedocles' death. When Hölderlin first conceived the project of this tragedy, he presented his hero under the sign of the great opposition between Oneness-wholeness and limitation, between plenitude and indigence, therefore under the sign of the impetuous élan toward the One-and-All. Empedocles then,

> [someone who], from long, by temperament and philosophy inclined to hate culture, to despise every special occupation, every interest in various objects, the mortal enemy of every settled existence, and for this reason, dissatisfied in the midst of really beautiful situations, indecisive, suffering because every situation is particular, because it brings him satisfaction only if experienced in the midst of a great agreement with the entire life—since in it he cannot live and love as a god, with a heart that wholly agrees with the present, free and expanding as a god, only because, no sooner have his heart and thought taken hold of the present than he falls prey to the law of succession (*SW,* 3:67),

Empedocles decides to throw himself into Etna's fire to experience again the great concordance therein with the entire living world. The destiny of Empedocles is therefore tied up with the nostalgia of omnipresence, on the path of the desire to be in everything, since in Etna's fire lives the One-and-All.

On this path, once more, language seems superfluous. Just as the young Hyperion considered words as clouds hiding the divinity, just as the hero of the definitive version of the novel says in celebration of the omnipresence of nature that "words are as the sound of the flame that rises up while leaving ashes behind it," likewise Empedocles in the first version of the tragedy repudiates language:

Divinely present nature
Is in no need of words. (*SW*, 3:150)

But a note added by Hölderlin at the end of the manuscript of the first version takes a stand against Empedocles' impetuosity and underscores its unilateral character, in the name of a difference that he no longer views as one soon to be overcome. Those sages, he says, only introduce purely general and insufficient distinctions, which is the reason why they assume that their return into pure Being places them in eternal nonopposition. It is possible to believe that under this enigmatic declaration, the correlation of plenitude and indigence is stressed once again. It is a fact that, while he was striving to reflect on the meaning of Empedocles' destiny, Hölderlin was led to lay the emphasis on differentiation, and to underscore that the "supreme fire," first described as the intimacy of undivided presence, of life, or of nature, is an excess exactly correlative of another excess, "the extreme of differentiation and indigence." At which point, he evokes a path leading to an intimacy of a more discreet kind (*SW*, 3:316–17).

Interestingly enough, in the second version of the work, neither boundless enthusiasm for undivided presence, nor the momentous opposition of nature and man's activity, is to be found. Far from contrasting the mortals' "narrow concerns" with the free unfolding of pure presence, or "dwelling down here" with life's holy and unfettered spirit, or the "fallacies of care" with the glory of the undying Oneness, Empedocles seems to say that presence, for man, has no way of coming to pass except by dint of the activities and words whereby the human being shapes and names what is:

Silent is nature

. . .

What would then be the earth and the sea,
and islands and stars, and everything offered to the eyes of men,
and what would also be
this inert lyre, if I did not give it sound,
and speech, and soul? What are the gods
and their spirit, if by me they are not proclaimed?
(*SW*, 3:194)

And the work is interrupted by the following monologue:

To work is man's duty,
the one who meditates must unfold,
around him must nurture, and release, Life;

For great Nature bears great presage
and surrounds the one heeding in readiness,
so that he may bring form.
So that Nature's spirit may be manifested,
he in his breast carries care and hope . . .
And much he can do, and magnificent is his word,
He who transforms the world. (*SW*, 3:195)

But then, Empedocles' message does not consist in calling for the fusion into the undivided presence of nature that would stand in opposition to human activity and speech, because, on the contrary, it is nature that requires their activity and speech in order to be manifested. It does not consist, either, in magnifying the autonomy of an activity dominating nature, because, as it is indeed man's duty to work, his work has no other meaning than revealing nature. In other words, the two aspects of fire previously encountered, one along the path of the élan toward the One-and-All, the other along the path of domination, have now faded away. What meaning does this confer upon Empedocles' destiny and his decision to throw himself into Etna?

This undoubtedly is the question motivating Hölderlin to inquire into the foundation of his tragedy, namely, into the meaning of this confrontation of nature and what he calls "Art," that is, human activity and speech. It results in an extremely dense text, namely, *Grund zum Empedokles (Groundwork For the Empedocles)*, in which the struggle of nature and art is deliberately inscribed in a process of absolute reconciliation of the opposites, which is described in terms of a circle exactly as in Schelling's contemporary essays. In it Hölderlin evokes the original unity, the pure life in the midst of which art and nature, the organic and the aorgic, harmoniously fuse, but he states that this "pure life" had to be shattered in order to be manifested and reach fulfillment.[6]

For this pure life to be grasped in knowledge, it is necessary that, as pure life first only present in feeling, it be divided in the excess of an intimacy in which opposites turn into each other, that the organic—after being excessively absorbed in Nature and forgetting its own being which is consciousness—take a radical step into autonomous activity, art, and reflection; and it is necessary, in contrast, that Nature radically move into the aorgic, the ungraspable, the unlimited—until both, which were were united formerly, now by dint

---

6. [*s'accomplir.*]

of the development of opposed reciprocal action, are for each other as originally, in the beginning. (*SW*, 3:321–22)

In this process what is finally initiated between them is an "infinite union," which is the dwelling "of the divine in their midst" (*SW*, 3:322). We have now reached a point very close to Schelling's speculations, very close to the ontotheology of absolute idealism. At this point, the third aspect of fire emerges: the fire of absolute reconciliation, of the identity of opposites, which provides the key to Empedocles' destiny. Tragedy, in this atmosphere of speculative thought, is, to use Hölderlin's words, "the metaphor of an intellectual intuition" (*SW*, 3:268). The hero's death strikes as a sort of speculative holocaust. It means that individuality does not measure up to the highest reconciliation, the Absolute described by Schelling at the same period, in terms amazingly close to Hölderlin's, as "the sanctuary where one single flame combines what, in life and action, and thus in thought as well, [was] eternally separated."[7]

But Hölderlin did not deem this path more satisfying than the two previous ones. In the attempt to implement these foundational reflections, Hölderlin confronted Empedocles with a rival of equal strength who refuses to unite the opposites and wants to preserve each one within its limit by connecting the reciprocal action and difference of each to "something firm and solid" (*SW*, 3:335). In Alleman's beautiful interpretation,[8] the firm and solid applies to institution, to rank, but also it applies to the rigor of words and of language, without which presence would be nothing but a devouring fire, and a light so intense that nothing would be manifested by it. With this theme of differentiation, and of the necessity to endure it firmly but confidently, at issue again is the theme of finitude. Being human, more or less said the young Hyperion, means holding oneself in between an unlimited aspiration and the welcoming of the limit; it means staying in a condition of perpetual absence, or in an unlimited project that exceeds everything that is, but whose meaning can be no other than opening up a world and giving us access to a presence.

Everything happens as though the path of nostalgia, the path of domination, and finally the path of the absolute reconciliation of opposites, could not acknowledge this difference inscribed in the heart of man, since he is dissatisfied with every limit and yet willingly keeps to them. The emergence of a world in its beauty, that is, in its Being or in its presence, was in the *Hyperion* drafts tied up with our finitude. Now Hölderlin discovers that it is tied

---

7. Schelling, *System des transzendentalen Idealismus*, in *Werke*, ed. K. F. A. Schelling, vol. 3, 628.

8. See Beda Alleman, *Hölderlin und Heidegger* (Zurich: Atlantis, 1954).

up with language, not with the everyday language that gives currency to what is already well known, but with the foundational language of the poet. For in this language it is still the ambiguity of finitude that finds its voice. The poet's Saying does not consist in forcing his access to the One-and-All, but in letting it be in its enigmatic presence, thus entailing that, constantly exposed to surprise, authentic speech is nothing but receptivity. But on the other hand, such presence would vanish if speech could not summon itself, and in that sense authentic speech is nothing but spontaneity. "Immediacy is impossible," would soon write the poet, "for the gods and the mortals" (*SW*, 5:276).

Hence, if one grants that, in each of the three paths followed, fire is linked to totality, to Being, to presence, first in the shape of undivided immanence, then in the shape of unconditional subjectivity, and finally in the shape of speculative reconciliation, must one conclude that, by rejecting them, Hölderlin dismisses the interest in omnipresence that entirely permeated his early itinerary? The answer is no, but from now on there remains open to him only one way of being faithful to presence and to the call that incessantly invests him: It is speech, guarded and restrained, which "holy sobriety" preserves from "ec-centric enthusiasm":

He whom the Fathers's fire does not consume,
He in the deepest elect, suffering the god's
sufferings, eternal heart, he still remains firm.[9]

---

9. Last stanza if "Wie wenn am Feiertage" ("As on the festival day . . . ") in *SW* 4:153.

# 7

# Art and Truth in Schopenhauer
# and Nietzsche

My purpose in this essay is to elucidate Nietzsche's aphorism "We have art so as not to perish from truth."[1]

Before trying to shed some light on this enigmatic sentence—and in order to do so—it is appropriate to recall the basic features of Schopenhauer's philosophy of art. Indeed, Nietzsche started shaping his own philosophy of art under the influence of Schopenhauer.

As Professor Philonenko put it in *Schopenhauer, une philosophie de la tragédie (Schopenhauer, a Philosopher of Tragedy)*, Schopenhauer is "the man of a single book, which he rewrote several times,"[2] namely, *The World as Will and Representation*. Philonenko argues that this book, in many respects, shows that Schopenhauer was the last great philosopher of German idealism. Indeed, his initial inspiration came from Kant; he found in Kant his key distinction between the thing-in-itself and phenomena, between ideas and concepts. Furthermore, the very structure of his book—its development through a theory of knowledge, a metaphysics of nature, a metaphysics of art, a theory of ethical life, and even its main topic—is comparable to the systematic structure of other post-Kantian philosophies like Fichte's, Schelling's, or Hegel's.

But such a kinship is meaningless if we do not realize that, in every respect, Schopenhauer aims at subverting the doctrine of all other German idealists. Whereas all other German idealists attempted to achieve and accomplish modern rationality, as conceived by Descartes and developed by

This paper was first published as "Art and Truth in Schopenhauer and Nietzsche," in *Man and World*, 1987, number 20, pp. 85–102.

1. Friedrich Nietzsche, *Der Wille zur Macht, (The Will to Power)* section 822.
2. Alexis Philonenko, *Schopenhauer, une philosophie de la tragédie* (Paris: Vrin, 1980), 9.

the Enlightenment, Schopenhauer instead was convinced that the prestige of reason—in whatever field, philosophy, natural sciences, political theory, theory of historical progress—is sheer deception.

Let us look at this matter closely. The very title of Schopenhauer's main book provides a clue. The title suggests that there is both a continuity and a discontinuity between will and representation. The world as will is not what the world as representation is, and still it is one and the same world. This deserves consideration.

The world as representation is the world as it appears, the world as a phenomenon. If the word *world* means, as it does in Schopenhauer as well as in classical philosophy, the totality of what is, then *world as representation* means the totality of what appears to us. What appears to us appears in *space* and *time:* this phenomenon here, this other one there, this one now, this other one later or earlier. According to Schopenhauer, in agreement with Kant, the spatial and temporal diversity of the phenomenal realm is articulated. It is not a chaos. It is an arrangement, an order. Two principles put the phenomena in an orderly arrangement: the principle of *individuation,* and the principle of *sufficient reason.*

By saying that the phenomena are ruled by the principle of individuation, Schopenhauer simply means that space and time individualize phenomena: This phenomenon here is not the same as that phenomenon there; this phenomenon now is not the one that just vanished in the past. And by saying that the phenomena are ruled by the principle of sufficient reason, Schopenhauer simply means that whatever appears to our senses is always explainable in terms of cause-effect sequences that provide a reason for it, or that account for its appearing this way or that way. Likewise, the events of our own lives all seem to have either an explanation in terms of causality or a justification in terms of motives and goals.

However, Schopenhauer claims that all this reasonable and rational order, which articulates the phenomenal field of our conscious life, is just a semblance. This orderly structure of the world as phenomenal representation is not true. It is a veil, the veil of Maya, covering a thoroughly different reality. The other reality hidden by the orderly structure of representation is the *will.* Representation seems to be the true and real. It is neither. The will is the real world, the true thing, the thing-in-itself, the *Ding an sich.* Whence and how do we find a way leading us to the real world? We find it while meditating upon what representation always presupposes without being able to know it in terms of representation. Obviously what representation as a phenomenon presupposes is a representing entity. Appearing as a phenomenon is appearing to, being perceived by, someone—*is being an object for a subject.* That subject is ourselves. Each of us is a knowing subject. Each of us articulates phenomena in terms of causality, or sufficient reason. But each knowing subject is individualized by a body. Now, a body is more than a perceiving entity. It also is a feeling entity. Here we do have a way to the real world. An individual's body, as perceived from without, is a phenomenon. But as felt from within, it opens the way to a realm that is beyond representation, namely, the will.

Of course, it is always possible to describe our will in terms of representations, which means that we seem to be entitled to justify our deeds, to prove that we had reasons to do what we did. But this image of the will as justifiable and reasonable is superficial and misleading. In its nature, the will escapes the scope of the principles of individuation and sufficient reason. And this is shown by our body life, as felt by us in pains and pleasures. Indeed, the repeated alternations of our expectations and disappointments, of our wishes and satisfactions, indicate that, instead of possessing a will as an individual ability, we are possessed by it as a transindividual and unjustifiable power. The will, in Schopenhauer's sense of the word, is a power that is beyond individuation and reason. Such a power is the very being of the world, an abyssal, groundless, unconscious power, aiming at its own perpetuation without any conceivable justification, and without any care for the individual entities emanating from it. This brief summary sheds some light on both the continuity and discontinuity I was evoking. Between will and representation there is discontinuity, since the features of the will (transindividuation and absence of reason) are strictly opposed to the features of representation (individuation and sufficient reason). But between will and representation there is also a continuity, in the sense that individuation and reason are like puppets with the help of which the will hides itself and perpetuates its own chaotic essence. In other words, when the world appears to us as ordered, when we claim to be able to know in a disinterested way the structure of the phenomenal realm, all our knowledge is illusory. Our supposed disinterest is a deception. Our critical mind is not really critical. Our neutrality is partial. Science as a whole is blindly submitted to the absurd momentum of the will. And because it is slave to the will, science is unable to see the nature of the will.

But what is necessarily ignored by science can be glimpsed by metaphysics, if and only if metaphysics does not approach the thing-in-itself, that is, the will, in the way science approaches phenomena. Scientific knowledge confirms the will, enhances its absurd self-perpetuation, by seeking reasons, causes, and laws. If metaphysics were looking at the thing-in-itself in terms of reason, then it would also confirm the will while covering its nature. In other words, metaphysics cannot perform its job, if it is conceived of as a superscience.

But, then, where is metaphysics going to find a model or an inspiration for approaching the thing-in-itself? The model is *art*. Whereas science—even when critical and full of doubt and suspicion—always plays the game of the will, art no longer plays such a game. How so?

Whereas science always works for the practical interests of the will, art is basically disinterested. Whereas science is *pragmatic*, and to that extent a form of the will, art is *contemplative*. By being detached, the artist is able to contemplate the nature of the will. Art is a *higher knowledge than science*. Science knows the world as phenomenon, and its supposed truth is a deception. Art knows the world in its essence; it perceives the will behind the phenomena; it grasps the phenomena as they *truly* are, as objectification of the will. To designate the essence as opposed to contingent appearances, Plato used the word *eidos*, "Idea." Art, in Schopenhauer's view, contemplates phenomena in their essences, or *ideas*, as specific types of objectification of the will. Allow me to quote:

> Whilst science, following the restless and unstable stream of the fourfold forms of reasons or grounds and consequents, is with every end it attains again and again directed farther, and can never find an ultimate goal or complete satisfaction, any more than running we can reach the point where the clouds touch the horizon: art, on the contrary, is everywhere at its goal. For it plucks the object of its contemplation from the stream of the world's course, and hold it isolated before it. This particular thing, which in that stream was a small part, becomes representation of the whole, an equivalent of the infinitely many in space and time. It therefore pauses at this particular thing; it stops the wheel of time; for it the relations vanish; its object is only the essential, the *idea*.[3]

Thus an idea is an immediate, intuitive presentation of the will. For Schopenhauer, nature as a whole objectifies the will. Likewise human history as a whole, all the deeds and words of humankind, objectify the will. Now there are grades or levels in the objectification of the will: Matter is an objectification of the will that is simpler than biological life; and in biological life there are different levels of objectification of the will, all of which are simpler than the objectification taking place in human and historical life. But of these various degrees there is an idea, an immediate intuitive presentation,

---

3. Arthur Schopenhauer, *The World as Will and Representation*, 2 vols., trans. E. F. S. Payne (New York: Dover, 1969), 1:185. Hereafter cited as *WWR*.

that is revealed by the fine arts. And those ideas reveal, in their own way, the groundless and conflictive nature of the will, of which each of us has an immediate perception in his or her emotional life.

Let me give a few examples.

*Architecture,* as a fine art, works with space and matter, or with a material content of space. But spatial matter as an object of study in empirical sciences, like physics or chemistry, is not identical to spatial matter as revealed by the work of architecture. The former is ruled by the principle of sufficient reason, the latter is not. Matter in empirical sciences is analyzed and divided into small entities, among which a network of causes and effects makes up a definite structure. The image of matter in empirical sciences is ordered, clear, measurable. It does not reveal matter as an expression of the groundlessness and inner conflict of the will. This is what architecture reveals. In architecture, gravity, cohesion, rigidity, fluidity, reaction to light, and so on, as universal properties of matter, are treated as phenomena expressing or objectifying the internal conflict of the will. Let me quote again:

> Even at this low stage of the will's objectivity, we see its inner nature revealing itself in discord; for, properly speaking, the conflict between gravity and rigidity is the sole aesthetic material of architecture; its problem is to make this conflict appear with perfect distinctiveness in many different ways. It solves this problem by depriving these indestructible forces of the shortest path to their satisfaction, and keeping them in suspense through a circuitous path; the conflict is thus prolonged and made visible. (*WWR*, 1:214)

Second example: *painting.* Schopenhauer liked very much the interior and daily scenes painted by the Flemish and Dutch painters. In those paintings the daily gestures and demeanor of human beings are represented: A woman is reading a letter, or playing a harpsichord; a group of people drink together or play cards. Those paintings seem merely to duplicate the world we experience in our daily life, that is, the world as representation, in which individuals are concerned with this or that particular goal and have reasons for doing this or that. But we all realize that it would be trivial to see such a painting in terms of the reasonable sequences and relations that organize our daily experience. While contemplating the picture, we realize, Schopenhauer insists, that "we no longer consider the where, the when, the why and the whither in things, but simply and solely the *what*" (*WWR*, 1:178). By showing a locus upon which our will has no grip, a moment that is no part of the temporal sequence in which our will pursues definite ends, by stabilizing the ephemeral disputes or pleasures of individuals without genealogy or heritage, the artist enables us to intuit individuation itself in its *idea,* namely, as an ephemeral objectification of the will.

The examples I just mentioned show that the fine arts mirror the world as will. But for mirroring the world as will, one must already be liberated from the will. Art, in other words, not only mirrors the will but provides to the contemplator of the will the energy required to overcome the will and the world. By showing the essence of the will, art leads us to deny the will. This interpretation of art in terms of asceticism and renunciation is at the core of Schopenhauer's theory of *tragedy* and *music*.

As for tragedy, Schopenhauer, who regards it as the summit of poetic art, sees in it the most complete unfolding of the highest grade of the objectification of the will. This highest grade is humankind. Tragedy reveals that the antagonism of the will with itself is the nature of humankind. By displaying the "wailing and lamentation of mankind, the dominion of chance and error, the fall of the righteous, the triumph of the wicked," tragedy reveals the absurdity of the will (*WWR,* 2:434). This revelation leads the spectator to realize that the world and life are not worth our attachment to them; it leads to resignation: "The summons to turn away the will from life remains the true tendency of tragedy, the ultimate purpose of the intentional presentation of the sufferings of mankind" (*WWR,* 2:435).

Music, however, better than the other arts, helps us contemplate the nature of the will. While all the other arts reveal the *Ideas,* which means the grades of the objectification of the will (matter, life, humankind), music instead reveals, discloses, the will itself, namely, the essence of all the Ideas, or the *essence of essences.* Since the other arts stimulate the knowledge of the Ideas—or objectifications of the will—by depicting individual things, they never pass over the world as phenomenon, which means that they are still attached to the manifold into which the Ideas enter by virtue of the principle of individuation. And they never pass over the Ideas, either. *But music passes over the Ideas,* and

> since it passes over the Ideas, (it) is also quite independent of the phenomenal world, positively ignores it, and to a certain extent, could still exist even if there were no world at all, which cannot be said of the other arts. Thus music is as *immediate* an objectification and copy of the whole *will* as the world itself is, indeed as the Ideas are, the multiplied phenomenon of which constitutes the world of individuals things. Therefore music is by no means like the other arts, namely a copy of the Ideas, but *a copy of the will itself,* the objectivity of which are the Ideas (*WWR,* 1:257).

In music, the a priori features of the will, its inner form and movement, its productivity together with its destructive character, its innumerable efforts, motions, expectations, satisfactions, repetitions, lacunae, are expressed, and we could just as well, Schopenhauer says, "call the world embodied music as embodied will" (*WWR*, 1:257ff.). Allow me to quote again, in order to suggest more concretely what Schopenhauer has in mind:

> A symphony of Beethoven presents us with the greatest confusion, which yet has the most perfect order as its foundation; with the most vehement conflict, which is transformed the next moment into the most beautiful harmony. It is *rerum concordia discors, the discordant concord of things*—i.e., a true and complete picture of the nature of the world, which rolls on in the boundless confusion of innumerable forms, and maintains itself by constant destruction. But at the same time, all the human passions and emotions speak from this symphony: joy, grief, love, hatred, terror, hope, and so on, in innumerable shapes—yet all, as it were, only in the abstract, and without any particularization; it is their mere form without the material, like a mere spirit world without matter. (*WWR*, 2:450)

In other words, *music discloses the contradictory essence of the will.* Hence music is a *true knowledge* of what in the world, beyond the phenomena, is foundational. Schopenhauer's metaphysics is nothing but an attempt to translate in ordinary language, in concepts, what music expresses intuitively. "Music and philosophy have the same topic, expressed in two different languages".[4]

However, aesthetic contemplation, or creation as an activity aiming at contemplating the true world, is not the ultimate in Schopenhauer's philosophy. Art reveals the truth, but it also conceals what it reveals.

If daily experience and empirical or formal sciences as well do not manifest the truth, it is because they are prisoners of the will, which objectifies itself through individuation and sufficient reason. For them, knowing is willing, and this is why they do not really know the truth, since they are unable to look backward at the will, which grounds their procedures as well as the phenomena they deal with.

Art discloses the truth insofar as artistic contemplation is a knowing that is disinterested, no longer under the pressure of the will. However, complete

---

4. Arthur Schopenhauer, *Sämtliche Werke*, ed. Paul Deusseh (München: R. Piper & Co. Verlag), vol. 10, p. 361.

disinterestedness is not within the scope of artistic contemplation. Though the artist is really disinterested, compared to the scientist for whom any knowledge is a form of power, he or she is still interested in contemplation itself. As Schopenhauer puts it,

> he is captivated by a consideration of the spectacle of the will's objectification . . . he sticks to this . . . he himself is the will objectifying itself. That pure, true and profound knowledge of the inner nature of the world now becomes for him an end in itself. (*WWR*, 1:267)

The highest disinterestedness is not an *aesthetic* one, but an *ethical* one: the asceticism of the saint who renounces all interests and so denies in himself or herself the will to live. In this disinterestedness, a state is attained that the spiritual writings of all ages and religions have called "ecstasy, rapture, illumination, union with God, and so on," a state that is a knowledge without any will, a state in which time and space, object and subject, all phenomena "are abolished with the will. No will: no representation, no world," only the "ocean-like calmness of nothingness" (*WWR*, 1:410–11).

Before considering Nietzsche's views about art and truth, let me summarize this quick and superficial survey of Schopenhauer's doctrine in light of the aphorism I quoted at the beginning of this paper:

We have art so as not to perish from truth.

Obviously Schopenhauer would never have said this. He would have said instead: *We have art in order to learn how to die, once we have overcome the deceptive order of representation, and contemplated the absurdity of the will.* In other words, nothing in Schopenhauer seems to justify Nietzsche's words.

However, there is no doubt that Nietzsche's philosophy grew in the shade of Schopenhauer. Let us look at this.

To be sure, unlike Schopenhauer, Nietzsche was not the man of a single book rewritten several times. However, he acknowledged that his first book contained the seeds of all the thoughts he was to develop later. Now, his first book, *The Birth of Tragedy*, is full of allusions to Schopenhauer and was obviously written under the influence of a close meditation on Schopenhauer's work. Consequently, we are invited to demarcate, in this first book, what belongs to Schopenhauer and what properly belongs to Nietzsche.

In the first edition, the complete title was *The Birth of Tragedy out of the Spirit of Music*. The main text was preceded by a preface to Wagner, of which I retain a basic idea: "[A]rt represents the highest task and the truly metaphysical activity of this life.''[5] Nietzsche's first book is an attempt to vindicate this claim.

How so? Allow me to recall the essential matter of the first page of the book. The point at issue in the book, Nietzsche says, is to

> perceive not merely by logical inference, but with the immediate certainty of insight, that the continuous development of art is bound up with the Apollinian and Dionysian duality. . . . The terms Dionysian and Apollinian we borrow from the Greeks, who disclose to the discerning mind the profound mysteries of their view of art, not, to be sure, in concepts, but in the intensely clear figures of their gods. Through Apollo and Dionysus, the two art deities of the Greeks, we come to recognize that in the Greek world there existed a tremendous opposition, in origins and aims, between the Apollinian art of sculpture and the non-imaginistic, Dionysian art of music. These two different tendencies run parallel to each other for the most part openly at variance; and they continually incite each other to new and more powerful births, which perpetuate in antagonism only superficially reconciled by the common term ''are;'' till eventually, by a metaphysical miracle of the Hellenic ''will,'' they appear coupled with each other, and through this coupling ultimately generate an equally Dionysian and Apollinian form of Art—Attic tragedy. (*BT*, 33)

On the face of it, this text could be considered a mere transposition of Schopenhauer. Indeed, further developments about the Apollinian and the Dionysian show that this duality is understood by Nietzsche according to Schopenhauer's duality between representation and will. Apollo, god of dreams and prophecies, but also sponsor of the art of sculpture and of the epic, is a deity that symbolizes the world of appearances, or phenomena, a realm of individualized entities between which there is a network of coherent and ordered relations. In other words, Apollo seems to symbolize what Schopenhauer called the ''world as representation,'' ruled by the principles of individuation and sufficient reason. As for Dionysus, god of intoxication and of orgiastic mysteries, but also protector of the arts that were performed during those mysterious celebrations, namely, an ecstatic music accompanied by an exalted dance—well, again, the symbolic meaning of this deity is

5. Friedrich Nietzsche, *The Birth of Tragedy* and *The Case of Wagner*, trans. Walter Kaufmann (New York: Vintage Books, 1967), 31–32. Hereafter cited at *BT*.

explained in terms of Schopenhauer's theory of the will. Dionysus, Nietzsche says, expresses the "Original Being," beyond individuation and causality. In other words, this deity symbolizes the will itself, beyond representation.

However, these similarities notwithstanding, the careful reader finds in the text several statements that would be inconceivable in Schopenhauer. For instance, Nietzsche says that, by contemplating appearances, or phenomena, the aesthetically sensitive man *"trains himself for life."* Further on, he says that the Apollinian arts "make life possible and worth living" (*BT*, 34–35). Further on still, he says that in the Dionysian festivals in which "the veil of Maya has been torn aside," nature (i.e., the will) celebrates what he calls "her reconciliation with man" or "a gospel of universal harmony" (*BT*, 37). Moreover, he says that the "Apollinian and its opposite, the Dionysian, are artistic energies which burst forth from nature herself" (*BT*, 38).

When, in addition to paying attention to those phrases, the careful reader realizes that the tonality of Nietzsche's text is entirely devoid of any regard to asceticism and renunciation, he or she is compelled to acknowledge that Nietzsche's philosophy of art is not at all identical to Schopenhauer's. In Schopenhauer, art has a metaphysical bearing insofar as it unconceals the will and the objectification of the will in phenomena. But in Schopenhauer, the arts attain their metaphysical significance by suspending—in the artist as well as in the aesthetic beholder—the spontaneous momentum of the will. This amounts to some form, even if limited, of renunciation of the interested movement of the will. In other words, it does not at all amount to a confirmation or affirmation of the will, since the will, for Schopenhauer, is entirely unartistic. In contrast, Nietzsche claims that the arts, as activities and works performed by human beings, confirm and affirm an artistic activity inherent in the will itself. *The will itself, beyond and prior to the artistic activity, is an artist.*

How do we understand this? As I suggested when dealing with Schopenhauer, art, according to Schopenhauer, operates a sort of redemption by turning away from the absurd voracity of the will to live. Nietzsche also talks of redemption. But redemption in Nietzsche's *Birth of Tragedy* no longer has the meaning it has in Schopenhauer. Since the will itself is an artist, it is in the movement of the will that there is a redemption, and not by renunciation of the will.

This Nietzschean redemption operates in two ways—Apollinian and Dionysian. The Apollinian, indeed, is an artistic energy bursting forth out of nature itself, which means that nature (or the will) justifies itself, again and again, within the coherent interaction of the individual entities that make up our daily environment. It justifies itself in the world as phenomenon. On the other hand, the Dionysian, as an artistic energy of nature, means the move by which the will justifies itself by overcoming or destroying the world as phenomenon. Here are the ways redemption operates within the world: production of individuals and of coherent relations among them, and destruction of these individuals and of their coherent interrelation.

Consequently, art, in the ordinary sense of a production of works by human hands, merely exposes in human artifacts either one or the other energy of nature. Thus the Apollinian arts, sculpture, architecture, epic poetry, which all celebrate the glory of the visible, far from suspending the will, magnify a need for appearances that belongs to the will itself. Whereas contemplation, in Schopenhauer's sense, redeems *us* by turning us away from the will, contemplation in Nietzsche's sense is that by which the will redeems *itself* in beautiful appearances. For Nietzsche as well as for Schopenhauer, there is an inner contradiction in the will; in it production and destruction, joy and suffering, alternate or even go together. Unlike Schopenhauer, Nietzsche does not claim that all the arts enable us to intuit an objectification of the contradictory nature of the will. The Apollinian arts (architecture, for example) do not, in Nietzsche's view, exhibit any form of conflict, they exhibit merely harmony. But though they cover the conflicting nature of the will, the Apollinian arts justify the contradictory essence of the will. Nietzsche writes: "The truly existent primal unity (of the will), eternally suffering and contradictory, also needs the rapturous vision, the pleasurable illusion, for its continuous redemption." And further: "Apollo . . . appears to us as the apotheosis of the *principium individuationis,* in which alone is consummated the perpetually attained goal of the primal unity (the will), *its redemption through mere appearance.* With his sublime gestures, he shows us how necessary is the entire world of suffering, that by means of it the individual may be impelled to realize the redeeming vision" (*BT,* 45). The Apollinian Greeks, in other words, as Nietzsche is going to say later in *The Gay Science,* were superficial out of profundity.

This profundity is what symbolizes Dionysus, the god who is both tortured and triumphant. What then is Dionysian art? Strictly speaking, there was only one Dionysian art, the exalted music performed during the Dionysian mysteries. This exalted music, which Nietzsche tried to imagine with the help of Wagner's music, was supposedly characterized by a sort of collapse of the principle of individuation in the "uniform flow of the melody," and by a similar collapse of the principle of sufficient reason in a harmony emanating from the conflict of opposites. By metamorphosing simultaneously the collapse of reason into a harmony, this music reveals that the will redeems itself even when it destroys the individual entities and their coherent network of relations. *Here pleasure is taken in the destruction of individuation and sufficient reason.*

I have recalled that, in Nietzsche's view, the summit of Greek art was reached in tragedy, which is equally Dionysian and Apollinian. Let me try to shed some light on this. The Apollinian component in the works of Sophocles and Aeschylus is present in the clarity of the character of the heroes, who are all like pure types without ambiguity, and who express firmly and lucidly their intentions. It is also present in the dialogues in which they vindicate their right to behave the way they do. It is also present in the plot, which is like a puzzle progressively solved by the poet. Finally, it is present in the cheerful atmosphere that seems to pervade the whole drama. On the other hand, there is a Dionysian component in the *chorus,* which we know was originally composed of satyrs (half beasts, half men); in the mythical content of the poem, which is extremely obscure compared to the clarity of the dialogues; and in the fact that, in spite of all their vindication, the characters are toys in the hands of a merciless fate. So tragedy combines and intertwines measure and excess, order and chaos, clarity and darkness. But this insurmountable tension, according to Nietzsche, was not at all perceived by the Greeks as an indictment of the will to live. Quite the contrary. Tragedy celebrated life in spite of this internal conflict. At this point, we are able to shed some light on the original title of Nietzsche's book: *The Birth of Tragedy out of the Spirit of Music.* As I suggested, Dionysian music generated a pleasure that is taken in the very collapse of individuation and sufficient reason. It is this pleasure that tragedy translates into words, that is, into a medium that is par excellence an Apollinian medium, and into images: the figures on the stage.

Let me quote again:

It is only through the spirit of music that we can understand the joy in the annihilation of the individual. For it is only in particular examples of such annihilation that we see clearly the eternal phenomenon of Dionysian art, which gives expression to the will in its omnipotence, as it were, behind the *principium individuationis,* the eternal life beyond all phenomena, and despite all annihilation. The metaphysical joy in the tragic is a translation of the instinctive unconscious Dionysian wisdom into the language of images: the hero, the highest manifestation of the will, is negated for our pleasure, because he is only phenomenon, and because the eternal life of the will is not affected by his annihilation. "We believe in eternal life," exclaims tragedy; while music is the immediate idea of this. Plastic art has an altogether different aim: here Apollo overcomes the suffering of the individual by the radiant triumphs over the suffering inherent in life; pain is obliterated by lies from the features of nature. In Dionysian art and its tragic symbolism, the same nature cries to us with its true, undissembling voice: "Be as I am!" Amid the ceaseless flux of phenomena, I am the eternally creative primordial mother, eternally impelling to existence, eternally finding satisfaction in this change of phenomena. (*BT,* 104)

Though Nietzsche, before this page, in the same section, quotes Schopenhauer, it is obvious that his understanding of both music and tragedy is far removed from Schopenhauer. *Music and tragedy, in Schopenhauer, bring a message of renunciation. In Nietzsche they affirm and confirm the will.*

We are now in a position to shed some light on Nietzsche's aphorism: "We have art so as not perish from truth." Does this sentence make sense in the context I have just recalled? It does. If applied to the philosophy developed in *The Birth of Tragedy,* the aphorism means approximately the following: For individuals who are attached to the phenomenal world, as an individuated and organized realm, the discovery of the true world, that is, of nature in its conflictual essence, entails fear, nausea, disgust. In other words, the first result of such a discovery is precisely a form of the renunciation that Schopenhauer was applauding. But for Nietzsche, unlike Schopenhauer, it is precisely the Dionysian art that saved the Greeks from any tendency to deny the will to live. It saved them by teaching them to affirm without reservation what could have led them to renunciation, pessimism, or nihilism. *The Greeks had art in order not to deny life as a result of the disclosure of the contradiction of the will.* Their Dionysian music, their tragedies, affirmed life in spite of its contradiction. Likewise, their Apollinian art affirmed life by concealing the contradiction of the will.

However, though this interpretation of Nietzsche's aphorism fits rather well with the context I have recalled, it does not yet reach the core of Nietzsche's thought about art and truth. Here, we must go a step further. *The Birth of Tragedy* is a book that does not deal only with Apollo and Dionysus. It deals also with a third character, namely, Socrates.

Socrates declared war against both Apollo and Dionysus, and above all against their reconciliation in tragedy. He won, and he was able to destroy tragedy. In the name of what did he fight that war? In the name of what Nietzsche calls "theoretical optimism." Theoretical optimism amounts to believing that reality in its ground is both good and intelligible. Consequently, theoretical optimism believes that evil and unreason do not belong to reality: They are appearances, they are unreal. Whereas tragical wisdom acknowledged in reality an insurmountable contradiction or tension between opposites, theoretical optimism overcomes this contradiction by declaring that is a mere appearance. Theoretical optimism replaces the ontological contradiction [either] by a dualism, which puts the true and real on the side of the good and the intelligible and declares that evil and the unintelligible are untrue and unreal, or by a dualism, which declares that the sensible is unreal, while the purely logical is the real. By holding to his theoretical optimism, Socrates discards both the Apollinian arts, because the Apollinian is attached to the sensible realm, and the Dionysian art, because it combines both the Apollinian appearances and the Dionysian contradictions.

In this war, Socrates takes side with the one against the manifold, with identity against differentiation, with eternity against time, with permanence against becoming.

Now, in Nietzsche's view, life itself as will is inherently characterized by a tension that cannot and should not be surmounted. In other words, in life the one cannot be dissociated from the manifold, identity cannot be dissociated from differentiation. Or, more concretely, invention or creation cannot be dissociated from destruction.

But then the denial of the manifold, of differentiation, of time, amounts to a denial of life itself. In other words, truth as it is conceived of by theoretical optimism—as pure intelligibility devoid of any contradiction and even of any ambiguity—amounts to some sort of death. The will to truth in that sense is denial of life.

This is what Nietzsche discovers in *The Birth of the Tragedy* by comparing the tragical wisdom of the Greeks with the theoretical aims of Socrates. It may be argued that all the further developments of his thought afterward— and they are very complex—amount to an ever more radical meditation on this discovery. Despite the complexity of these developments, it is the discovery made in *The Birth of Tragedy* that provides continuity. In this further critique of all the forms of afterworld, of all the forms of denial of tension and conflict, as well as in his attempts to operate a transvaluation of all the values inherited by our tradition, Nietzsche was in some sense merely drawing the conclusions of his early discovery. However, in this double task— critical and reevaluating—he was to realize more and more intensely that his early discovery had been obscured by what he was initially borrowing from Schopenhauer. Indeed, if life or will is an insurmountable tension, then all dualisms, not only Socrates' or Plato's dualism of the appearances and the Ideas, but also Schopenhauer's dualism of representation and thing-in-itself, are to be denounced. The theoretical optimism of the former and the ethical pessimism of the latter are but two forms of one and the same denial.

This allows me to put in a new light the sentence with which I began. The Greeks of the tragical age had art in order not to perish as a result of their insight into the Dionysian truth. We, in the modern age, have art in order not to die from the type of truth that was claimed by Socrates and Plato, then transmitted to the Christian age of faith and metaphysics, and is still preserved today in the modern age of science. This amounts to saying, as Nietzsche in fact said, that art is the antinihilistic movement par excellence, or that it intensifies life instead of letting it perish. There are three items at issue here: *Truth* (which from Socrates forward was to become the correlate of science, at first as a metaphysical proceeding and later on as an empirical proceeding), *art,* and *life.* In an attempt at self-criticism that was written fifteen years after the publication of *The Birth of Tragedy,* Nietzsche bound up those three terms in the following way: "[M]y much older, a hundred times more demanding, but by no means colder, eye had not become a stranger to the task which this audacious book dared to tackle for the first time: *'to look at science in the perspective of the artist, but at art in that of life' " (BT,* 19). This comment suggests that in order to get the right understanding of the aphorism by which I began this paper, we must get the right understanding of Nietzsche's notion of life. We have seen so far that life, or will, needs appearances, and also that in satisfying its need for appearances, the productivity of life does not stop, which means that life again and again destroys what it produced, to the benefit of new appearances.

Appearance, as I suggested, is characterized by an organization, a measure, an order. This measure or order is what Nietzsche in his mature writings was to call "perspective." Life is perspectival, and a living being could not live without continuously projecting perspectives that are all active interpretations of itself and its surroundings. Moreover, Nietzsche said, the more life is active or living, the more it is able to invent perspectives, to renew them, to multiply them. This renewed invention, which implies an overcoming of the acquired, is at the core of what Nietzsche in his maturity calls the "will to power."

This actively perspectival nature of life is the light in which Nietzsche looks at art. The value of art lies in the new perspectives it opens. Therefore, it does not have to be looked at, as in Schopenhauer, in terms of pure, disinterested contemplation; it has to be considered in terms of *action,* or *creation of perspectives.* Nietzsche insisted many times that art has to be understood from the viewpoint of the artist, which means from the perspective of an attitude for which the extant works of art do not deserve absolute consecration, for the perspectives opened up by them are valid only if they inspire other and new perspectives.

From this we can understand why Nietzsche often criticizes artists and their opinions. If the works of art entail the conviction that they are indisputable, we are, when facing them, like museum keepers. The artist who claims that his or her inspiration opens him or her to an afterworld takes sides with the subterranean nihilism that is inherent in any dualistic view of the world. If his or her work generates nostalgia, it instigates reaction instead of action, somnolence instead of living affirmation.

But we can also understand, the other way around, why at several points Nietzsche seems to give back to science—and to religion and morals as well—what he seems to deny to them in other respects.

Let me conclude by trying to elucidate this. Already in *The Birth of Tragedy* Nietzsche suggests that there are perhaps incompatible sides in the proceeding of Socrates. What is thoroughly hostile to life in Socrates is his attempt to contemplate a fully intelligible ground of reality. If, however, Socrates' theoretical undertaking is considered in its movement, as a dynamic search more than a static contemplation, then perhaps we may say "that he cared more for the search after truth than for truth itself" (*BT*, 95). In this respect, Socrates, when he repeats time and again that he does not know, is perhaps an artist in his own right. Indeed, Nietzsche at least suggests that, like an artist, Socrates, as "theoretical man, finds an infinite delight in whatever exists." The only difference, then, between the theoretical man as a searcher and the artist would be that "whenever the truth is uncovered, the artist will always cling with rapt gaze to what still remains covered even after such uncovering, (whereas) the theoretical man enjoys and finds satisfaction in the discarded covering, and finds the highest object of his pleasure in the process of an ever happy uncovering that succeeds through his own efforts" (*BT*, 94). But this amounts to saying that his theoretical enterprise would not exist "if it were concerned only with that one goddess of truth and nothing else" (*BT*, 95). Which in turn means that Socrates himself had another goddess, namely, life in its metamorphoses, in its becoming, in what the later writings of Nietzsche call its "perspectivalism."

Now we can note that, in the light of life, art and science—in Nietzsche's sense—are open to two readings. The first reading instills suspicion. If one takes the view that the artist's inspiration puts that individual in touch with an afterworld, then there are seeds of death in the artistic undertaking. The same goes for the scientist, if he is interpreted as coming face to face with the one goddess of truth. The second reading, on the other hand, amounts to acknowledging, in science as well as in art, perspectivalism, movement, becoming. In the former reading, both art and science deny life. In the latter, they celebrate it. Consequently, the sentence by which I began may be reformulated as follows: We have both art and science, as living perspectives, in order not to perish from immobilization of life.

# 8

# The Hegelian Legacy in
# the Heidegger's Overcoming
# of Aesthetics

In the epilogue to the essay "The Origin of the Work of Art," Heidegger calls attention to the fact that the pages of the text proper "are concerned with the riddle of art, the riddle that art itself is." Then we read: "They are far from claiming to solve the riddle. The task is to see the riddle."[1] What is the import of these sentences? Are they simply repeating one and the same thing? But why is such stress put on the "riddle"? If the entire essay itself focuses on the riddle and only prepares the reader to welcome it, why now this denial of any pretension to ever solve it? Why such an insistence on the rejection of this claim, if not because the essay itself, at least in some respects, had subscribed to it? It is difficult not to read these words of the epilogue without suspecting an ambiguity at the very core of the essay, the indication of a tendency to oscillate between the exposure to the riddle and something very different: a solution proposed to a problem. I find this conjecture confirmed by the publication of the addendum a few years after the epilogue. In it we read the following caveat: "What art may be is one of the questions to which no answers are given in this essay. What gives the impression of such an answer are directions for questioning (Cf. the first sentence of the Epilogue)" (*OWA*, 80).

Is the essay an approach to the riddle of art, or does it supply an answer to the philosophical question about the essence of art? Such is the ambiguity—one at the same time acknowledged and kept at bay—with respect to

First published in *Recoupements* (Brussels: Editions Ousia, 1982).
1. "The Origin of the Work of Art" in *Poetry, Language, Thought*, trans. Albert Hofstadter (New York: Harper & Row, 1971), 79. Hereafter cited as *OWA*.

which we are invited to read the essay. Yet how are we to attempt this reading? What help in our effort can this ambiguity—hardly detected so far—provide? Perhaps the following pages of the epilogue will help us to unravel the impact of such an ambiguity,[2] detected so far only in the beginning of the text.

Two other topics determine the unfolding of the epilogue: The first is aesthetics; the second is the destiny of Western art. *Aesthetics* is the name given to a specifically modern discipline that considers works of art solely as *objects* of sense apprehension, that is, objects of what this discipline conceives as a modality of subjectivity, the *Erlebnis*, or lived experience. By virtue of such an approach to works of art, *Erlebnis* is granted an ultimate normative status; it determines the essence of art, it becomes "the standard not only for art appreciation and enjoyment, but also for artistic creation" (*OWA*, 79). By the same token, the riddle—which the work is—is threatened. The riddle consists in this, that the work works, like speech speaks, world worlds, time temporalizes, or Being is. With reference to *Erlebnis*, the work stops working. The enigmatic consistency of its identity and differentiation dissolves and is transformed in enjoyment, emotion, and vital excitement. These are stimulations that indeed endorse the unexpected, but in which the "subject" does nothing but expand its own empire and gain self-certainty. The aesthetic imperialism of *Erlebnis* raises, therefore, the question of the destiny of art. It is impossible to come to terms with this question—the last topic in the epilogue—without addressing Hegel's words: "Die Kunst ist nach der Seite ihrer höchsten Bestimmung für uns ein Vergangenes . . ." (Art is . . . for us, as regards its highest vocation, something of the past)" (*OWA*, 80). If it is true that *Erlebnis* reigns free and that in it the riddle is dissolved, then Hegel is right: Art is for us a thing of the past, its death is under way.

Here the articulation of the ambiguity detected earlier begins to unfold. Recognizing the riddle of art means attempting to overcome aesthetics, the modern figure of metaphysics. Yet recognizing that the empire of subjectivity over art is not an invention of aesthetics, but the expression given by aesthetics to the principle that really rules over modernity, amounts to validating aesthetics under its most metaphysical figure—the one found in Hegel's *Lectures on Aesthetics,* which provides "the most comprehensive reflection on the nature of art that the West possesses—comprehensive because it stems from metaphysics" (*OWA*, 79).

---

2. [*les implications de cette ambiguité.*]

Overcoming aesthetics and yet validating it, such is the formula that captures the ambiguity in regard to which I propose to reread "The Origin of the Work of Art." The question brought to the forefront by the recognition of this ambiguity might perhaps be formulated in the following abrupt manner: What makes the essay escape Hegel's thought? Immediately after recalling Hegel's point on the modern death of art and stressing the impossibility of escaping its verdict, the epilogue adds:

> The question remains: Is art still an essential and necessary way in which that truth happens which is decisive for our historical existence, or is art no longer of this character? If, however, it is such no longer, then there remains the question why this is so. The truth of Hegel's judgment has not yet been decided; for behind this verdict there stands Western thought since the Greeks, which thought corresponds to a truth of beings that has already happened. Decision upon the judgment will be made, when it is made, from and about this truth of what is. Until then the judgment remains in force. But for that very reason the question is necessary whether the truth that the judgment declares is final and conclusive and what follows if it is. (*OWA*, 80)

Even though the essential words of this text can be interpreted in two different ways (truth in the sense of *alētheia*, and truth in the sense of absolute certainty of oneself; history in the sense of the development of the absoluteness of Spirit and in the sense of the history of Being), the overlapping of the two is obvious and deserves questioning. How can the attempt to think art nonaesthetically, that is, nonmetaphysically, intersect with—and validate—Hegel's philosophical position (even though such validity still remains provisional and not yet decided) when clearly Hegel's original formulation is based on an approach to art that is entirely aesthetic and metaphysical? The last sentences of the epilogue stress that the intersection with Hegel is not fortuitous, but lies at the core of the Heideggerian questioning into art:

> In the way in which, for the world determined by the West, that which is, is the real, there is concealed a specific concordance of beauty and truth. The history of the nature of Western art corresponds to the change of the nature of truth. This is no more intelligible in terms of beauty taken for itself than it is in terms of experience (*Erlebnis*), supposing that the metaphysical concept of art reaches to art's nature. (*OWA*, 81 modified)

In punctuating a situation of overlapping with Hegel, these words unveil, so to speak, what is presupposed in the question about the validity of Hegel's verdict on the death of art. Heidegger pointed out earlier that behind Hegel's position "stands Western thought since the Greeks, which thought corresponds to a truth of beings that has already happened" (*OWA*, 80). The last sentences of the epilogue invite us to recognize that this truth of beings, such as it has already been unfolding for the moderns, is actuality, *Wirklichkeit*. To be sure, this word plays a major role in Hegel, who takes it in the strong sense of achievement and result of implementation. Actuality in the Hegelian sense is that which results from an implementation, or setting-into-work, of the Spirit. Actuality is fully achieved in those works where the Spirit, seeking implementation, encounters nothing that eludes such a setting-into–work, finds nothing else but itself—a situation that, to use a different language, exhibits the identity of the worker, the work, and the working. Full actuality is exhibited in modern times and is that toward which the history of the world has been developing, by presupposing it from the outset. The proposition that "for the world determined by the West, that which is, is as the real (actual)"[3] is therefore a Hegelian assertion. It is no less Hegelian to maintain that this Western unfolding of actuality includes "a specific concordance of truth and beauty (*OWA*, 81 modified). This unfolding, according to Hegel, is indeed the Western maturation of actuality, and Western history is the process of its gestation.

At the dawn of Western history—without considering its Oriental antecedents—the Greek world indeed had grasped actuality, but under a form that is far from corresponding to its completion, to its truth. To the fact that the Greek world grasped beings as actuality, that is, as a setting-into-work of the Spirit, Hegel testifies by arguing that such a world is entirely artistic. It honors the Being of beings under the guise of works of art, in which Spirit (that is, its Greek form) understands its own operation. But it is the same point that also reveals the deficiency of this apprehension. Because the Greek world honors the Being of beings in works of art, it reveals that the actuality it apprehends is burdened with matter, with immediacy, with sensibility. The truth of actuality is the identity of the worker, of the work, and of the working. The Greek modality of actuality does not raise itself to such an identity, it loads this identity with a difference that it is incapable of overcoming. The specifically Greek concordance of beauty and truth is contained for Hegel in the fact that beauty reached there its full measure but that truth was affected with a deficiency. For the Greeks, he says, "beauty is the veil that hides truth." To

---

3. In the original text, the German word for "real" is *wirklich*.

this deficiency, with regard to the truth of actuality, Greek philosophy itself bears witness. *Wirklichkeit* is the word by which Hegel translates the Aristotelian *energeia*. By his thinking of *energeia* as *entelecheia*, Aristotle, according to Hegel, proves that he understood it as "in itself goal and realization of the goal." *Energeia* provides Aristotle with a way of grasping the speculative identity of actuality, "the pure actuality that originates within itself" and "negativity focussing on itself."[4] But because in Aristotle this notion is subordinated to an entirely positive philosophy of nature, it fails to acknowledge negativity and mediation, and is credited by Hegel only with reaching the first level of the self-movement of the Spirit.

The overcoming of this first level entails the overcoming of nature, of immediacy, of sensibility, in a process at the end of which actuality in its modern form accomplishes its truth: namely, the Spirit being certain of itself within its own actuality. From truth as harmony with a given nature, the Spirit has progressed to truth as absolute self-certainty. At the end of this process, we find the specifically modern concordance between beauty and truth. It is the inverted form of the Greek concordance, because truth, which has now reached its full measure, manifests the deficiency of beauty. From now on, beauty is nothing but an elementary modality of self-certainty, a situation exhibited by modern art according to Hegel, in that it makes a game of every form and content.

It is therefore possible to lend a strictly Hegelian interpretation to Heidegger's claim that "to the transformation of the essence of truth corresponds a history of the essence of Western art (*OWA*, 81 modified). Since the point at issue in this history of the essence of Western art is the manifestation of Being as actuality, in a development that after the summit of Greek art is for Hegel one of decline, the last sentence of Heidegger's epilogue also lends itself to a Hegelian reading: The full measure of the essence of art is revealed neither by beauty as an abstract concept, nor by the psychological effects that works of art spark in the lived experience of individuals.

This close kinship between Heidegger and Hegel and the importance it has in the very text of the essay "The Origin of the Work of Art" is what we now proceed to interrogate. As it turns out, its importance has manifested itself in our previous analysis of the epilogue. Before actually returning to the text itself, let us bring together the manifold ways in which this importance emerges by articulating these questions: What unites or separates the meditation on the riddle and the theory of the essence of art? What unites or sep-

---

4. G. W. F. Hegel, *Sämtliche Werke*, (Berlin: Verlag von Dunckes und Humbold, 1832–45) 18:321. Hereafter cited as *SW*.

arates the overcoming of aesthetics and its metaphysical completion in speculative dialectics? What unites or separates the history of Being and the history of the Spirit? It can be argued that these three questions point to a fourth one that is more fundamental: Concerning art, what unites or separates the setting-into-work (or *energeia*) of *alētheia* in the Heideggerian sense and the setting-into-work (or *energeia*) of the Spirit in the Hegelian sense?

To address these questions, the end of the epilogue gives a guideline. By stressing that neither beauty considered in itself nor the lived experience (*Erlebnis*) gives the measure of the essence of (Western) art, this text calls to mind the methodological outline found at the beginning of the essay. These considerations of methodology now require our attention.

It has sometimes been noticed that, because of the similarity of their central themes, these considerations of methodology bear a relation, at least formally, to Hegel's introductory remarks at the beginning of his *Lectures on Aesthetics*. In both the central theme is circularity.

Heidegger's very provisional stance among the "common ideas" allows him to undermine their evidence by gradually highlighting something to which they are blind: the circular movement of the questioning into the origin of the work of art. If one asserts that the origin of the work of art is the artist, one must add—immediately and conversely—that the work is the origin of the artist, since without the work his title would be undeserved. Here we have the first, still elementary, figure of circularity, which immediately rebounds by virtue of a third term. "Artist and work *are* each of them by virtue of a third thing which is prior to both, namely that which also gives artist and work their names—art" (*OWA*, 17). But if we investigate the essence of art understood as the origin of both artist and work, we cannot fail to notice another, more deeply rooted, figure of circularity: "What art is should be inferable from the work. What the work of art is we can come to know only from the nature of art" (*OWA*, 18). Thus we have a circle that "common sense" compels us to avoid, but into which wakeful thinking is bound to enquire:

> This is neither a makeshift nor a defect. To enter upon this path is the strength of thought, to continue on it is the feast of thought, assuming that thinking is a craft. Not only is the main step from work to art a circle like the step from art to work, but every separate step that we attempt circles in this circle. (*OWA*, 18)

Undermining the evidence of common ideas, the emergence of circularity to broad daylight now allows us to discard two antithetical forms of philosophy of art: The first derives the essence of the work of art from cumulative empirical symptoms, the second derives it from higher concepts. Both are equally blind to the figure of circularity without which, however, no inquiry could be pursued. This double rejection, which furthermore is akin to the phenomenological reduction of the natural attitude, is Hegelian in style—because of what it discards, because of its insistence on circularity, and because of the manner in which circularity is approached.

It is indeed easy to isolate in Hegel the two figures of circularity that we have just identified in Heidegger. The first one—the reciprocity of the artist and of the work, itself founded on a third term extending over both—is the theme of the individual figure of consciousness that the *Phenomenology* names "the spiritual animal kingdom and deceit, or the 'matter in hand' itself."[5] This figure describes the creator who erects his own individuality into an absolute. In the consciousness of this individual, the determined character of his nature is perceived not as a limitation, but as a universal element inside which his nature unfolds without obstacle and is "pure reciprocal relationship with itself in its actualization" (See *PhS*, section 396). In this actualization, a differentiation emerges that affects the simplicity of his original nature: This consciousness sets a *goal* for itself, represents to itself the *means* of realizing it, and achieves it in a *work*. But these differences do not shatter the simplicity of that consciousness; they are inessential and rather confirm it in its circularity, in its pure act of relating itself to itself. No matter what the nature of the consciousness, the circumstances that it finds at its disposal, its goals, its means, its works, all elements produce a pattern of circularity with that consciousness at the center: "There is nothing for individuality which has not been made by it, or there is no reality (actuality) which is not individuality's own nature and doing, and no action, nor in-itself of individuality that is not real (actual)" (*PhS*, section 403, p. 242). Yet this circularity of the individual and of its work is only the animal anticipation of a deeper and properly spiritual type of circularity of the individual and of its work is only the animal anticipation of a deeper and properly spiritual type of circularity that exceeds the confines of this individual. The experience pursued and undergone by the individual shows the deceptive character of the circularity to which that consciousness is linked. Deeper than this elementary circularity, the "matter in hand" that inevitably confronts such an experience is a third element: This element shatters the simple reciprocity of elementary circularity and foreshadows within the individual, and beyond him or her, the true circle of the Spirit.

5. G. W. F. Hegel, *Phenomenology of Spirit*, trans. A. V. Miller (Oxford: Oxford University Press, 1977), sections 397–418, pp. 237–52. Hereafter cited as *PhS*.

For in the work the individual does not claim to accomplish anything but its singularity. But as soon as the work exists, the individual creator from whom it came and who thought that nothing except this person's individuality had been brought into it, undergoes the realization that, inasmuch as it is being offered to others, the work lends itself to operations other than its creator's. The work is thus exposed to a transindividual operation that causes a shift and opens a new process of becoming. Facing this process, the individual creator experiences the contingency of what he or she originally felt compelled them and contained a necessity—his or her talent, the goal pursued, the circumstances, the means available, even the work. Since the work turns out to be ephemeral, consciousness dissociates itself from it and erects its concept as the perdurable. The true work, therefore, is not this product, which from now on turns out to be contingent, but the "matter itself" (*Sache selbst*) as the identity of Being and setting-into-work.

The true thing, the matter at issue, the *Sache*, is not the work, but art. But as soon as the individual creator raises the issue of art, he or she either tends to reduce it to a kind of universal predicate unifying the various aspects of the creator's operations, or turns the issue of art into a pure abstraction without any possible determination as he or she dismisses the accusation of merely pursuing self-interest in such works. As a consequence, the artist oscillates between two fallacies, one being the false reduction of the universal to the singular, and the second being the false dissociation of the universal and the singular. Since the cause that this consciousness invokes is in fact nothing without the operation of everybody, including its own operation, this individual consciousness experiences that the matter is neither an abstract universal, the predicate of individual species, nor a pure ideal.

> It is rather substance permeated by individuality, subject in which there is individuality just as much qua individual, or qua this particular individual, as qua all individuals; and it is the universal which has being only as this action of all and each. (*PhS*, section 418, p. 252).

Concerning the second figure of circularity—in which art is grasped exclusively from the work, yet every reception of a work presupposes the understanding of the essence of art—we only need to recall that it plays a fundamental role in the introduction to the *Lectures on Aesthetics*. To be sure, the first pages of this lecture course take great care to stress that the train of thought about to unfold does not provide us with the full measure of the essence of art, because the circularity characterizing the essence of art at the most essential level cannot be sufficiently clarified in the narrow framework of a lecture course. In order for a theory of art to be fully philosophical, or scientific, in the Hegelian sense, it must satisfy the "highest scientific need which requires that, even though an object exists, its necessity be nevertheless demonstrated."[6] Hegel remarks that regarding the object of any science, two points must be taken into consideration, "first, that such an object *is*, and second, *what* it is" (*LA*, 1:11). In the ordinary sciences, which in this regard are aligned with the common notions, the existence of such an object is tantamount to an absolute beginning, to a point of departure from which the sciences proceed toward the appropriate essence. Thus, the point of departure of ordinary aesthetics consists in the fact that some works of art can be "shown." From this one assumes that an appropriate method can be found to determine the essence of these works. But in a science worthy of the name (only the whole of philosophy—the encyclopedia of philosophical sciences—is granted such a status in Hegel), nothing must be accepted as pure and simple fact subjected to the so-called contingencies of existence. That there are works of art is not a factual occurrence that philosophy should take for granted from the outset. For philosophy, the occurrence of works of art is more than a fact, it exhibits a necessity that can and must be demonstrated. This necessity is derived from the concept, or essence, of art—and this concept itself results and derives with utmost necessity from the Spirit itself. Therefore aesthetics has the status of a science only when it is understood as a sphere inserted as a broader circle of the system that explicitly demonstrates the necessary unfolding of the Spirit in its totality. In science, thus understood as system,

> there is so to speak no absolute beginning. By absolute beginning, what is often meant is an abstract beginning, a beginning that would be *nothing else but* a beginning. But since philosophy is a totality, as such its beginning is everywhere. Now, essentially this beginning is everywhere a result. It is necessary to conceive philosophy as a circle coming back upon itself. (*LA*, 20)

But the *Lectures on Aesthetics* cannot exhibit the connection between the various spheres of the system and clarify its circularity by demonstrating how the phenomenal production of works follows a necessity of essence arising from the Spirit—and how, conversely, their production was necessary in order for the Spirit to complete its essence. As a result, the *Lectures on Aes-*

---

6. English text translated from *Leçons d'esthétique,* Vol. 1, trans. S. Jankelevitch (Paris: Aubier, 1979) 11. Hereafter cited as *LA*.

*thetics* take their departure in ordinary notions and the common theories associated with them: "First of all, we have to consider only one thing, i.e., that there are works of art. Such a consideration is appropriate to give a sound starting point" (*LA*, 14). From this ordinary notion, we must gain access to the circle and show how the latter is at the same time presupposed and ignored by the common representation.

It is at this juncture that the introduction to these *Lectures* and the very beginning of Heidegger's essay intersect and overlap. Both cases involve the rejection of empiricism and of intellectualism. In addition, these rejections are for the same reason: Both approaches fail to recognize circularity. According to Hegel, empiricism is flawed because it leads either to negative results—there is no essence of art—or to very abstract and general definitions: for instance, that art aims at eliciting pleasurable sensations. Moreover, not only can these definitions be simply contradicted by antithetical ones, but their realm is so vast that it can extend to many other domains. In no way can empiricism remedy this void or expansion without surreptitiously and contradictorily permeating its approach with a nebulous view of the essence.

Against all this, Hegel draws on Plato: "One must consider not particular objects, that are called beautiful, but the Beautiful." The idea is what provides us with the right beginning. Yet this new beginning would be as misleading as that of empiricism if it only consisted in holding the idea as a unique ethereal principle antithetically opposed to the self-proclaimed concreteness of the sensible, or as the pure intelligible entity heterogeneous to phenomenal production. This notion, in effect, too, would fail to recognize circularity. Hence the idea in the Hegelian sense cannot be set apart from its setting-into-work. It is essential for the idea "to differentiate itself, to particularize from within itself, by developing into the variety, the multiplicity, into the differences, into the many and different forms and figures of art" (*LA*, 19).

From the previous assessment, we see that it is a Hegelian, as much as a Heideggerian, proposition to assert that neither lived experience (*Erlebnis*) nor beauty taken in itself proves equal to the essence of art. Yet one can object that it is not the same kind of circularity that is at stake in both cases: Hegel's is the speculative circle; Heidegger's, the hermeneutic circle. Thus it is toward a comparison of these two figures of circularity that we must strive. It is such a conparison that will guide our questioning.

The circularity of the question of art in "The Origin of the Work of Art" is reminiscent of another circularity previously treated by Heidegger, namely, the circularity of understanding. Insofar as the question of art entails the "understanding" of the essence of art, the circularity of this question presents itself as a particular instance of the hermeneutic circle mentioned in section 32 of *Sein und Zeit.* This circle was announced as early as the "exposition of the question of the meaning of Being." In order to be taken up expressly as a problem, this question requires, indeed, a preliminary elucidation of the entity that is taking the problem up and of this entity's mode of being. Heidegger stresses that this circular procedure does not beg the question, but rather acknowledges that an understanding of Being is what the entity that we are has always already been involved in.

This analysis acknowledges the "remarkable 'relatedness backward or forward' which what we are asking about (Being) bears to the inquiry itself as a mode of Being of an entity."[7] This ambiguous connectedness between the inquiry and what is under inquiry is essential in the hermeneutic circle.

The existential structure of this ambiguous relatedness is what the analytic of *Dasein* exhibits. The analytic stresses that every interpretation moves within a circle. Yet this point is not tantamount to saying merely that there must be an antecedent, in the form of pretheoretical understanding, to every interpretation that adopts a theoretical comportment in the attempt to explain a given being in the light of its properties. The elucidation of any being as such certainly depends on an everyday mode of being of the entity that we are. This mode of being has always already been grounded on the basis of a prior understanding of the manifestation of the world and has always already produced perspectives and meanings, if not anticipated new ones. However, this circle of interpretation and antecedent understanding is only the expression of a deeper circle whose source originates in the circular ontological structure of *Dasein* itself.

To refer the hermeneutic circle to *Dasein*'s structure amounts to associating the latter to the existential triad of thrownness-in (situation), understanding, and fallenness. Such a triad shows a circular structure, because there is an overlapping of all the terms: Every thrown situation is understood as such, every understanding is engaged in a situation, yet neither is free from obliteration, and thus both allow for the emergence of fallenness—which consists in forsaking their inalienable character. This structure is ontologically circular, because the mutual overlapping of these terms discloses *Dasein* as a *project* of Being always already *thrown* into the openness of Being—yet a project such that it is always in danger of letting this openness be obliterated, hidden from itself, and masked by the public and everyday evidence of beings present-at-hand (*Vorhandenes*).

---

7. Martin Heidegger, *Being and Time*, trans. J. Macquarrie and E. Robinson (New York: Harper & Row, 1962), 28 Eng./8 Germ. Hereafter cited as *BT.*

The hermeneutic circle announced in the exposition of the question of the meaning of Being unfolds its existential structure in the analytic of *Dasein*. But the analytic only exhibits the foundation of this circle when the existential components[8] of interpretation, provided that they are held together in the unitary structure of care, lend themselves to an originary interpretation that, while integrating the results of the analytic, reveals temporality as the ontological meaning of *Dasein*, and time as the transcendental horizon of the question of the meaning of Being. Accordingly, the foundation of the hermeneutic circle turns out to be the knot tying together the three ecstasies of finite temporality. The phenomenon of care, in which *Dasein* maintains itself open to its ownmost possibility of Being, reveals that *Dasein* is always self-preceded, inasmuch as it presupposes its inscription in the openness of Being. In other words, *Dasein*'s coming to itself (future) matters to it only inasmuch as it has already been (past). And we can say that there is reciprocity between these two dimensions, because every recasting entails an anticipation and vice versa. "Eigentlich Zukünftig *ist* das *Dasein* eigentlich *gewesen* . . . Dasein kann nur eigentlich *sein*, sofern es zukünftig ist" (As authentically futural, *Dasein is* authentically as *having been*. . . . Only so far as it is futural can *Dasein be* authentically [as having been]) (*BT*, 373/326). At the intersection of anticipation and repetition, a relation to the present takes place. It is also this chasm that the relation to the present always threatens to obliterate, when that present—antecedently dissociated from its ec-static foundation—is granted a primordial status.

If such is indeed the teaching of *Sein und Zeit* regarding the circle of understanding, one can justifiably conclude that its circularity excludes any privileging of the present and precludes its hypostasis as eternal *nunc stans*. The privileging of the present can only bear witness to the obliteration of circularity. The second conclusion is that understanding, which is grounded upon the finite temporality of *Dasein*, is not amenable to a totalization that is not finite. It is not amenable to a totalization that would trespass the limits of the intrinsically mortal project constitutive of *Dasein*, as well as the limits assignable to the interaction of finite projects whose radical historicality is a dimension precisely not totalizable in any global history.

If one now pays attention to the fact that we have an understanding of Being inasmuch as it is no being, one could conclude finally that the circle at issue is intrinsically differentiated. It is not enough to say that the project is always a cast-forth project, that anticipation is always retrospective; one must

---

8. [*existentialia.*]

also add that the movement of transcendence constituting *Dasein* emanates not so much from *Dasein* itself as from what transgresses all entities, namely, from Being, of which the entity existing ec-statically is itself nothing but the ''–there.'' In other words, in the circularity of understanding, we detect the insurmountable, originary, and ever-present difference between Being and beings, a difference that supports the ec-static nature of *Dasein,* but that the latter does not constitute.

These three points show that the hermeneutic circle is heterogeneous to the speculative circle. Recall the famous proposition by which the speculative circle is presented in the *Phenomenology of Spirit:* ''[The true] is the process of its own becoming, the circle that presupposes its end as its goal, having its end also as its beginning; and only by being worked out to its end, is it actual'' (*PhS,* Section 18, p. 10). This circle grants a privilege to the present, to totalization and to saturation. It entails the privilege of the present, because in the *Phenomenology* this self-becoming is nothing but the phenomenal or temporal succession of the moments of the Spirit. But the present is privileged also in the sense that the phenomenal or temporal moments, defined by their contribution to the increasing actualization of the Spirit, exhaust their effectiveness in their own contribution and are thus linked to a determined epoch, representing a determined degree in the maturation of the Spirit: After or beyond such a degree, the past no longer offers the possibility of retrieval or repetition (*Wiederholung*), but only of commemoration (*Erinnerung*). Finally, the present is granted a privilege, in the sense that the goal both presupposed and sought by the self-becoming— the Spirit certain of itself, or the concept knowing itself as such—eliminates the form of time, that is, the succession of presents, in order to be actualized in the *nunc stans* of the full presence, ''the eternal Idea that is in and for itself eternally actualizing itself and reaching its goal in absolute spirit'' (*Encyclopedia,* section 577). This form of circularity entails totalization: It is the same thing to say that ''the true is its own self-becoming'' and to say that ''the true is the whole.'' Here understanding what is true amounts to totalization. In particular, understanding calls for the totalization of the meaning of history and of the institutions that came into existence in its process. It is equally obvious that this form of circularity also entails saturation: In Hegel differentiation never has a primordial status; it is only a preface to identity, identity's provisional alienation, the element through which the equality of self-sameness makes itself absolute.

If such are indeed the respective consequences of the hermeneutic circle and the speculative one, then the methodological similarities that we identi-

fied earlier—the rejection of empiricism and of an intellectualistic a prior-
ism, the preliminary detection of a double circularity (the first regarding the
work and of the artist with reference to art as a middle term, the second concerning the work and of the essence of art), the progression toward circularity
on the basis of common notions—these similarities contain absolutely no evidence of a core kinship between these two approaches. In every respect there
is heterogeneity between the fundamental features of each form of circularity
toward which each path progresses independently.

However, the question remains open as to what treatment is given by the
essay "The Origin of the Work of Art" to the three consequences of the
hermeneutic circle. In other words, we still have to ask what its own circular
progression can assert regarding the privilege of the present, totalization, and
the excess of Being over beings. It is only by investigating the treatment of
these topics that we shall be able to clarify the ambiguity that set this inquiry
in motion: How does the Heideggerian overcoming of aesthetics, as a figure
of metaphysics, come to intersect and overlap Hegel's aesthetics, which is the
most metaphysical aesthetics of all?

So far, only in the epilogue did we find a more or less implicit acknowledgment of this overlapping. However, another text, roughly of the same period as the essay, expressly recognizes and underscores this recognition to
such an extent that this very overlapping now seems to result in the abolition
pure and simple of the heterogeneity between the hermeneutic and the speculative circles. I have in mind an important text of the 1936 course on Nietzsche, "The Will to Power as Art." The text in question bears the title "Six
Basic Developments in the History of Aesthetics."[9] These developments—
brought together by Heidegger at the time of his debate with the Nietzschean
interpretation of the essence of art—are said to "characterize the essence of
aesthetics, its role in Western thought and its relation to the history of Western art" (N, 79–80). Of the six alleged facts or developments, the first four
are of central interest to us, because their very formulation acknowledges the
overlapping we are investigating.

Let me reintroduce them:

1. "The magnificent art of Greece remains without a corresponding
cognitive-conceptual meditation on it, such meditation not having to be identical with aesthetics" (N, 80).

2. "Aesthetics begins with the Greeks only at that moment when their
great art and also the great philosophy that flourished along with it comes to

---

9. Martin Heidegger, *Nietzsche*, Vol. 1, trans. David Krell (New York: Harper & Row,
1979), 77ff. Hereafter cited as *N*.

an end. At that time, during the age of Plato and Aristotle, in connection with the organization of philosophy as a whole, those basic concepts are formed which mark off the boundaries for all future inquiry into art. One of those basic notions is the conceptual pair, *hylē-morphē, materia-forma*, matter-form'' (*N*, 80). To this first pair is associated the next one: *technē-physis*. The first pair owes its origin to Plato's determination of beings in view of their appearing: *eidos*, or idea. As in other texts of the same period, here as well Heidegger insists on the fact that *eidos* (originally only an effect of *physis*), as soon as it became predominant as a determination, by virtue of the fact that it had acquired a founding and normative status with respect to *physis*, not only detached itself from its origin but obliterated the pre-Platonic sense of *physis* as the unconcealment of the totality of beings (*alētheia*). Since the distinction *hylē-morphē* is regulated by the priority of *idea*, it starts to function in the context of an obliteration of *physis* (or *alētheia*). It was to *alētheia* that the initial use of the word *technē* was connected, designating the knowledge by means of which man, immersed in *physis*, orients himself, goes about his activities, and copes with beings according to what they let be revealed out of themselves. But by associating itself with the *hylē-morphē* distinction, now regulated by the new priority of *idea*, *technē* "loses this primitive force of meaning" (*N*, 82 modified) and undergoes an interpretation which gives it the sense of the aptitude to confer a form upon a material. As soon as we notice, says Heidegger, that this aptitude does not belong to the realm of the fine arts but to the realm of the fabrication of tools, we are bound to be overcome by serious doubts concerning the relevance of the fundamental concepts of the philosophical questioning of art.

3. "The third basic development is the beginning of the modern age. Man and his unconstrained knowledge of himself, as of his positions among beings, become the arena where the decision falls as to how beings are to be experienced, defined, and shaped" (*N*, 83).

The *cogito me cogitare* acquires the highest-court status for judging all beings. "I myself, and my states, are the primary and genuine beings. Everything else that may be said to be is measured against the standard of this quite certain being" (*N*, 83). At this juncture, in close connection with the modern metaphysics of subjectivity, aesthetics is born: It is the discipline specifically devoted to the study of the beautiful in art, inasmuch as the beautiful is related to the emotional states of man as to an exclusive normative principle. "A mode of observation (is recognized) for which the way had long been paved" (*N*, 83), Heidegger stresses. It presupposes indeed the Platonic heritage evoked earlier and consists essentially in a transposition: " 'Aesthetics' is to be in the field of sensuousness and feeling precisely what logic is in the area of thinking" (*N*, 83)—logic that had been born out of metaphysics, and that since its birth has bound truth to enunciation and to judgment and its rules.

Therefore, the third fact is the birth of "aesthetics" as the modern discipline conceived as a logic of sensibility. In this discipline, "the artwork is posited as the 'object' for a 'subject'; definitive for aesthetic consideration is the subject-object relation, indeed as a relation of feeling" (*N*, 78).

It is concerning this third fundamental fact that the question of the intersecting and overlapping that we are pursuing is presented with the utmost clarity. Heidegger writes:

> Parallel to the formation of aesthetics and to the effort to clarify and ground the aesthetic state, another decisive process unfolds within the history of art. Great art and its works are great in their historical emergence and Being because in man's historical existence they accomplish a decisive task: they make manifest, in the way appropriate to works, what beings as a whole are, preserving such manifestation in the work. Art and its work are necessary only as an itinerary and sojourn for man in which the truth of beings as a whole, i.e., the unconditioned, absolute, opens itself up to him. What makes art great is not only and not in the first place the high quality of what is created. Rather, art is great because it is an "absolute need." Because it is that, and to the extent it is that, it also can and must be great in rank. For only on the basis of the magnitude of its essential character does it also create a dimension of magnitude for the rank and stature of what is brought forth.
>
> Concurrent with the formation of a dominant aesthetics and of the aesthetic relation to art in modern times is the decline of great art, great in the designated sense. Such decline does not result from the fact that "quality" is poorer and the style less imposing; it is rather that art forfeits its essence, loses its immediate relation to the basic task of representing the absolute, i.e., of establishing the absolute definitively as such in the realm of historical man. (*N*, 83–84).

I hope to be forgiven for this long quote. Even though no mention is directly made of Hegel, no great familiarity with speculative aesthetics is required to recognize the obvious echo of the Hegelian concept of great art. It is more than an echo, because the expression *absolute need*—put in quotation marks by Heidegger—is clearly borrowed from Hegel. He thought that art is great, is art fully, only when it comes as the response to the "absolute need" to manifest the "unconditioned" or the "absolute"; for him, this need was historically connected to the Greek world, because only in it was art truly "necessary." Hegel also claimed that the period of blossoming of great art preceded the birth of philosophy—with Socrates and Plato—a birth that would soon spell the demise of Greek art. Because of the fact that the sequence of the first three fundamental facts advanced by Heidegger is pivotally centered on the idea that the only "great art" was Greek, and more precisely pre-Socratic, and also because of the fact that it expressly subscribes to the Hegelian definition of great art as the necessary response to the absolute need to exhibit the absolute with its speculative connotation, for these reasons this sequence is a very close duplication of the Hegelian succession of the ages of the history of art:

1. The great Greek art, without corresponding conceptual reflection;
2. The Greek end of great art at the time of the birth of metaphysics with Socrates and Plato, within which is foreshadowed and announced at a distance the advent of aesthetics;
3. The properly modern decline of great art at the time when metaphysics moves into the era of subjectivity, thus making possible the birth of aesthetics proper.

Therefore, it is not surprising that the fourth fundamental fact advanced by Heidegger should be formulated by him in the very same terms that Hegel used:

> The achievement of aesthetics derives its greatness from the fact that it recognizes and gives utterance to the end of great art as such. The final and greatest aesthetics in the Western tradition is that of Hegel. . . . There the following statements appear: ' . . . In all these relations art is and remains for us with regard to its highest determination, something of the past.' (X:1. 16)

> The magnificent days of Greek art, like the golden era of the later Middle Ages, are gone. (X:1. 15–16) (*N*, 84)

It is extremely surprising, however, that this sequence of fundamental facts should endorse a properly metaphysical concept of art without questioning it, at the same time as, in the wake of a meditation on the most primordial semantic units of Greek thinking, it points toward a nonmetaphysical essence of art. What an amazing tangle! For what could be more metaphysical than to assign to the fine arts the essential task of exhibiting "the truth of beings as a whole, that is to say the unconditioned, the Absolute" (*N*, 84)? What could be more surprising than to hear that only Greek, pre-Socratic art took upon itself this properly metaphysical task for which it alone deserves "greatness," at the very same time as it is stressed that the most significant words found in the pre-Socratic thinkers and poets—*alētheia* and *physis*—point not toward an unconditional and supreme being as the ground of beings as a whole, but toward the twofold unity of revealing and reserve at the very core of Being? What could be more amazing than the fact that Heidegger points out, at the same time, that the Greek word *technē* initially referred not to making, to fabricating, to the imposition of a form upon a material—but to a knowledge, to an opening to the twofold unconcealment of *physis*, to a know-how involved in dealing with it, in co–responding to its very twofold nature.

What are we to make of this intertwining? One may wonder whether it does not constitute the unthought of the Heideggerian overcoming of aesthetics and whether it does not create—within his texts devoted to art—a tension that they never overcame.

Before detecting the evidence of such a tension, let us first remark that, inasmuch as the Heideggerian conception of the history of Western art expressly endorses the Hegelian definition of great art, it is led to discard the three consequences of the hermeneutic circle upon which we insisted earlier on. Indeed, the recasting of that Hegelian definition entails the privilege given to the present, the totalization of history, and the reduction of Being on the level of beings or of their beingness. A privilege is given to the present with the notion that once, during the Greek dawn, there had been a time—a present—when art was art fully. There is also a totalization of history in the sense of the sequence of the four fundamental facts mentioned previously, a sequence that furthermore is complemented with a fifth development: the Wagnerian aspiration to the integral work of art in the unfixed, evanescent, and measureless element of blind and superficial *Erlebnis;* and finally a sixth: the Nietzschean reaction against that nihilistic vertigo with the notion of art as an intoxication of the will willing its own overcoming, that is, its everrenewed intensification. These last two facts cannot indeed be found in Hegel, but they confirm and continue a series whose style we may identify as Hegelian because they imply that in this present–day and age of planetary technology—whose metaphysical essence Nietzsche anticipated in the twin doctrines of the will to power and of the eternal return—art does nothing but perpetuate its nonessence. This sequence of facts entails the abolition of the difference between Being and beings, which can easily be understood by noticing that the Hegelian concept of "great art" that regulates it derives its meaning not from the twofold unity of revealing and reserve at the core of *alētheia,* but rather from the manifestation of an unconditioned and absolute foundation of the totality, in short from a supreme being.

Yet, as we saw, the book *Nietzsche* combines this purely metaphysical concept of art with a nonmetaphysical one, and this fusion generates in it an internal tension whose signs we can now attempt to detect in the essay "The Origin of the Work of Art."

It is remarkable that in it we should also find the expression *great art.* At the beginning of the second section of the essay, Heidegger stresses the fact that "only great art is under consideration here" *(OWA,* 40). The immediate context of that sentence leaves no doubt on the Hegelian origin of this expression. Not only does the expression aim, as it does in Hegel, at the Greek world and the Christian Middle Ages (Heidegger evokes the Aegina sculptures, Sophocles' Antigone, the temple in Paestum, but the Bamberg cathedral, too), but also in a very Hegelian style it evokes both worlds as irrevocably gone, their works being no longer what they were as a result of the collapse of their worlds and, more importantly, of the fact that we, moderns, approach them as we do objects, by means of representation *(Vorstellung).*

Heidegger writes:

> World-withdrawal and world-decay can never be undone. The works are no longer the same as they once were. It is they themselves, to be sure, that we encounter there, but they themselves are gone by. As bygone works, they stand over against us in the realm of tradition and conservation. Henceforth, they remain merely such objects. Their standing before us is still indeed a consequence of, but no longer the same as, their former self-subsistence. Their self-subsistence has fled from them. The whole art industry, even carried to the extreme and exercised in every way for the sake of works themselves, extends only to the object-being of the works. But this does not constitute their work-being. *(OWA,* 41)

It is difficult not to hear in these words the echo of Hegel's words in the *Phenomenology of Spirit* that evoked the collapse of Greece and "the disappearance of the works of the Muses":

> So Fate does not restore their world to us along with the works of antique Art, it gives not the spring and summer of the ethical life in which they blossomed and ripened, but only the veiled recollection of that actual world. Our active enjoyment of them is therefore not

an act of divine worship through which our consciousness might come to its perfect truth and fulfillment; it is an external activity—the wiping-off of some drops of rain or specks of dust from these fruits, so to speak—one which erects an intricate scaffolding of the dead elements of their outward existence—the language, the historical circumstances, etc.—in place of the inner elements of the ethical life which environed, created, and inspired them. All this we do, not in order to enter into their very life but only to possess an idea of them in our imagination. (*PS*, section 753, pp. 456–57)

Once more it is in close agreement with Hegel that after stressing that the works of the great art are no longer for us moderns "what they were (*die Gewesenen*)," Heidegger claims that "as work, [the work] belongs uniquely within the realm that is opened up by itself. For the work-being of the work is present in, and only in, such opening up" (*OWA*, 41). The privilege of the present lies in this: The works of the great art were truly works only within the realm that they opened up in a bygone age; only then were they truly present. For us now, they no longer actualize that opening, for they have changed to objects.

Another affinity with Hegel lies in the particular choice for the work of art selected to apprise the reader of the advent of this opening: the Greek temple. Such a choice brings in a special load of meaning, for it unmistakably presupposes that the works that truly work—that is, the works of great art—can be nothing but sacred, that the world that they erect is the one in which a "people" embraces the seal and figure of its destiny, and also it supposes that they remain works only "as long as the god has not fled from them" (*OWA*, 43). Hegel, likewise, maintained that art was fully art only in the artistic religion of the Greek people and as long as this religion remained alive.

Yet, striking though it is, this parallelism cannot be extended too far. Even though the Heideggerian description of the features characterizing the work as opening up a realm is reminiscent of Hegel, it nevertheless escapes the Hegelian ascendancy. At the same time as the work erects and consecrates a world, it manifests from the very depths of that world that there is something that the world cannot absorb: the earth, another name for *physis*. What the work manifests, arranges, administers, and organizes, is consequently referred and entrusted to something ungraspable, to an enigma, to a secret. Such is the polemical essence of the work, which Hegel indeed recognized in the great art of Greece, but in which he sought to acknowledge nothing but a provisional conflict, the tension between substance and subject before the absorption of the former by the latter. Nothing of the like is to be found in Heidegger. The earth, or *physis*, is not the substance that the Spirit is called upon to dissolve in the process of acquiring total self-certainty. More importantly, the earth is the unfathomable reserve at the core of what is disclosed, for which it is the ever-presupposed and ever-renewed resource.

At this juncture comes to the fore the tension between the Hegelian theme obscurely espoused by Heidegger and another theme that escapes it. It is one thing to maintain, in line with Hegel, as we read in *Nietzsche*, that great art corresponds to the absolute need to exhibit "the truth of beings as a whole, that is to say (of) the unconditioned." It is quite another thing to say that it brings into the open the struggle between earth and world.

In this struggle, by virtue of which only the work is truly work, the polemical nature of *alētheia* is at stake. *Alētheia* is what sets itself to work in the work. But the meditation on the nature of *alētheia* is precisely what shatters the first superficial evidence of the notion of "great art," along with the entire network of Hegelian echoes brought in the wake of this notion.

Let me call attention to the indications of such a shattering. The simple fact that a painting by Van Gogh should be entrusted with the mission of conveying an example of the setting-into-work of *alētheia* is not compatible with the Hegelian connotations present in the Heideggerian concept of the great art. Which "historical people" could possibly be summoned to embrace its historic destiny by this modern painter whose works were frowned upon by his contemporaries? Yet the peasant's shoes painted by Van Gogh are granted the virtue of making reliability (*Verlässlichkeit*) manifest, that is, of manifesting the link between the world and the earth, more profoundly rooted than the readiness-at-hand of equipment. Moreover, the very meditation on *alētheia* to which the description of the Greek temple leads, entails a relativization of the aletheic privilege of Greek *Dasein,* and thus shatters the artistic privilege of Greece. Indeed, Heidegger writes:

> The nature of truth as *alētheia* was not thought out in the thinking of the Greeks, nor since then and least of all in the philosophy that followed after. Unconcealedness is, for thought, the most concealed thing in Greek existence, although from early times it determines the present of everything present. (*OWA,* 51)

The sequence (a. artistic but nonphilosophical Greece; b. philosophical but no-longer-artistic Greece), Hegelian in origin, is therefore not the last word, since *alētheia* remained concealed to those very thinkers of the artistic—not yet philosophical or metaphysical—age of Greece, even though it did "flash out" through their most pregnant linguistic coinages. Their Saying, therefore, is less the vestige of a treasure to which they had privileged access than a constellation of signs that have been awaiting, up to this very day, a meditation that always is to come.

There is more. This meditation on *alētheia*, on unconcealedness, proceeds along a way that avoids all normative application. At the core of this meditation it turns out that "the clearing in which beings stand is in itself at the same time a concealing [*Verbergung*]" (*OWA*, 53) and that the latter rules over beings as a whole in a double mode—in the mode of the refusal or concealing, which we best reach when "we can say no more of beings than that they are" (*OWA*, 53), and in the mode of displacement, that is, of dissembling (*Verstellen*), which occurs when, inside the clearing (*Lichtung*), something in a being masks something else of that being or passes itself off as something that it is not. Of this double mode Heidegger writes:

> Concealment can be a refusal (*Versagen*) or merely a dissembling (*Verstellen*). We are never fully certain whether it is the one or the other. Concealment conceals and dissembles itself. (*OWA*, 54)

And further on:

> Truth occurs as itself in that the concealing denial, as refusal, provides its constant source to all clearing, and yet, as dissembling it metes out to all clearing the indefeasible severity of deception. (*OWA*, 55, modified)

Here indeed the most severe shattering of the Hegelian theme is expressed: How can one convincingly talk about great art, and consequently suggest a clear distinction between great and inferior, if one cannot decide whether concealment—inseparable as it is from unconcealment—is encountered by us in the mode of refusal or in that of dissembling? How then could it be possible to distinguish, in Hegel's manner, between the age of art's greatness and the age of its decline?

Isn't Heidegger's position worlds apart from the Hegelian "greatness," worlds apart from the exhibition of the unconditioned, worlds apart from the monumentality, the resolute and given unanimity of a historical people, when he writes later on in the essay the following assessment?

> The simple *factum est* wants to be held forth into the Open by the work: namely this, that unconcealedness of what is has happened here, and that as this happening it happens here for the first time; or, that such a work *is* at all rather than is not. . . . Precisely where the

artist, the process and the circumstances of the genesis of the work remain unknown, this thrust, this "*that* it is" of createdness, emerges into view most purely from the work. (*OWA*, 65)

And further:

The more solitarily the work, fixed in the figure stands on its own and the more cleanly it seems to cut all ties to human beings, the more simply does the thrust come into the Open that such a work *is*, and the more essentially is the extraordinary thrust to the surface and the long-familiar thrust down. (*OWA*, 66)

It is at this point, a point almost characterized, one might say, by insignificance, since it resists all knowledge and all power—when the work simply offers itself and reveals the enigma that it is, rather than is not—that the Heideggerian meditation is radically irreducible to the speculative circle.

Therefore, there is present in the text of "The Origin of the Work of Art" a tension between the terms we singled out at the beginning: On the one hand, attention is given to the enigma; on the other hand, we have the suggestion of a solution to the philosophical problem of the essence of art. It is true that the language of the essay remains questioning throughout, in contradistinction to that of *Nietzsche*, which is massively assertive. Consequently, the weight of speculative circularity is less predominant in it than in *Nietzsche*. However, the speculative circle is still present, and it reemerges implicitly when the essay expressly reiterates what the hermeneutic circle teaches in relation to art. I have in mind here the pages of the third section, dealing with poetry (*Dichtung*) conceived as the essence of art:

The nature of poetry [*Dichtung*], in turn, is the founding of truth. We understand founding here in a triple sense: founding as bestowing [*Schenken*], founding as grounding [*Grunden*] and founding as beginning [*Anfangen*]. Founding, however, is actual only in preserving. Thus to each mode of founding there corresponds a mode of preserving. (*OWA*, 75)

This is, the text adds, "the structure of the nature of art." The fact that we are dealing here with a variant of the hermeneutic circle, of the circle of the cast-forth project that understanding is, such a fact is unmistakably indicated in the text by the qualification of *Dichtung* as "poetic projection," which opens up "that into which human being as historical is already cast" (*OWA*, 75). The inclusion within the structure of the *Dichtung* of the previously analyzed characters of the hermeneutic circle is undeniable, because the *bestowing* here evoked designates the excess of Being over beings, because the *founding* here evoked consists in entrusting that which is instituted by the work of art to the already-there of the earth, or *physis,* and because the *beginning* also evoked consists in opening a space of safekeeping and retrieval. In a way, such a circle is untotalizable, because in it we face the ever-renewed intersection of the three ec-stases of time, that is to say an ad-vent (*Geschehen*) that preserves itself at the very core of what happens. One can suspect, however, that the shadow of speculative circularity looms within the meditation on this ad-vent, which is the very history of Being. Isn't it this shadow, which at a distance in the text rules over Heidegger's outline for art history, articulated along three major epochs: Greek, medieval, and modern? Isn't it the same shadow, most importantly, that makes it necessary to construe each of these eruptions of history as the "awakening of a *people* to what it has been entrusted to accomplish"? Isn't it also the same shadow that compels Heidegger to ask at the closing of the essay whether art can still be today an "origin" or "whether it is to remain a mere appendix and then can only be carried along as a routine cultural phenomenon"?

Beyond the text that we have just scrutinized, two other signs give additional testimony to the fact that the shadow of the speculative history of Spirit is brought to bear on Heidegger's meditation on art. The first sign is the precipitation with which Heidegger confined the adventure of contemporary art within the limits of technology, that is, of what he called *Gestell,* taken to be the completed figure of metaphysics—as we can see both in the 1967 Athens conference and in the posthumous interview by *Der Spiegel* magazine. Why such precipitation, when the lecture *The Question Concerning Technology* seemed to suggest quite a different approach? This lecture indeed first undermined the naive certainties about the instrumental conception of technology and then proceeded to show how contemporary technology, which is the achievement and the completion of the modern metaphysics of subjectivity, still remains—in the midst of the generalized challenge that constitutes it—a mode of unconcealing, that is, of *alētheia.* Its essence, therefore, is ambiguous: At the same time as the *Gestell* entails the ruling of the darkest forgetfulness of Being, because beings are reduced to their availability for manipulations and calculations, it contains the way Being has of calling us to attention while preserving its secret. The kinship between danger and saving power, says Heidegger, is comparable to the two sides of a coin. Precisely because of this ambiguity, the essence of technology is not at all technological. Heidegger then draws the consequence that an "essential reflection upon technology and decisive confrontation with it must happen in a realm that is, on the one hand, akin to the essence of technology, and, on the other, fundamentally different from it. Such a realm is art."[10] Is he here contemplating art in the morning of Greece? Perhaps. But if so, why would a privilege be given to Greece if it were not by dint of some unquestioned Hegelian reemergence? Why couldn't contemporary art itself testify to this "ambiguous essence"? Even acknowledging that contemporary art invents and exhibits itself under the mode of challenge and defiant provocation—an acknowledgment that in my opinion should be made without hesitation or condition—doesn't the very fact that such works are offered to the public eye amount to letting others glean the enigma that they are, and therefore detect the ambiguous essence that appeared to the thinker on the lonely path of the meditation on Being?

The second sign is the insistence with which Heidegger stresses that aesthetics, the offspring of the modern metaphysics of subjectivity, turns the work of art into an "object" of private experience, of *Erlebnis*. Precisely because art has now moved into the horizon of aesthetics thus circumscribed, it is destined to a decline of its essence—an essence that consists in setting *alētheia* into work. Yet Heidegger himself taught us to recognize that one aesthetics, at least, one properly modern philosophy of subjectivity, escapes such a characterization: the Critique of Judgment (*N*, 1:109). He called attention to the fact that, when Kant characterizes the attitude by which we receive the beautiful thing as favor (*Gunst*), in a sense Kant causes the collapse of the modern correlation of subject and object, because such a favor stands beyond any possible conceptualization, any purposefulness, and any subjective complacency, and is rather the pure openness to the unconcealed as such. The surprising thing is that this profound reading of Kant is in no way integrated by Heidegger in his meditation on the history of art, insofar as the history of art is linked to the history of aesthetics. Everything happens as if, in his acceptance of the various epochs of that history, determined though they might be by the increasing forgetfulness of Being and not by the *parousia* of the Spirit, Heidegger is taking Hegel as the only guide. In Kant, however, we find—in strict conformity with the doctrine of favor—an invitation to cast another look on the history of art, one that would amount to considering it not in terms of progress or decline, but as "a domain of originality," that is, of an enigmatic irruption of nature that does not cease to be renewed in the interplay with the tradition that inspired it. This view is akin to a Kantian approximation of the hermeneutic circle: The past of art is not something dead, merely handing down the remnants of bygone ages; it is a

---

10. Martin Heidegger, *The Question Concerning Technology*, trans. William Lovitt (New York: Harper Torchbooks, 1977), 35.

myriad of signs pregnant with future possibilities. This approximation of the hermeneutical circle in Kant is not brought to the fore by Heidegger. Had he pointed in its direction, he might have been led to concede that the modern ushering of art inside the horizon of aesthetics is less the sign of a decline or of a terminal captivity inside the closing of subjectivity than of a new opening to the enigma of unconcealment.

9

# The Origin of "The Origin of the Work of Art"

I remember Heidegger saying in passing during the Zähringen seminar held in September 1973 that the meditation on the origin of the work of art had played a decisive role in the *Kehre*, the turn, that occurred in his thought in the thirties. In this essay I would like to elucidate in a provisional way in what sense and to what extent the texts dealing with the question of the origin of the work of art bear evidence to a turn, or at least a shift, in Heidegger's thought.

In what texts are we to look for such an evidence? As it turns out, we now have three texts about the origin of the work of art. In chronological order, they are these:

1. The first elaboration of the text of the lecture given by Heidegger on 13 November 1935 at the Society for the Sciences of Art of Freiburg im Breisgau. This text is now available in the last issue of *Heidegger Studies*.[1]
2. The second elaboration of the same lecture, which came out in France in 1987 together with a translation into French, by Emmanuel Martineau, based upon a photocopy of the typewritten transcript of Heidegger's own manuscript. This second elaboration constitutes the text of the lecture as

---

This essay is the revised version of a paper read in English at the centenial of Heidegger's birth at Loyola University in Chicago, September 1990. That paper is now included in the collection of essays, *Reading Heidegger*, ed. J. Sallis (Bloomington: Indiana Press University, 1992).

1. Martin Heidegger, *Heidegger Studies*, 1989, vol. 5. The text is published in that journal under the title "Vom Ursprung des Kuntswerk, Erste Ausarbeitung" (First elaboration).

it was actually pronounced by Heidegger in November 1935 and repeated without change in January 1936 at the University of Zürich in Switzerland under the title *Vom Ursprung des Kuntswerkes.*[2]

3. Finally, we have a third elaboration of the topic with the text of the three lectures offered in November and December 1936 at the Frei Deutsche Hochshift in Frankfurt am Main. This version was published in the fall of 1945 in the *Holzwege* under the title "Der Ursprung des Kunstwerkes."[3]

My purpose in this essay will be to take literally what Heidegger suggested in 1973 and to look for evidence of a shift in the various texts dealing with the origin of the work of art. More precisely, I propose to search for such evidence by comparing the two 1935 versions to the 1936 version. But before proceeding, tentatively of course, to sketch out a comparison, a short investigation about the place of art in Heidegger's writings before the fall of 1935 would be helpful.

## Fundamental Ontology

If we consider the writings and the now-published lecture courses of the period of fundamental ontology, we might say that although art, taken in the sense of the Greek word *technē,* is everywhere present as a topic, in no way is it originary, *ursprünglich.* Let me try to clarify this point.

The project of fundamental ontology is intended to prove that there is only one focus for understanding the various meanings of Being, namely, the finite time of the being that we ourselves are, *Dasein.* Proving that the question of the meaning of Being finds its answer in the finite and mortal time that each *Dasein* is at bottom amounts to taking the very Being of *Dasein* as the ground of ontology. It amounts to making the ontology of *Dasein* the basis of fundamental ontology. The publication or widespread diffusion of the lecture courses offered by Heidegger in Marburg before the publication of *Being and Time,* particularly the lecture course on Plato's *Sophist*[4] and the lecture

---

2. Martin Heidegger, "De l'origine de l'oeuvre d'art" trans. E. Martineau (Paris: Authentica, 1987). This unauthorized publication, which contains both the German text and Martineau's French translation of it, is the only available version of the second elaboration. Hereafter cited as *SE*.

3. Martin Heidegger, "Des Ursprung des Kuntswerkes," in *Holzwege* (Frankfurt A.M.: V. Klostermann, 1945). Hereafter cited as *UKW*. The English translation of *UKW* is by Albert Hofstadter, in Martin Heidegger, *Poetry, Language, Thought,* trans. Hofstadter (New York: Harper and Row, 1971). Hereafter cited as *OWA*.

4. Martin Heidegger, *Gesamtausgabe, Platon: Sophistes* (Frankfurt am Main: V. Klostezmann, 1922).

course *The Basic Concepts of Greek Philosophy,* today allows us to realize that Heidegger discovered the articulation of his fundamental ontology primarily as a result of a decade-long meditation on Aristotle—more specifically as a result of a particular reappropriation of the *Nicomachean Ethics,* a work indeed that, for Heidegger at that time, was the first ontology of *Dasein.*

Now art, or *technē* in Greek, is among the topics of the *Nichomachean Ethics.* How does it deal with art? Aristotle's treatise scrutinizes the dianoetic excellences or intellectual virtues in order to determine their rank. The intellectual virtues have two levels: On the lower level are the deliberative virtues, on the higher level are the epistemic virtues. *Technē,* art, is an intellectual virtue, yet it is located on the lowest level of the deliberative virtues. It is an intellectual virtue in the sense that it is a way of disclosing, of discovering, of *alētheuein,* of revealing. It is thus a way of knowing truth. However, as a way of knowing truth and even of being-in-truth, *technē* is strictly linked to a specific activity, the activity of producing, *poiēsis,* which consists in setting-into-work (*energein*) what *technē* reveals. In the Aristotelian framework, the origin of the work of art (i.e., of the *ergon* of the *technitēs*) is *poiēsis* (i.e., the productive activity), but the productive activity itself has its origin in art, in *technē,* as a way of unconcealing, of *alētheuein.* "The origin of the work of art is art" is a strictly Aristotelian statement. Likewise, it is strictly Aristotelian to state that the essence of art lies in a happening of truth. However, in Aristotle's *Ethics,* both art and the activity ruled and permeated by it (i.e., *poiēsis*) suffer from an intrinsic deficiency. They are deficient because the end, or the *telos,* of the productive activity ruled by *technē* is not in the agent, but outside him. To be sure, the principle for the production process is within the agent (it is the model the agent has in view), and to that extent it is an excellence. But it is a deficient excellence, since its end is a product, or *ergon,* outside the agent.

Such a deficiency does not characterize the highest deliberative excellence, namely, *phronēsis,* a way of *alētheuein,* of unconcealing, that is adjusted to the activity that is no longer *poiēsis,* but *praxis,* action in the sense of the conduct by an individual of his life among, and in the presence of, other individuals. *Phronēsis,* practical judgment, is the highest deliberative virtue insofar as neither its principle, its *archē,* nor its end, its *telos,* fall outside the agent himself. Indeed the principle of *phronēsis* is a prior option of the agent for acting well, its end is the acting-well of the agent. *Phronēsis* is nothing other than his resoluteness to act well.

For Aristotle, however, *phronēsis* is not at all the highest excellence. Both *technē* and *phronēsis* are linked to the realm of the perishable in general. And *phronēsis* is strictly confined to the realm of human affairs, which cannot be the highest realm, since, because of their mortality, human beings are not what is highest in the world. Higher than the *aion*, the finite time of mortals, is the *aei*, the imperishable that is forever what and how it is.

Two dianoetic excellences, or virtues, are concerned with the *aei*. They are the epistemic virtues, *epistēmē* and *sophia*. Both virtues are adjusted to a way of behaving that is higher than *poiēsis* and *praxis*. Such a way of behaving is *theoria*. The two disclosing or unconcealing virtues of *theoria* have nothing to do with the perishable. Indeed, *epistēmē* is concerned with unchangeable entities, like the mathematical figures. And *sophia*, the highest intellectual excellence, is concerned with the ontological structure of the totality of beings and with the highest being, the prime mover that is the principle of all the movements among the beings of *physis*. According to Aristotle, the contemplation of that immutable realm is for a mortal being the most authentic way of being. As long as such a contemplation lasts, the mortal spectator comes close to the divine. He reaches *eudaimonia*, or authenticity, in the sense of being himself with excellence.

Heidegger's fundamental ontology is both a reappropriation and a critique of Aristotle's views. He thoroughly agrees with Aristotle's distinction between *technē* as a mode of disclosing adjusted to the production of artifacts or of effects, and *phronēsis* as a mode of disclosing adjusted to the conduct of human life. In other words, he agrees with Aristotle's distinction between art as adjusted to production and *phronēsis* as adjusted to *praxis*. But he reappropriates the distinction in ontological terms, whereby it is metamorphosed in the distinction between, on the one hand, an everyday way of being—concerned with and preoccupied by ends to be attained by utensils and their readiness-to-hand and previously revealed by a specific circumspection—and, on the other hand, an authentic way of being that cares for the very Being of *Dasein*'s existence and is illuminated by resoluteness.

Heidegger's reappropriation also includes an agreement with Aristotle about the privilege of *theoria*. But this reappropriation once more implies an ontological metamorphosis.

What is at stake in Aristotle's concept of the highest form of *theoria* is the knowledge of the Being of beings; such knowledge in Aristotle is conflated with the science of the highest being, theology. This view, Heidegger claims, involves both an equivocation and an indeterminacy. There is an equivocation because the science of Being (ontology) gets confused with the science of the divine (theology); there is an indeterminacy because for Aristotle, as for all the Greeks, the meaning of Being is limited to *ousia*, presence in the sense of *Vorhandenheit*, presence-at-hand, a presence whose privilege, moreover, presupposes that only one mode of time has been taken into account. The aim of fundamental ontology is to overcome both the equivocation and the indeterminacy. It overcomes equivocation by showing that the eternity of the prime mover is but a concept derived from everydayness, in which indeed our art—our know-how, the circumspective and projective disclosure of our environment—constantly requires a permanence, that is, the stable persistence of nature. But such interest and fascination for permanence, claims Heidegger, is nothing but a way of escaping our own Being, a falling away from our own existence and its finite time. In contrast, it is by taking into account our own finite time as originary—a time in which the projection upon a future and the retrieval of a past are essential features—that fundamental ontology also overcomes what remains indeterminate in the meaning of Being, when the latter is limited to sheer presence.

This schematic presentation is enough, I trust, to show that in the framework of fundamental ontology, art is in no way originary, although it is understood as a mode of unconcealment. On the contrary, art (i.e., *technē*) and the activity of setting-into-work ruled by it, are secondary; they are derived, they are in a position of fallenness with respect to what is our own, our existence and its finite time.

We find confirmation of this, as far as the fine arts are concerned, in the way in which Heidegger deals with *The Notebooks of Malte Laurids Brigge* in the 1927 lecture course, *The Basic Problems of Phenomenology*. Heidegger's commentary proves that for him, at that time, the poet cannot be of the same rank as the thinker. The poet cannot go beyond an improper or inauthentic understanding of existence, because while he has the presentiment of what existence is, he either projects existence upon things or projects upon existence the mode of being of things.[5]

## The Rectoral Address

Hence, in fundamental ontology *technē* as a whole is minimized and downgraded. There is no significant change concerning this topic until the 1933 *Rectoral Address*. But with the *Address* things change dramatically. In it, we are presented, indeed, with a major correction to the hierarchy of the ranks of active life as articulated in *Being and Time,* a major correction concerning *technē. Technē,* which formerly was narrowly confined within the inauthentic realm of everydayness, now suddenly reaches to the top of the ladder of authenticity. Let us consider this transformation more closely.

---

5. Martin Heidegger, *The Basic Problems of Phenomenology* (Bloomington: Indiana University Press, 1982), 171–73, 289.

At the beginning of the *Address*[6], Heidegger evokes the following points, in strict agreement with Aristotle and in continuity with what he had already developed in the Marburg period about philosophy as the highest way of existing, and the authentic principle of individuation: The Greeks, he says, conceived of *theoria* as the "implementation of the highest form of *praxis*" (*SDU*, 12). Aristotle indeed, and Plato before him, conceived of *theoria* as a *bios*, a way of existing, a way of behaving, namely, a *praxis*. There is nothing new in Heidegger's statement of the matter. But in the same context, Heidegger brings to mind an old Greek legend according to which Prometheus was reportedly the first philosopher, and he calls attention in this context to the words of Prometheus in Aeschylus's tragedy, *techné d' anagkes asthenestera makro*. Heidegger translates this as "Knowing [*Wissen*] however is much weaker than necessity."

> This means that all knowledge concerning things is first of all delivered to the overpower [*Übermacht*] of destiny and falters in front of such overpower. That is precisely why, if it is to genuinely falter, knowledge must display the highest challenge, in front of which only the power of concealment of beings is erected (*SDU*, 11).

Hence philosophy, as the highest knowledge, the knowledge of the Being of beings, is both *theoria*, which is the highest form of *bios* or *praxis*, and *techné*, which obviously means a mode of disclosing adjusted to a peculiar *poiésis*, that is, to some setting-into-work over which it rules. This is quite a correction to the previous hierarchy.

Does it mean that the link formerly established between *techné* and fallen everydayness disappears? Not at all. Indeed a distinction has to be made between a low form of *techné* unable, ontologically speaking, to overcome *Vorhandenheit* (or presence-at-hand) and a superior form of *techné*, adjusted to the unconcealment of the Being of beings. Concerning this superior form of *techné*, we find developments and precisions in the two lecture courses offered by Heidegger immediately after the Rectorate period, namely, in the first lecture course on Hölderlin (1934–35 winter semester) and in the lecture course *An Introduction to Metaphysics*, offered during the 1935 summer semester, that is, immediately before the elaboration of the first lecture, "The Origin of the Work of Art" (Vom Ursprung des Kunstwerkes). Let me present these developments very briefly.

---

6. Martin Heidegger, *Die Selbstbehauptung der deutschen Universität* (*The Self-Affirmation of the German University*) (Frankfurt A.M.: V. Klostermann, 1983). Hereafter cited as *SDU*.

# First Lecture Course on Hölderlin and
## The Introduction to Metaphysics

Concerning the first lecture course on Hölderlin, it seems obvious to me that its articulation stems directly from fundamental ontology, in the sense that it is entirely dominated by the contrast between fallen everydayness and resolute authenticity. This reading of Hölderlin proposes to discard right away the various figures of fallen everydayness that were described in *Being and Time* as obstructing the question, Who is *Dasein*? The difference with *Being and Time* is that the *Dasein* at stake is no longer the individual, but "the authentic gathering of individuals in a community."[7] Hölderlin's poetry raises the question, "Who are we?" (*GA*, 39:48), not as individual beings, but as this singular German people, to whom the poet addresses himself. In order to appropriate the question "What about the Being of this very people?" (*GA*, 39:22), one should, insists Heidegger, be capable of withdrawing from everydayness (*GA*, 39:22) and of maintaining what the *Rectoral Address* called an " attitude of radical questioning" over against the "they" who immediately object: not questioning, but "the answer is what is decisive" (*GA*, 39:41).

Now how does Heidegger here characterize everydayness? The answer is, in terms of *technē*—in the sense, of course, of a circumspection dedicated to the management of an environment. A rigorous opposition, he says, should be preserved between, on the one hand, "the authentic Dasein," as "exposed to Being" and, on the other hand, "the everyday operations of productive man, who then uses his products and contributes to the progress of culture" (*GA*, 39:38). This lower level of *technē* includes, in the context of the lecture course on Hölderlin, the everyday life of the Nazi regime: cultural activism, subordination of thought and poetry to specific political needs, the rulings of ministries. But on the level of authentic *Dasein*, there is place for a quite different *technē*. Once again what is at stake in this reading of Hölderlin is no longer the finite time of individuals but the "historical Dasein of a people, experienced as the authentic and unique being, from which the fundamental position towards beings in their totality grows and owns its articulation" (*GA*, 39:121–22). Now there is a difference between the finite time of individuals and the ownmost time of historicality of a people: Each individual can temporalize the former; only a few individuals can temporalize the latter. Those few are the creators.

---

7. Martin Heidegger, *Gesamtausgabe*, "Hölderlins Hymnen "Germanie" und "Der Rhein" " (winter semester lecture course of 1934–5) (Frankfurt A.M.: V. Klostermann, 1980), vol. 39.

In his interpretation of Hölderlin's sacred mourning (i.e., the awareness that the gods have disappeared), Heidegger tries to show that such a basic mood, *Grundstimmung*, reveals the truth of the German people "and opens it to the decision of standing already in the acceptance of a return of the divine" (*GA*, 39:102). In this context he writes the following:

> The *Grundstimmung*, and this means the truth of the Dasein of a people, is originally instituted by the poet [*gestiftet*]. But the Being of beings thus disclosed is understood and articulated, and thus opened up for the first time by the thinker. Thus understood, Being is posited in the ultimate and original seriousness of beings, which means within a determinate [*bestimmt*] historical truth, by this only: that the people is brought to itself as a people. This occurs only thanks to the creation by the State-creator of a specific state adjusted to the essence of that people. . . . These three creative powers of the historical Dasein are the ones who set-to-work that which solely deserves to be acclaimed as great. (*GA*, 39:144)

This triad of the creators—the poet, the thinker, and the state-founder—embodies the Promethean *technē* evoked in the *Rectoral Address*. Insofar as they are aware of the over-power of destiny, they are aware of finiteness. Insofar as they take this awareness as the incentive to the highest challenge, they rise to the level of the demigods. The Promethean *technē*—the superior *technē* of the poet, thinker, and state-creator—is thus separated by an abyss from the low and petty *technē* of everydayness.

The lecture course *An Introduction to Metaphysics* focuses upon the same topic in the light of the Pre-Socratics. We already know that there is no *technē* without *poiēsis*, without a production of a work, without a setting-into-work (*energeia*) of what *technē* discloses. As a result of the elevation of a peculiar *technē* to the highest ontological level, the convergences that Heidegger now detects between Parmenides, Heraclitus, and Sophocles can be summarized in the following way:

> Being human determines itself from out of a relationship to beings as a whole. The human essence shows itself here to be the relation which first opens up Being to man. Being human, as the need for apprehending and gathering a being-driven into the freedom of undertaking *technē*, of the setting-into-work of Being, a setting-into-work which is itself knowing. This is History [*Geschichte*].[8]

---

8. Martin Heidegger, *An Introduction to Metaphysics*, trans. Ralph Manheim (New Haven: Yale University Press, 1959), 130. Henceforth cited as *EM*.

In other words, there is now an ontological compulsion or assignment to *technē*, and to setting-into-work what *technē* knows. Why such a necessary assignment to *technē?* Because Being itself (*physis*) is essentially polemical. It is an unconcealment that, on the one hand, remains within itself, and that, on the other hand, in its very appearing is constantly threatened by sheer appearance, deception, illusion. Being itself is "an intricate struggle" (*EM*, 81) between powers, Being is an over-power requiring a "creative self-assertion [*Selbstbehauptung*]" (*EM*, 81), an over-power that places man before a "constant decision" (*Entscheidung*), that is, a "separation in the togetherness of Being between unconcealment and appearance, Non-Being" (*EM*, 84). Such a decision is the way man is called to be responsive to the over-power of Being. And because this over-power is violence, he can rise to its challenge by being himself *the* disrupting and *the* violent one. The issue for him is to operate "a taming and ordering of powers by virtue of which beings open up as such when man moves into them. This disclosure [*Erschlossenheit*] of beings is the power that man must master in order to become himself amidst beings, i.e., in order to be historical" (*EM*, 120). In the context, "himself" means "the wielder of power," the one "who breaks out and breaks up, he who captures and subjugates" (*EM*, 120).

This violent activity is that of *technē* in the superior and essential sense. Heidegger writes:

> It is *technē* which provides the basic trait of *deinon*, the violent; for violence is the use of power against the overpowering: through knowledge, it wrests being from prior unconcealment into the manifest as Being. (*EM*, 122)

Thus understood, *technē* is also what it was during the Marburg period, a knowledge and a power. But the difference is that *technē* in Marburg was reduced to everydayness and was therefore dominated by presence-at-hand and confined to a position of fallenness with regard to authentic *Dasein*. By contrast, *technē* reinterpreted with the help of the Pre-Socratics turns out to be the countermovement against the falling tendency of everyday and petty *technē*. The *technē* that is now acclaimed is great *technē* as opposed to petty *technē*. As a knowledge, instead of being limited by the present-at-hand, it is "the initial and persistent sight looking beyond what is directly given before the hand [*Vorhanden*]" (*EM*, 122). And as a power, it is the "capacity to set-into-work Being as a being which each time is so and so" (*EM*, 122) and consequently the work stemming from *technē* is a "manifesting implementation [*Er-Wirhen*] of Being in beings (*EM*, 122)."

This great *technē*, as opposed to the petty business of the many, or the "they," had three fundamental modalities: artistic, philosophical, and political. Heidegger writes:

> Unconcealment occurs only when it is achieved by work: the work of the word in poetry, the work of stone in temple and statue, the work of *polis* as the historical place in which all this is grounded and preserved. (*EM*, 146)

These works are those of the creators celebrated in the first lecture course on Hölderlin: the poet, the thinker, and the state-creator. In addition, there is now the architect of the temple and the sculptor of the gods of a people. Only the works of these creators deserve the qualification of greatness, insofar as they are foundational.

The state-creator grounds the *polis*, that is, "the place, the There, wherein and as which historical Dasein is." He is the one who first creates "institutions, frontiers, structures, and order" (*EM*, 126). The great poet is the one who is dedicated to the "original institution [*Stiftung*] of the historical Dasein of a people" (*EM*, 126). And "great poetry is that by which a people enters into history" (*EM*, 131). The great thinker is the one who takes upon himself the essence of philosophy, namely, "a thinking that breaks the paths and opens perspectives of the knowledge that sets the norms and hierarchies, of the knowledge in which and by which a people fulfills itself historically and spiritually" (*EM*, 8).

> It is the genuine function of philosophy to challenge the historical Dasein and hence, in the last analysis, Being pure and simple. Challenge [*Erschwerung*] restores their weight (Being) to things, to beings. How so? Because challenge is one of the essential prerequisites for the birth of all greatness, and in speaking of greatness we are referring primarily to the destiny of a historical people and to its works. There is destiny, however, only where a truthful knowledge about things dominates Dasein. And it is philosophy that opens up the paths and perspectives of such knowledge. (*EM*, 8)

Heidegger even suggests that it is because of that foundational role with regard to his people that his own work up to then deserved the title of "fundamental ontology" (*EM*, 133). In this context, Heidegger liked to quote, in full agreement, Hegel's words in the first page of the preface of his 1812 *Logic:* "A people without a metaphysics is like a temple without a holy of holies."

Concerning the artistic setting-into-work of *alētheia,* we find the following:

> The Greeks called art in the true sense and the work of art *technē* because art is what most immediately brings Being (i.e., the appearing that stands in itself) to stand in something present in the work. . . . It is through the work of great art as a given being that everything else that appears and is to be found, is first confirmed and made accessible, explicable, and understandable as being or not being. Because art in a preeminent sense stabilizes and manifests Being in the work as a being, it may be regarded as the ability pure and simple to set-into-work, as *technē*. (*EM,* 122)

Such is the background of the lecture of November 1935 on "The Origin of the Work of Art."

All the key words and topics of the actual lecture, as well as its first undelivered draft, are already present in the first lecture course on Hölderlin or in the *Introduction to Metaphysics.* These topics are the historical *Dasein* of a people, the struggle at the heart of Being and at the heart of the work, the setting-into-work of unconcealment, the instituting (*Stiftung*) of history by the work, the greatness of such instituting with its three basic modalities, the necessity of a decision (*Entscheiden*) "for Being against Not-Being, and thus of a struggle with appearance" and "against the continuous pressure of involvement in the everyday and commonplace" (*EM,* 128), the necessity of preserving the unconcealment against cloaking and concealment" (*EM,* 133), the obligation—since art is disclosure of the Being of beings and not the representation of the beautiful in the sense of the pleasing—to fight aesthetics and to "provide the word 'art' with a new content" on the basis of a "*recaptured originary relation* to Being" (*EM,* 101, emphasis added). Even the topic of the origin is a decisive one in the *Introduction to Metaphysics.* Indeed, in the preliminary considerations on the basic question of metaphysics, we read that the question "Why are there beings rather than nothing?" recoils upon itself, and "has its ground in a leap through which man thrusts away all the previous security of his life." And Heidegger adds: "The leap [*Sprung*] in this questioning opens up its own source. . . . We call such a leap, which opens up its own source or origin [*Ur-Sprung*], the finding of one's own ground" (*EM,* 5).

On the basis of what I have called attention to, the preliminary discussion about the origin of the work of art that took place before the fall of 1935 and started with the *Rectoral Address* does not yet indicate any turn in Heidegger's thought. On the contrary, the introduction of a distinction between petty *technē*, which is blind toward Being and trapped within every-

dayness, and a great *technē*, which sets-into-work Being itself as unconcealment, not only leaves untouched, but even reinforces, the articulation of fundamental ontology, namely, the contrast between the inauthentic and the
authentic or, more deeply, between vulgar time and originary time. For that
matter, the fact that the *Dasein* at stake is now the *Dasein* of a people does not
introduce any significant discontinuity with respect to the early problematic
of fundamental ontology. The *Dasein* of the people, either Greek or German,
is still understood in light of the key sentence of fundamental ontology, *Das
Dasein existiert umwillen seiner.*[9] Instead of introducing a discontinuity, the
modifications I just mentioned even bring fundamental ontology to a sort of
metaphysical climax. To be sure, Heidegger introduces in his approach to the
Greek world several discrepancies between the Pre-Socratics, on the one
hand, and Plato, on the other. He thus seems to take sides with them against
Plato. But this, in a sense, is perhaps just a semblance, insofar as he obviously takes from Plato the assertion that philosophy is not only the true principle of individuation, but the foundational work by which the thinker
conceptually discloses the totality of beings taken in its ground, and claims to
be able to be a ruler for a people. In other words, Plato's *Republic* is still, in
spite of several corrections, one of the most inspiring texts at the core of
Heidegger's thought.

## The Lecture of November 1935

What about the lecture of November 1935, *Vom Ursprung des Kunstwerkes* (On the Origin of the Work of Art)? As I said, there are two versions
of it. Because they follow one another within a short time, one can surmise
that the first is the draft of the second. And because both are separated from
the lecture course *An Introduction to Metaphysics* by a very short time, one
may surmise that they both continue the train of thought developed in that
lecture course. However, the weight and the legacy of fundamental ontology,
including the modification I have mentioned, are more obvious in the draft
than in the script of the actual paper. The issue here is not, as will be the case
much later on, to "see the enigma of art," but, as Heidegger insists at the
very beginning of the draft, "only to prepare an alteration of the basic stand
[*Grundstellung*] of our Dasein towards art." (*UKW*, 2) (The same sentence is
already present in the *Introduction to Metaphysics*.)

---

9. Martin Heidegger, *Vom Wesen des Grundes*, (Frankfurt am Main: Vittorio Klostermann,
1965), 38; *The Essence of Reasons*, trans. T. Mallick, (Evanston: Northwestern University Press,
1969), 85. The *Dasein* exists for the sake of itself.

The preparation of such an alteration entails an overcoming of the approach to works of art in terms of *Vorhandenheit*, presence-at-hand. Such an approach is blind to the very meaning of the word *origin, Ur-sprung,* primal leap. Because *origin* simply means the cause of the art product in the psychological processes of the artist, it does not let the work be itself. And when the usual approach seems to do so, it treats the work as an object for an artistic business in which the works are explained, maintained, restored, criticized, and enjoyed. The work, however, is neither an object nor a product. By seeing it in such a way, we miss its origin. We approach the origin only by a leap away from the public agitation of the *Kunstbetrieb*. Clearly, the leap is here understood as a move away from the publicity of the 'they' (*das Man*) of everydayness. This shows the continuity between this lecture and fundamental ontology. And indeed, as soon as Heidegger in the first part of the first draft considers the artwork as work, he stresses that the being-manifest of the work has nothing to do with its availability to the public. He writes: "The only relation of the work towards the public, where there is one, is that the former destroys the latter. The greatness of a work is measured by this destructive power" (*UKW,* 3). In other words, what is at issue here, as in fundamental ontology, is the distinction between everydayness and authenticity, between presence-at-hand and existence. This is confirmed by the way in which Heidegger describes the two basic features of the work's Being, namely, world and earth. The world that is set up by the work is neither the sum of the present-at-hand, nor the frame of it, nor an object in front of us. It is like an escort (*Geleit*) that is more being than all the things present-at-hand and graspable "amid which in everydayness we believe to be at home. World is the every unfamiliar [*Unheimlich*]." What is at work in the work, as it sets up a world, is the "rejection [*Abweisung*] of the usual present-at-hand" (*UKW,* 4).

The other feature is the pro-duction (*Herstellung*) of the earth. The earth here is described as the "unison of an unsurpassable fulness" that is "both a ground and an abyss which essentially closes itself" (*UKW,* 5–6). But it is also a harshness (*Härte*), which, because it is in a trial or conflict (*Streit*) with the world, requires, in order to come to the fore, the counterharshness of what is usually called a "form," a "sketch" (*Riss*). Such dispute opens a space of dis-play, a There (*Da*) "in which a people comes to itself." The works thanks to which such a There is opened are the *temple* around the *statue* of the god and the poems in which "are pre-coined [*vorgeprägt*] for a people its great concept of the totality of beings." Poetry is thus the anticipation of philosophy, as it was in Hölderlin's *Hyperion* or in Hegel's chapter on the "Religion of Art" in the *Phenomenology of the Spirit.*

This description of the work of art gives Heidegger the opportunity to criticize the classical approaches to the work in terms of matter and form, which are concepts adjusted to utensils, not to artworks. Likewise, the approach to the work in terms of representation (*Darstellung*) is rejected. In such a notion, no matter how elaborated, "the presence-at-hand of everyday things operates as a standard" (UKW, 9). And at the conclusion of this description, in continuity with a basic scheme of Fundamental Ontology, Heidegger stresses the "solitude" (*Einsamkeit*) of the work of art, over against the "common reality" (*UKW*, 9), which is shaken and frightened by it.

The second part of the first draft deals with the origin. The origin is art considered in its essence. Taken in its essence, in its origin, art is the very historicality of truth, its *Geschehen*. Here, too, we face an obvious continuity with both the earlier fundamental ontology and its broadening to the *Dasein* of a people. Heidegger insists that setting-into-work is a necessity because truth occurs only with and thanks to the work. And it occurs only within the work, because truth has to be projected. In other words, the aletheic and historical traits that in *Being and Time* were the properties of authentic *praxis*, or fully temporal existence, now turn out to be also properties of the recently discovered superior forms of *poiēsis* and *technē*.

But this poietic project—*Dichtung* in Heidegger's German—requires a locus that itself is what it is, following the impact of the work of the poietic project. This locus is the *Dasein* of a people, which means that the There (i.e., the very openness of truth, or truth itself in its historicality) has no other locus than the people. Ultimately, therefore, there is a knowledge of the essence of art insofar as the people decides to win "clarity as to who we are and who we are not." This clear knowledge taken as a will is also a decision as to "what is great and what is petty, what is brave and what is cowardly, what is durable and what is transitory, what is Lord and what is Slave." This clear knowledge, taken to be the decision by which a people wills itself, is "the decisive leap into the proximity of the origin" (*UKW*, 13).

Up to this point, I cannot detect in the texts any significant admission of a turn. To be sure, the opening of the There, its grounding character is rooted in a "dark abyss," in the earth itself which is for a people "its earth" closing itself and resisting open-ness. To be sure, "the leap of the origin essentially remains a secret." But in spite of several new words, all of this is already present in *Vom Wesen der Wahrheit* and *Vom Wesen des Grundes*. And I find it highly significant to read at the end of the first draft the following sentence, which sounds as an echo of the 1929 essay on truth: "The origin is a mode of that ground whose necessity we have to call *Freedom*" (*UKW*, 14).

There is no adumbration of a turn, either, in the actual lecture of 1935. A few sentences suffice to show it: "The world is that in which a people comes to itself." (*SE*, 26). The world is never anybody-and-everybody's world, the world of universal humankind; it is "world for one people, the task which is assigned to it" (*SE*, 36). "The open-ness of the 'there,' Truth is only as History. And only a people can be historical, as projected upon its future by retrieving what it is. The people takes over the task to be the There" (*SE*, 36). "Truth occurs only insofar as it has thus decided, thereby grounding new domains of decision" (*SE*, 44). "The work is a leap ahead [*Vorsprung*] pointing toward what a people decides to be" (*SE*, 48).

## The 1936 Lecture

Thus, instead of being attentive to the enigma of art, both versions of the 1935 lecture turn out to be voluntarist proclamations in the name of the German *Dasein*. However, those who know or knew "The Origin of the Work of Art" only on the basis of the third version will probably object that the tone of voluntarist proclamation to a people is not obvious in this third version. They are right. Although questioning is claimed to be a central issue in all the texts I have mentioned, starting with *The Self-Assertion of the German University*, it is obvious in the very tone of those texts that self-assertion prevails upon questioning. Not so in 1936. This change of tone, occurring in the final version, deserves consideration.

To be sure, the "people" is still taken up as an issue along with its gods, and "greatness" is still mentioned along with the state-creator. Likewise, decision is still taken up as an issue. But all these topics seem to have lost the harshness of the former versions. Or at least their harshness seems to be diluted by a tone that is more meditative than assertive or proclaiming, and certainly not Promethean. Moreover, the circle that was emphasized in the early versions was in the last analysis a means of showing the circular character of *Dasein*, as a being existing for its own sake and becoming what it always already was. By contrast, the circle considered in 1936 loses the voluntarist connotation and now seems to mean that Being is neither beings, nor without them, and that human beings are concerned with the difference between both. In addition, the previous contempt for everydayness and its pettiness has almost vanished. It is highly significant that the first third of the final version should be devoted to the question, What is a thing in its thingly character?

In the framework of fundamental ontology, paying attention to the Being of things was clearly not a central issue for the task of thinking. Things did not deserve questioning, because their Being had nothing enigmatic. This character was defined either by presence-at-hand or by readiness-to-hand. Such easy answers are no longer made. Instead it is now said that

> the unpretentious thing evades thought most stubbornly. Can it be that this self-refusal of the mere thing, this self-contained independence belongs precisely to the nature of the thing? Must not this strange feature of the nature of the thing become what a thought that has to think the thing confides in? If so, then we should not force our way to its thingly character. (*GA*, 5:17)

In other words, everydayness is no longer "the familiar, all too familiar" that resoluteness has to avoid and overcome. It is now strange, though familiar. Likewise the tool previously defined once and for all by its readiness-to-hand now turns out by virtue of its very reliability to bear witness to the deepest truth, that is, to the interplay of unconcealment and concealment. Obviously, if the unpretentious character of things and tools now deserves meditation, it no longer makes sense to despise everydayness and its petty *technē*.

We can now observe a remarkable shift in the second third of the final version. Formerly, *alētheia* was connected with the There that a people is entrusted to take upon itself, thus making the *Dasein* of a people the locus of truth. This characterization now disappears. *Dasein* is no longer the locus of truth. Unconcealment is now taken to be a *clearing* in the midst of beings, a clearing to which humans belong and are exposed, rather than one instituted by them. Consequently, resoluteness also undergoes a deep change of meaning: It forsakes its initial call to the will, to its decision, to its project to be a self. It now becomes dis-closure of exposure to the reserve that is at the core of clearing. By the same token, truth itself is no longer a matter of human decision between Being and not-Being, or between unconcealment and mere appearance. And if it is no longer a matter of human decision, the reason is that the very distinction between concealment and deception or mere appearance has now become undecidable. "Concealment can be a refusal or merely a dissembling. We are never directly certain whether it is the one or the other. Concealment conceals and dissembles itself" (*GA*, 5:41). The word *decision*, to be sure, is still used. But the decision now belongs to Being, no longer to *Dasein*.

Finally, the last section of the final version deals with creation, but in a tone from which the Promethean inspiration has disappeared. What is seen as most essential in the work inasmuch as it is created, what is valued as most extraordinary in it, is no longer its capacity for anticipating in a leap what a people wills to be, and for affixing in the register of greatness what its rank and standards should be. Much more modestly, what is most essential in it, as created, is this, "that such a work is at all rather than is not" (*OWA*, 65). The most essential feature is now "this '*that* it is' of createdness" (*OWA*, 65). In other words, the coming to presence now seems almost to erase the previous privilege of futural projection.

As for the creator, what he sets-into-work is still a striving, the struggle of world and earth, but he himself is no longer a struggler. Creating, Heidegger says, is "receiving and borrowing within the relation to Unconcealment" (*OWA*, 62). Indeed, such verbs contain nothing Promethean.

# 10

# The Thinker and the Painter

The title of my presentation, "The Thinker and the Painter," is intended to suggest that in Merleau-Ponty's eyes there was a link between the activity to which, as a philosopher, he had devoted his life and the activity to which painters devote theirs.

Such a proximity calls for a clarification and an explanation. It needs to be both clarified and explained because it does not go without saying. I need only to recall that for the founder of the Western philosophical tradition those two activities are antithetical. Plato, one recalls, strongly maintains in the *Republic* that to paint amounts to refuse to think and that the activity of thinking requires a sort of detachment from perception and the perceived, which is the very element to which the painter is attached. To paint is to refuse to think, because for Plato the painter is par excellence the one who takes sides with appearances, which are labeled adverse to Being. He copies appearances without ever taking into consideration the essence (or he deals with copies without ever being concerned with their models). He celebrates the shadowy lights—the *clair obscur*—of the sensible realm as well as the equivocities that surface throughout it, and he fails to recognize that, beyond this confused area, it is possible for the eyes of the mind to have access to the clear and peaceful ordering of intelligible Ideas provided that the mind be detached from the sensible realm. This access to Being beyond appearance, or more precisely this access to appearances devoid of the ambiguities of the sensible, is reserved for the thinker. It allows him to understand with total clarity that what the painter prides himself on is worthy only of disdain: The work to which he devotes so much effort is in vain as, at the time when the painter believes he captures what truly is, he lets something that is nonbeing lead him

This chapter was originally published in *Merleau Ponty Vivant*, ed. M. C. Dillon (Albany: SUNY Press, 1991), 195–212.

astray. Although he wants to raise sensible things to the glory of a pictorial radiance, he achieves only the flimsy fabrication of nonreal copies of entities that are themselves devoid of being and truth because the sensible realm is not the medium within which the true aspect (*eidos*) of things is apprehended. The sensible aspects of things are nothing but the distorted reflection of their true physiognomies. Fascinated by the sensible appearances of things, the painter therefore produces only reflections of reflections.

Now is not the time to question the transformations undergone by the Platonic conceptions throughout the history of philosophy, nor even to evoke their persistence, under different forms, in the writings of philosophers of painting.

Those writings are relatively scarce, because only at the beginning of the nineteenth century, with Hegel and Schopenhauer, does one find philosophers of the first rank producing elaborate analyses of pictorial works.

Let me restrict myself to mentioning that, even when those analyses grant considerable attention to painting and seem to bestow upon it the privileged status of a form of thought, they continue to function within the space of those bimillennial oppositions elaborated by Plato: the thing itself and its copy, the real and the imaginary, the sensible diversity and the intelligible unity, the body and the mind. In other words, what those analyses seem to give to painting with one hand, they take back with the other. Thus Hegel, in contrast to Plato, entertains the notion that art is the manifestation of the idea. But he immediately adds, in perfect accord with the Platonic distinction between the sensible and the intelligible, that the element within which art produces its works, the sensible, is not adequate for a genuine manifestation of the idea.

Likewise Schopenhauer, also in contrast to Plato, maintains that the idea is manifested by art, which does not mean that art manifests the rational character of the Idea as Hegel thinks, but instead, that it manifests the profoundly absurd character of the thing-in-itself, the insatiable will. Yet there is also a profound agreement between Schopenhauer and Plato. This agreement emerges when Schopenhauer specifies his general thesis with the claim that art—even though it is an eminent form of thought because it exhibits the truth of reality; that is, the truth that reality is absurd—still is not adequate to think what it attempts to grasp. The reason for this inadequacy is simple: Art continues to entangle us in sensible phenomena (and therefore in the emanations of the will to live) at the very moment when it shows the absurdity of these emanations.

Schopenhauer, in spite of the abyss that separates him from Hegel, agrees with the latter, and finds himself in profound agreement with Plato when he says that the flaw of art is that it rivets us to the sensible. And both continue to maintain with Plato that, in the final analysis, thinking and being attached to the sensible are antithetical attitudes and terms.

Such an antimony is precisely what Merleau-Ponty, from the beginning until the end of his work, never stopped denouncing. To think, for Merleau-Ponty, does not mean to turn away from the perceived; rather it means to grant it the status of a first ground, to dwell within its boundaries, to listen to its echoes, to interrogate it, to always go back to it. Now it is precisely because thinking for him was fundamentally attracted to the perceived that thought, in the sense he gave to it in his own work, has to free itself from the dichotomies in which the philosophical tradition was trapped.

## Perception

To what degree does the perceived invite thought to rid itself of these dichotomies if thought takes the perceived as its privileged theme of meditation? Exactly to the degree that the dualistic oppositions that originated in Plato are not applied to the perceived. Already the Husserlian descriptions, whose importance and innovative character Merleau-Ponty had been quick to acknowledge, stood for him in contrast to the Platonic heritage carried along and transformed by Descartes to fashion the scientific project of the modern *mathesis;* those Husserlian descriptions were able to show that the phenomenal character specific to the perceived brings about a constant overlapping of those terms deemed antithetical and heterogeneous in the tradition. The tradition of modern philosophy, whether it be rationalistic, empiricist, or Kantian, finally relegated the perceived to the realm of pure multiplicity and diversity. Such a tradition maintained that the perceived as such is recalcitrant to unity and identity.

It is against this notion that Husserl reacts. He shows that it is not beyond the diversity of its aspects—the famous Husserlian profiles—or above them, that the perceived thing acquires its unity and its identity. These two features do not occur to the thing from the exterior and after the fact by virtue of a synthetic act of the understanding or an associating repetition. It is at the very core of the diversity of those profiles that, from the outset, the unity of the perceived thing emerges. In the perceived realm, the unity is not heterogeneous to multiplicity, rather it is folded within the multiplicity of the thing and is even required by it. Likewise the identity of the thing is not the antithesis of a difference. The perceived entity would lose its perceptual density, its incarnated existence, and would cease to be perceived if the aspects that are presented by it did not announce other aspects, which are not yet offered to sight. These latent sides form the horizon hidden by the first ones. A thing perceived from all sides would not be a perceived thing. In a rather similar manner, the realm of perceived entities does not fall prey to the classical antinomy between the particular and the general.

The perceived never presents itself as some strictly individual feature, some singular form, some incomparable color. At the outset, as the Gestalt psychologists discovered at the beginning of the century, perception generalizes: We do not see this particular white as strictly particular but as an example of whiteness. At the outset, too, perception stylizes: We see at the same time this singular tree as singular and as a token of the type "tree;" together with its singular form, we apprehend the type that connects it to all other trees.

In addition to an overlapping of the particular and the general, the perceived attests to a surprising overlapping of our fellow beings and the "I," a pluralistic interweaving of subjects. From the start, I am aware that the profiles of a thing—which remain latent for me so long as I remain within a given vantage point—are manifest to others who see the thing from another point of view. And even the aspects given to me do not present themselves as private images that occur within the solipsistic theater of my states of consciousness, but as aspects of the thing that bear witness to the thing's constitution and that cannot be denied by the person next to me. On this point, the descriptions given by Merleau-Ponty can claim as theirs Husserl's motto: "We see and we understand not simply as an individual among other individuals, but as individuals along with others [*miteinander*]."

To those various overlappings that allow the perceived to overcome the classical dichotomies, one should also add analogous overlappings on the side of the perceiving subject and in the very relation that this subject maintains with the perceived.

According to a traditional and established way of looking at things, vision and movement are heterogeneous: It is one thing to see, it is another thing to be in motion. As a consequence, the perceiving subject is more or less spontaneously interpreted as a spectator who, in addition to the capacity for seeing, has the unrelated capacity to move around. But such a distinction is shattered by phenomenology. Phenomenology requires that one recognize in the one who sees—qua seeing, and not by virtue of some extrinsic accident—"an intertwining of vision and movement,"[1] such that to see is, at the outset, to be able to come within proximity of what is seen, to hold it at arm's length and to come within closer range. As Merleau-Ponty says so well, "the

---

1. Maurice Merleau-Ponty, *L'Oeil et l'esprit* (Paris: Gallimard, 1964), 16; henceforth cited as *OE*, "Eye and Mind," trans. Carleton Dallery, in *The Primacy of Perception*, ed. James M. Edie (Evanston, Ill.: Northwestern University Press, 1964), 162; henceforth cited as *EM*.

map of the visible overlaps that of my intended motions" and "this extraordinary overlapping . . . makes it impossible to consider vision as an operation of the mind that erects in front of it a representation of the world" (*OE*, 17; *EM*, 162). But this overlapping of vision and motion, which blurs the traditional opposition of contemplation and action, goes hand in hand with another "intertwining," the one between vision and visibility. What such an intertwining of vision and visibility calls in question is another traditional distinction that has always been taken for granted: the distinction of activity and passivity, more precisely of spontaneity and receptivity. The point is that the being who enjoys both vision and movement is an integral part of the visible: While seeing the visible, the perceiving being is at the same time visible and in the act of seeing. Moreover, that being's moving body, which is itself part of the visible, is at the same time moved and self-moving, in the same manner as it touches things and is touched by them. By virtue of that fact, the body is at the same time decentered and centralizing. It is paradoxically the same thing to say that, "as visible and self-moving, my body is to be counted among things, is one of them" and, in apparent conflict, also to say, "Since [the body] can see itself and move itself around, things are maintained in a circle around it, are encrusted within its flesh as part of its full-fledged definition, and the world is made of the very stuff from which the body is made" (*OE*, 19; *EM*, 163). Those intertwinings, those overlappings, have the effect of dismantling a great many traditional oppositions; furthermore, they move as a barrage against the classical notion of reflection as *cogito me cogitare*, as the presence to itself of the *cogitatio* within its *cogitatum*. The teaching of the phenomenological analysis of perception is that, in contrast to the classical notion, a reflective capacity exists at the very core of perception, but this reflection does not allow us to see perception as a "thought of seeing" in the sense that Descartes used to give to the expression. Because it is linked to "the impossibility of dividing the being who sees from the seen entity," the reflexivity that arises at the very core of perception is one of a flesh caught by fleshly ramifications at the very same time it becomes a self.

In all this, there is an interiority that, as Merleau-Ponty says, "does not precede the material arrangement of the human body" (*OE*, 20; *EM*, 163) because the interiority occurs thanks to that arrangement, yet does not result from assembling various parts for the sake of an intended sum total. To say that the interiority precedes the arrangement of the body would make it as enigmatic as a spirit descending into some automaton and would be equivalent to saying that "the body itself is without inside or 'self.' " To say that the interiority results from the arrangement of the body is to conceive that this interiority is the aftereffect of the disposition of the parts of the body. It would be necessary therefore to conceive this arrangement as *partes extra partes* without granting to the body itself—taken as parts, whole, and interaction of parts and whole—the possibility of reflecting upon itself. It is true that,

> if our eyes were made so that not one part of our body could fall within our purview, or if some tricky arrangement made it impossible for us to touch our own bodies without affecting how we move about things—or simply if we had lateral eyes that do not produce an overlapping of the visual fields as some animals do—such a body, unable to reflect upon itself, would then be incapable of feeling itself; such a body almost as rigid as stone, which would not quite be flesh, could not be the body of a man, and would be devoid of humanity. (*OE,* 20; *EM,* 163)

But this does not mean that corporeal reflexivity is produced by the spatial disposition of organs in which each has a strictly determined function, because that disposition as such, precisely because it would be *partes extra partes,* would also be without overlappings, without intertwinings, without the interwoven reality of fleshly existence. One must therefore grant that it is an interweaving, an intertwining that must count as the basic datum for which no mechanical theory of the body will ever give a proper account.

## Thought

The phenomenal features specific to the perceived and to perception cast a light on the activity of thinking, inasmuch as the account of thinking that seeks to give them full justice and follow them closely is very different from the account of thinking that emerged from the Platonic tradition or the tradition of modern classical philosophy. This contrast is highlighted in the preface to *Signs,*[2] which dates back to the same period as the essay on *Eye and Mind.*

According to the Cartesian tradition, thought is a pure activity that penetrates with light anything that appears to it and that is revealed to itself free of any shadows in the mode of a pure presence to itself. Such a notion is rejected by a thought that takes the primacy of perception so seriously as to define itself in terms of the phenomenal features already present in percep-

---

2. Maurice Merleau-Ponty, *Signes* (Paris: Gallimard, 1960). *Signs,* trans. Richard C. McCleary (Evanston, Ill.: Northwestern University Press, 1964).

tion. "The philosophy of the overview," Merleau-Ponty says in memorable words, "was an episode, and it is now over" (*Signes*, 20; *Signs*, 14). To the question 'what is thinking?' one who has turned the world of perception into his dwelling place cannot answer in the manner of Descartes or Plato. Valéry somewhere in his work uses the expression "flesh of the spirit."[3] Two themes allow Merleau-Ponty to stress the appropriateness of this remark: time and language. It is the intrinsic link between thought and both time and language that compels thought to be defined, as perception was defined, in terms of intertwinings and overlappings. To think, in the Cartesian sense, means to intuit a clear and distinct idea at the present time: Thought is performed exclusively in the present. And as that thought is pure intuition, language is not essential to it; it is nothing more than an instrumental means destined to preserve some former intuitions that, as such, transcend language.

In contrast to the Cartesian perspective, Merleau-Ponty stresses the intrinsic link, not between thought and the present, but between thought and the nonpresent, the nonactual. If thought is alive, he says, it is "by virtue of the sliding motion which pushes it outside of the present into the non-actual" (*Signes*, 21; *Signs*, 14). Thinking indeed always means to rest on some previously acquired thought that by definition is always a past, but that, instead of being just obsolete, opens "a future for thinking, a cycle, a field" (*Signes*, 21; *Signs*, 14). In the activity of thinking thus understood, what is successive and what is simultaneous are not contradictory terms as they would be for Descartes. They overlap. Thus Merleau-Ponty writes: "If I think, it is not because I step outside of time into an intelligible world, nor is it because I recreate meaning out of nothing, but rather it is because the arrow of time pulls everything else along with it and causes my successive thoughts to emerge, in a sense, as simultaneous or at least as legitimately overlapping each other" (*Signes*, 21; *Signs*, 14). On a closer inspection, what takes place here is a double overlapping: that of the successive over the simultaneous and also that of the past (the acquired) over the future (the field of thought that calls for an exploration). And on even closer inspection, to those two overlappings several others are linked. The time to which the activity of thinking is linked is not constituted by the thinker who would rule over it: The thinker receives it, is receptive and sensible to it. To say that "my thought is nothing but the other side of my time [*l'envers de mon temps*]" amounts therefore to saying that it is "the other side of my passive and sensible being" (*Signes*, 22; *Signs*, 15). But to acknowledge that is also to acknowledge that I cannot think without remaining assigned, affixed to the sensible at the very time I

3. "*corps de l'esprit.*"

distance myself from it to reflect on it. It is to acknowledge also that the solipsism of the *ego cogito* is nothing but an abstraction. It is true that one must isolate oneself to think, but within that very isolation others remain included. There is therefore both an overlapping of the sensible on thinking and of the others on the one who thinks. Merleau-Ponty condenses these overlappings in a superb formula: "But if it is true that my thought is nothing but the reverse of my time, of my passive and sensible being, then whenever I try to understand myself, the whole fabric of the perceptible world comes too, and with it come the others who are caught in it" (*Signes,* 22; *Signs,* 15).

Thinking does not require that one leave the sensible to move to the intellectual, it requires that the individual reflect and retrieve the intertwining structures that are the very ones at work in the sensible. Just as to see is already to have seen and yet to remain open to what remains to be seen, likewise to think is always already to have thought and to be open to what remains to be thought. In both cases the same connection with time comes into play. Spontaneously we have the tendency to believe that perception is nothing but a spatial relationship of a "here" that is perceiving to a "there" that is perceived. But time is secretly involved in that relationship. The thing that I perceive, I see as being already there, before my eyes set down upon it, and in that sense it is past. But at the same time, it offers itself as belonging to the future, as a "hoped-for thing" ("*la chose espérée*" in Merleau-Ponty's expression); that is, as arousing the power I have of exploring it, of investigating it from all sides. My perception is therefore the overlapping of two dimensions: the present and actual with the nonpresent and nonactual, or in other words, *the visible and the invisible.* Other individuals are involved in such an overlapping, because what is invisible for me is from the outset apprehended by me as visible to those who face the perceived things from another side. To appear perceptually is at the outset to appear, not only to one single being, but to several beings. And just as the most insignificant perception bears witness to the plurality of human beings, the most unpretentious thought bears witness to the presence of other thinking individuals. Indeed, what is it to think but to be in a dialogue with oneself? In such a dialogue we are carried along by words of which we are not the authors and that others have transmitted to us.

The connecting bond of time, the bond weaving thought to language, confirms the appropriateness of Valéry's phrase of "the flesh of the spirit." Similarly, the fact that one cannot think without talking to oneself, albeit silently, the fact that words give rise to thoughts, constitutes an overlapping that makes us suspicious of the appropriateness of the Cartesian idea of thought that in its own solitude gains and retains the position of a universal legislator.

This overlapping is something quite different from a parallelism between two levels of reality, both of which are construed as complete and comprehensive, the level of ideas and meanings and the level of the code that expresses them. On this subject, Merleau-Ponty writes: "The weakness of every brand of parallelism is that it takes for granted correspondences between the two levels and masks from us those operations which produced them in their overlapping" (*Signes*, 26; *Signs*, 18). Just as my vision of the object at a distance finds in my body a correspondence in my ability to acquire a closer vision of it, in the same way it is my being immersed within the existing body of concrete words—upon which I depend when I speak and that I received from a tradition of speakers of the same language—that connects me with the art of thinking what still remains to be thought. But in these conditions, the position of the thinker has nothing in common with the regal condescension of Plato's philosopher or with the solitude of the Cartesian *cogito*. Just as to perceive is first and foremost to be caught by the visible, that is, to be included in it, in the same way, to think is first and foremost to be caught "by a Speech and a Thought which we do not own, but which own us" (*Signes*, 27; *Signs*, 19). Whereas the thought of the overview "held the world subdued at its feet" (*Signes*, 31; *Signs*, 22), in contrast the thought that takes root in the various overlappings just recalled is capable of accounting for what Merleau-Ponty calls the "verticality" of the world.

## Painting

I trust that I have provided enough context that we may now turn our attention to painting.

But before doing so, because the notion of overlapping has played a major role in my exposition, I would like to be allowed a few words to illustrate that notion with an example familiar to everybody that will clearly indicate the deficiency of the classical alternatives. What I have in mind is the intersection of two gazes. When two gazes, two pairs of eyes, intersect and meet, there is an overlapping of the one who looks and the one who is seen. The philosophy of reflection—which first posited the "I think" as a principle— cannot take this into account, as it moves within the asserted duality of the same and the other, of the *cogito* and extension, or, as Sartre, a Cartesian, puts it, of nothingness and Being. For the philosophy of reflection, what is at stake here is a juxtaposition such that either one of the two conscious beings relegates the other to the status of being an object, or is so relegated by the other, in such a way that there is "only one *cogito* at any given time" (*Signes*, 24; *Signs*, 17). The alternative postulated by reflection is simple: Either I cast my gaze on the other individual and then I am the subject and the other is the object; or else it is the other's gaze that is cast on me and then I am the object and the other person the subject. What this reflection fails to understand is that the crossing of the two gazes surmounts that antinomy: What happens is that there is indeed an adjustment of one individual to the other, or as Merleau-Ponty says, "two gazes, one inside the other [*deux regards l'un dans l'autre*]."

The idea central to Merleau-Ponty's meditation on painting, in particular in the essay "*The Indirect Language and the Voices of Silence*"[4] and "The Eye and Mind," is that all the problems of painting concern the overlappings that, as I have suggested, led Merleau-Ponty to define thought itself in terms of overlappings.

Painters, for example Dürer, have often said that the outline of their paintings had been derived by them from an inspection of the things in nature, out there; but no less frequently they would say conversely that this outline had been found within themselves. Thus I may invoke Cézanne, who used to say that "nature is inside,"[5] but I could also mention the classical advice of a Chinese painter who used to say that to paint a bamboo, one must first be able to grow it inside oneself. Taken together, these suggestions indicate that the painter paints not only what is visible, but the intertwining of the visible with the seeing. I proposed the view that the dimensions of the visible are inseparable from the seeing individual, from the echos that they provoke in our bodies inasmuch as it is our bodies that gather those dimensions. Such echoes are what each painting makes noticeable. In this regard, Merleau-Ponty asks: "That internal equivalent, the carnal formula for their presence which things spark in me, why in turn wouldn't they give rise to an outline, still in the visible realm, inside of which any other seeing eyes will uncover the motifs which sustain their own inspection of the world?" And then he answers: "Thus emerges something visible to the second degree, the carnal essence or the icon of the first" (*OE*, 22; *EM*, 164). There is an aphorism of Paul Valéry's that Merleau-Ponty used to like: "The painter brings in his own body." This seems a trivial point: One cannot conceive of an individual as capable of seeing a motif, of mixing colors, of handling a brush, unless that individual had a body. But the aphorism ceases to be trivial if it is taken to mean that the painter is the one who expresses on his canvas the schema of one of the manifold relationships of overlapping that the sensible realm weaves with our body.

---

4. In *Signes*, 49–104; *Signs*, 39–83.
5. Quoted by Merleau-Ponty (*OE*, 22; *EM*, 164).

If this analysis gives us a faithful description of the phenomenon of painting, a picture is never a *trompe l'oeil*, a fake of a thing, or a double, or a copy; painting is never a system of elements, or fragments, or "visual data" borrowed from the world, the so-called real world, to envisage reality in its absence, as Plato used to think in antiquity or Descartes and Pascal at the beginning of modernity.

The picture is not an unreal double of reality; it manifests to our gaze the unmistakable schema of the life of things within our bodies. Even Giacometti, one of those artists whose works might seem at first to be only remotely related to common perception, can write: "What I am interested in when I look at any painting is the resemblance." And he adds as if to emphasize that this resemblance has nothing to do with the phenomenon of *trompe l'oeil:* "that is to say what for me is resemblance: what allows me to discover a little bit of the external world" (*OE*, 24; *EM*, 165).

Under these conditions, the work of the painter comes to disrupt the standard distinction between the real and the imaginary (the latter being conceived as unreal or fictional). What the artist's work brings under our gaze is not the unreal double, the fictional copy of the real, but what Merleau-Ponty calls without contradiction "the imaginary texture of the real." Hence the overlapping of the visible world and the seeing individual must now be associated with a second overlapping: the one between the real and the imaginary. This overlapping is often expressed by the creators who apparently are most prone to giving free rein to fantasy. The words of Max Ernst, for example, might well stand as a manifesto for all surrealists: "The role of the painter," he said, "is to project what is visible and seen within himself" (*OE*, 30–31; *EM*, 168). Color also attests to this overlapping, if it is true that, already in the everyday visual field and to a greater extent in painting, each color is inseparable from the symbolic or cultural significance invested in it and is never ultimately a pure "sensorial datum," except in the laboratory of the psychologist.

It might be objected that this schema that things evoke in the body of the painter belongs strictly speaking to him or her alone, that it is the artist's private world and therefore has no reality. But the paradox is precisely that this supposedly private world, as soon as it is expressed, becomes constitutive of a common world. Thus the schema that became a picture and a painting elicits echos in different individuals and imposes upon each one a specific way of looking at the world. In his novel, *Remembrance of Things Past*, Marcel Proust notices that shortly after the time when Renoir's paintings of women were the targets of sarcasm and reprobation because of their supposed failure to look like real women, people began to look at women in light of

Renoir. One could say almost the same thing concerning Modigliani's paintings or the drawings and cutouts of Matisse. Strange though they were when they were first released, those works were quickly seen as awakening echos in all of us and eliciting carnal recollections, thus allowing us to recognize a collective schema of femininity.

Thus the intertwining of the visible and seeing blends the overlapping between real and imaginary together with the intertwining of the private and the shared. It is as if painting attested to a generalized overlapping function. But let us return to the intertwining of the visible and the one who sees. It works indeed in two directions: the visible, as we just said, elicits in the seeing individual a carnal schema of what the visible realm is; but in addition, the seeing individual is part of the visible realm, too. This notion was expressed by a variety of painters who, as Merleau-Ponty observed with regard to Paul Klee, liked to say that they felt "looked at by things" (*OE*, 31; *EM*, 167). This is also what, as early as the classical period, painters expressed in an iconographic manner either by depicting themselves in the process of painting (Matisse does this in some drawings) or, as in many Flemish and Dutch interiors, by installing some sort of onlooker in the form of a mirror in which the entire scene is reflected. The mirror, as Merleau-Ponty says, functions "as a pre-human gaze that is the symbol of the gaze of the painter." And he adds: "The mirror appears because I am seeing-visible, because there is a reflexivity of the sensible; the mirror translates this reflexivity and redoubles it." And further on: " . . . It is the instrument of a universal magic which transforms things into spectacles, spectacles into things, myself into someone else and someone else into myself" (*OE*, 33–34; *EM*, 168). If Merleau-Ponty speaks here of magic, it is not of course because of some exotic taste for the irrational, but instead because he wants to highlight the contrast between the actual vision and its reconstruction by analytical thinking in a philosopher of reflection such as Descartes, for example. Such a reflection in principle refuses the promiscuous contact of the seeing individual and of the visible to such an extent that "a Cartesian does not see *himself* in the mirror: he sees a mannequin, the 'outside' of a being" which for him is not the carnal appearance of his flesh, rather it is a simple "image"—upon which his thought makes the judgment that it is the mechanical reflection of his own body, a reflection to which his thought in a second move grants, in the same way as to an effect, some resemblance to its cause (*OE*, 38–39; *EM*, 170).

These intertwinings are far from being the only ones expressed by painting. Indeed, what painting expresses most forcefully is the reciprocal overlapping of all the dimensions of the sensible—light, shadows, colors, reflections, lines. For a thought of the Cartesian type, it goes without saying that line and color are distinct just as much as form and content are different: The line determines the contour of a thing, or its envelope, which color then fills up. But a distinction of that kind, which is not problematic for the understanding, is precisely what painting brings into question. A few lines, and only lines, are sufficient for the prehistorical painters of the cave of Teruel in Spain to make us see a group of hunters. Merleau-Ponty recalls that Leonardo da Vinci in the *Treatise of Painting* proposed as a task for each painter to discover within each object "the unique and specific curve woven in it which permeates throughout its extension as its generating axis" (*OE,* 72; *EM,* 183). To take a more contemporary example, Paul Klee is a painter for whom one single line is enough to set up in front of us the character of a "Timid Brute" and more generally to make visible a kind of genesis of things. This shows that, instead of being a limit, a line can express the entire thing and paradoxically function as a "total part." What is true of line is also true of color: it, too, functions as a total part capable by itself, without any lines, of presenting the object in its specific form and voluminous character as in Cézanne who used to say, "When color is at a perfection, form is at its fullest."

No less indicative of the overlappings that I am talking about is the fact that often good painters—I am thinking of Degas, Picasso, and Matisse— also turn into good sculptors, in spite of the fact that the manipulations and processes required to be a sculptor are very different from those required by painting. In this, Merleau-Ponty sees "the proof that there is a system of equivalences, a *Logos* of the lines, of lights, of reliefs, of masses, a presentation without any concept of universal Being" (*OE,* 71; *EM,* 182). Painting shows, he says somewhere else, "a polymorphism of Being."

It is again the notion of overlapping that guides Merleau-Ponty's meditation on style in his essay on André Malraux's book on Art, *The Voices of Silence.*

One meaning of style is the structural cohesion achieved by an individual work, a cohesion with which the spectator quickly becomes familiar and that allows him or her to recognize as works of painter X or Y paintings he or she has never seen before. On this topic, Malraux mentions a "coherent deformation" and he talks as if the shaping into a form effected by the artist was purely arbitrary with regard to the visible in the sense that style creates its own system. More precisely, he speaks as though styles were imposed from the top by the artist, without any prior anticipation in the visible. "The plastic arts," he writes, "are never born out of a way of looking at the world, but of shaping it." It is this voluntarist stand, this idea of a sovereignty, this a— cosmic attitude, to which Merleau-Ponty objects. And what he objects to in those notions is the fact that they are based on the previous dichotomies and dualities. In sum, Malraux confronts us with a choice between the visible world and the spiritual world of the creator; and as the artistic world has no antecedent in the visible one, the victory of a style seems to imply the abdication of the many who live in the visible in favor of the sovereign genius of the creator. There is no abdication, Merleau-Ponty objects, but only recognition. Recognition here is based on the fact that a style imposes itself simply because it adheres to the visible and somehow or other finds in the sensible its own antecedents; precisely because of this, a style is accessible to others, it is interindividual and does not emerge *ex nihilo* from the stormy solitude of the genius (*Signes,* 67–68; 72–73; *Signs,* 53–55, 57–59). From the perspective of others, the painter can sometimes appear as the creator of a counterworld, but for the painter at work there is but one world, and this world is what beckons him or her to work in a call to which the work will never stop responding.

One last mode of intertwining remains to be investigated. Not only do painters respond to what the visible world elicits in them, rather than merely continuing the task instituted by their own beginnings, they also inscribe themselves within a tradition of painting that overlaps on their work, just as their work is intertwined within the tradition. Here again the debate with Malraux is instructive. Malraux insists that painting forms a unique temporal adventure such that there is an affiliation among past and present painters, some kinship of present and past in the pictorial problems and solutions, in short, a sort of unity of painting as such. But that unity is expressed by him in such terms that it appears to be only retrospective, that is, made present and visible, and constituted after the fact, only by virtue of the modern phenomenon of the museum. In this view, the unity of painting seems to be transhistorical, and in the actual history Malraux sees nothing but scattered disunity, the struggle of each painter against others, forgetfulness, failure to be acknowledged. It is to such a duality—the unity created by the museum on the one hand, and historical dispersion on the other—that Merleau-Ponty objects. To say that the unity of painting is retrospective amounts to failing to recognize that, just as to see is always to see more than one sees (for it provides access to a fringe of invisible features that have no place within the totality of strictly visual data), in the same way to paint is always to paint more than one paints. As soon as there was painting, it was in excess of itself. At the same time as it offers a field that goes beyond the given picture, the perceptual power of the painter is doubled with a prospective power. So, rather than oppose the nontemporal unity of the museum to the scattered character of actual history, the point is to understand actual history in terms of temporal overlappings. By virtue of these overlappings, neither the acquired nor the new can be regarded as entirely acquired or entirely new, and "the idea . . . of a totalization of painting . . . is meaningless" (*OE*, 90; *EM*, 189).

If it is true that such overlappings constitute the roots and the resourcefulness of thought, and if it is true on the other hand that painting itself has its roots and its resourcefulness in analogous overlappings, then one understands why Merleau-Ponty could speak of a "mute thought of painting" (*OE*, 91; *EM*, 189).

But by the same token it is evident that Merleau-Ponty stands oceans apart from the philosophers who, ever since Plato, have been proclaiming in one guise or another that there must be an overcoming of painting—whether this be in the name of Platonic or Cartesian ideas, in the name of the history of the Spirit, in the name of material praxis, in the name of the absurdity of the will, or in the name of the history of Being. The reason for this notion of an end of art is that the attention of those philosophers, when they happen to be concerned with things pictorial, never dwells on the specificity of the visible. If one grants the visible realm its own full rights, then—against the pronouncements made by those grand narratives that, starting with the Myth of the Cave, proclaimed the death of art—one should be able to maintain: "Should the world still last millions of years, for painters, if some are still left, that world would still remain to be painted and will end before being completely captured" (*OE*, 90; *EM*, 189).

# Index

Abraham, 101
absolute agreement (conforming objects/
  representations), 26
agreement (unity) vs. cleavage, 32
Aegina, 145
*aei*, 156
Aeschylus, 158
aesthethics: (conscious intuition) vs.
  teleology (unconscious intuition),
  30; judgment (vs. three types of judgment), 10, 57–60; absorbing ethics
  and logic, 53; purism, 61. *See also*
  subjectivity and *Erlebnis*, 128,
  142, 151
*agora*, 3
*aion*, 156
*Alētheia*, 129, 132, 141, 144, 147–48,
  151, 163, 168. *See also*
  unconcealment
*alētheuein*, 155
Alleman, Beda, 109
Aphrodite, 65, 92, 100
Apollo, 4, 7, 65; vs. Dionysus, 119,
  122–23
*archē*, 155
Aristotle, vii, 12, 13, 75, 131, 141,
  155, 156, 158; connection of poetics
  and politics, 9; *Nicomachean Ethics*,
  155; *Rhetoric*, 6
art (tranquilizer of the will), 33
artist vs. artisan, 2
artistic production (autonomous), 62;
  antiartistic manifestations, 67–68
arts: plastic—vs. literary—and musical, 66

asceticism, 116
Athena, 65

Bamberg cathedral, 145
baroque art, 74
beauty (soothing vs. energizing, *sinnlichen Trieb* vs. *Formtrieb*), 87; birth
  of Love from, in *The Symposium*, 92,
  100, 104
Berlin, 67
*bios*, 158
Bloch and Von Wartburg, 73
body (centralizing, decentered), 175

Cassirer, Ernst: *Kant's Life and
  Thought*, 23, 35
Cézanne, Paul, 62, 180, 183
circularity of the understanding (obliterated), 138
Christianity, 48–52, 65, 66
*clair obscur*, 171
classicism, 48
cleavage (disjunctive apprehension) vs.
  unity, meaning (synthetic reception),
  33–37, 39
*cogito*, 141, 175, 178, 179
Cohen, Hermann, 35–36, 39; *Kants
  Begründung der Ethik*, 35–36; *Kants
  Theorie der Erfahrung*, 39
conceptual artists, 63
concordance (affinity), 60
corporate body of the general will, 43
corporate orders (*Stände*), 50
creators (triad of), 162
cubism, 62